BEST-LOVED
STORIES OF THE LDS
PEOPLE
VOLUME 1

BEST-LOVED
STORIES OF THE LDS
PEOPLE
VOLUME 1

Edited by Jack M. Lyon, Linda Ririe Gundry,
and Jay A. Parry

DESERET BOOK COMPANY
SALT LAKE CITY, UTAH

Also available from Deseret Book
BEST-LOVED POEMS OF THE LDS PEOPLE
BEST-LOVED HUMOR OF THE LDS PEOPLE
BEST-LOVED STORIES OF THE LDS PEOPLE, VOLUME 2

Library of Congress Cataloging-in-Publication Data

Best-loved stories of the LDS people / edited by Jack M. Lyon, Linda
Ririe Gundry, Jay A. Parry.
    p.   cm.
Includes bibliographical references and index.
ISBN 1-57345-266-1 (hardcover)
    1. Church of Jesus Christ of Latter-day Saints—History—19th
century—Sources. 2. Mormon Church—History—19th century—Sources.
3. Mormons—History—19th century—Sources. I. Lyon, Jack M.
II. Gundry, Linda Ririe. III. Parry, Jay A.
BX8611.B36   1997
289.3'32—dc21   97-24195
                                                                      CIP

Printed in the United States of America   72082-4604D
10 9   8   7   6   5   4   3

CONTENTS

⌒

Protection

"Someone Laid His Hand upon My Head"

Healing

Missionary Work

Love

Humor

PREFACE

⌒

The history of The Church of Jesus Christ of Latter-day Saints is filled with stories—accounts of faith, conversion, protection, revelation, and healing. Some of these stories are told over and over again, in books, articles, talks, and lessons, because they make a point, touch the heart, or in some way define what it means to be a Latter-day Saint.

The purpose of this volume is to bring together in one place the stories that have been perennial favorites among members of the Church. If you have a favorite story from Church history, chances are you'll find it in this collection. Still, we have undoubtedly missed some stories. Although we have tried to be thorough, there are so many wonderful stories that it would be almost impossible to include them all.

We acknowledge our debt to other compilers and editors, including Hyrum G. and Helen Mae Andrus, Alma P. and Clea M. Burton, George Q. Cannon, Kate B. Carter, Leon R. Hartshorn, Bryant S. Hinckley, Andrew Jenson, N. B. Lundwall, Truman G. Madsen, Preston Nibley, B. H. Roberts, Eliza R. Snow, Edward Tullidge, and Orson F. Whitney.

We also express our appreciation to the officers and publishing staff of Deseret Book Company, and particularly to Ronald A. Millett, Sheri Dew, Jennifer Pritchett, Patricia J. Parkinson, and Ronald O. Stucki.

THE
RESTORATION

THE FIRST VISION

JOSEPH SMITH

I was born in the year of our Lord one thousand eight hundred and five, on the twenty-third day of December, in the town of Sharon, Windsor county, State of Vermont . . . My father, Joseph Smith, Sen., left the State of Vermont, and moved to Palmyra, Ontario (now Wayne) county, in the State of New York, when I was in my tenth year, or thereabouts. In about four years after my father's arrival in Palmyra, he moved with his family into Manchester in the same county of Ontario—

His family consisting of eleven souls, namely, my father, Joseph Smith; my mother, Lucy Smith (whose name, previous to her marriage, was Mack, daughter of Solomon Mack); my brothers, Alvin (who died November 19th, 1823, in the 26th year of his age), Hyrum, myself, Samuel Harrison, William, Don Carlos; and my sisters, Sophronia, Catherine, and Lucy.

Some time in the second year after our removal to Manchester, there was in the place where we lived an unusual excitement on the subject of religion. It commenced with the Methodists, but soon became general among all the sects in that region of country. Indeed, the whole district of country seemed affected by it, and great multitudes united themselves to the different religious parties, which created no small stir and division amongst the people, some crying, "Lo, here!" and others, "Lo, there!" Some were contending for the Methodist faith, some for the Presbyterian, and some for the Baptist.

For, notwithstanding the great love which the converts to the different faiths expressed at the time of their conversion, and the great zeal manifested by the respective clergy, who were active in getting up and promoting this extraordinary scene of religious feeling, in order to have everybody converted, as they were pleased to call it, let them join what sect they pleased; yet when the converts began to file off, some to one party and some to another, it was seen that the seemingly good feelings of both the priests and the converts were more pretended than real; for a scene of great confusion and bad feeling ensued—priest contending against priest, and convert against convert; so that all their good feelings one for another, if they ever had any, were entirely lost in a strife of words and a contest about opinions.

I was at this time in my fifteenth year. My father's family was proselyted to the Presbyterian faith, and four of them joined that church, namely, my mother, Lucy; my brothers Hyrum and Samuel Harrison; and my sister Sophronia.

During this time of great excitement my mind was called up to serious reflection and great uneasiness; but though my feelings were deep and often poignant, still I kept myself aloof from all these parties, though I attended their several meetings as often as occasion would permit. In process of time my mind became somewhat partial to the Methodist sect, and I felt some desire to be united with them; but so great were the confusion and strife among the different denominations, that it was impossible for a person young as I was, and so unacquainted with men and things, to come to any certain conclusion who was right and who was wrong.

My mind at times was greatly excited, the cry and tumult were so great and incessant. The Presbyterians were most decided against the Baptists and Methodists, and used all the powers of both reason and sophistry to prove their errors, or, at least, to make the people think they were in error. On the other hand, the Baptists and Methodists in their turn were equally zealous in endeavoring to establish their own tenets and disprove all others.

4

In the midst of this war of words and tumult of opinions, I often said to myself: What is to be done? Who of all these parties are right; or, are they all wrong together? If any one of them be right, which is it, and how shall I know it?

While I was laboring under the extreme difficulties caused by the contests of these parties of religionists, I was one day reading the Epistle of James, first chapter and fifth verse, which reads: *If any of you lack wisdom, let him ask of God, that giveth to all men liberally, and upbraideth not; and it shall be given him.*

Never did any passage of scripture come with more power to the heart of man than this did at this time to mine. It seemed to enter with great force into every feeling of my heart. I reflected on it again and again, knowing that if any person needed wisdom from God, I did; for how to act I did not know, and unless I could get more wisdom than I then had, I would never know; for the teachers of religion of the different sects understood the same passages of scripture so differently as to destroy all confidence in settling the question by an appeal to the Bible.

At length I came to the conclusion that I must either remain in darkness and confusion, or else I must do as James directs, that is, ask of God. I at length came to the determination to "ask of God," concluding that if he gave wisdom to them that lacked wisdom, and would give liberally, and not upbraid, I might venture.

So, in accordance with this, my determination to ask of God, I retired to the woods to make the attempt. It was on the morning of a beautiful, clear day, early in the spring of eighteen hundred and twenty. It was the first time in my life that I had made such an attempt, for amidst all my anxieties I had never as yet made the attempt to pray vocally.

After I had retired to the place where I had previously designed to go, having looked around me, and finding myself alone, I kneeled down and began to offer up the desires of my heart to God. I had scarcely done so, when immediately I was seized upon by some power which entirely overcame me, and had such an astonishing influence over me as to bind my tongue so that I could not speak. Thick darkness gathered around me, and it seemed to me for a time as if I were doomed to sudden destruction.

But, exerting all my powers to call upon God to deliver me out of the power of this enemy which had seized upon me, and at the very moment when I was ready to sink into despair and abandon myself to destruction—not to an imaginary ruin, but to the power of some actual being from the unseen world, who had such marvelous power as I had never before felt in any being—just at this moment of great alarm, I saw a pillar of light exactly over my head, above the brightness of the sun, which descended gradually until it fell upon me.

It no sooner appeared than I found myself delivered from the enemy which held me bound. When the light rested upon me I saw two Personages, whose brightness and glory defy all description, standing above me in the air. One of them spake unto me, calling me by name and said, pointing to the other—*This is My Beloved Son. Hear Him!*

My object in going to inquire of the Lord was to know which of all the sects was right, that I might know which to join. No sooner, therefore, did I get possession of myself, so as to be able to speak, than I asked the Personages who stood above me in the light, which of all the sects was right (for at this time it had never entered into my heart that all were wrong)—and which I should join.

I was answered that I must join none of them, for they were all wrong; and the Personage who addressed me said that all their creeds were an abomination in his sight; that those professors were all corrupt; that: "they draw near to me with their lips, but their hearts are far from me, they teach for doctrines the commandments of men, having a form of godliness, but they deny the power thereof."

He again forbade me to join with any of them; and many

other things did he say unto me, which I cannot write at this time. When I came to myself again, I found myself lying on my back, looking up into heaven. When the light had departed, I had no strength; but soon recovering in some degree, I went home. And as I leaned up to the fireplace, mother inquired what the matter was. I replied, "Never mind, all is well—I am well enough off." I then said to my mother, "I have learned for myself that Presbyterianism is not true." It seems as though the adversary was aware, at a very early period of my life, that I was destined to prove a disturber and an annoyer of his kingdom; else why should the powers of darkness combine against me? Why the opposition and persecution that arose against me, almost in my infancy?

Joseph Smith–History 1:3–20.

THE ANGEL MORONI

JOSEPH SMITH

On the evening of the . . . twenty-first of September, after I had retired to my bed for the night, I betook myself to prayer and supplication to Almighty God for forgiveness of all my sins and follies, and also for a manifestation to me, that I might know of my state and standing before him; for I had full confidence in obtaining a divine manifestation, as I previously had one.

While I was thus in the act of calling upon God, I discovered a light appearing in my room, which continued to increase until the room was lighter than at noonday, when immediately a personage appeared at my bedside, standing in the air, for his feet did not touch the floor.

He had on a loose robe of most exquisite whiteness. It was a whiteness beyond anything earthly I had ever seen; nor do I believe that any earthly thing could be made to appear so exceedingly white and brilliant. His hands were naked, and his arms also, a little above the wrist; so, also, were his feet naked, as were his legs, a little above the ankles. His head and neck were also bare. I could discover that he had no other clothing on but this robe, as it was open, so that I could see into his bosom.

Not only was his robe exceedingly white, but his whole person was glorious beyond description, and his countenance truly like lightning. The room was exceedingly light, but not so very bright as immediately around his person. When I first looked upon him, I was afraid; but the fear soon left me.

He called me by name, and said unto me that he was a messenger sent from the presence of God to me, and that his name was Moroni; that God had a work for me to do; and that my name should be had for good and evil among all nations, kindreds, and tongues, or that it should be both good and evil spoken of among all people.

He said there was a book deposited, written upon gold plates, giving an account of the former inhabitants of this continent, and the source from whence they sprang. He also said that the fulness of the everlasting Gospel was contained in it, as delivered by the Savior to the ancient inhabitants;

Also, that there were two stones in silver bows—and these stones, fastened to a breastplate, constituted what is called the Urim and Thummim—deposited with the plates; and the possession and use of these stones were what constituted "seers" in ancient or former times; and that God had prepared them for the purpose of translating the book.

After telling me these things, he commenced quoting the prophecies of the Old Testament. He first quoted part of the third chapter of Malachi; and he quoted also the fourth or last chapter of the same prophecy, though with a little variation from the way it reads in our Bibles. Instead of quoting the first verse as it reads in our books, he quoted it thus:

For behold, the day cometh that shall burn as an oven, and all the proud, yea, and all that do wickedly shall burn as stubble; for they that come shall burn them, saith the Lord of Hosts, that it shall leave them neither root nor branch.

And again, he quoted the fifth verse thus: *Behold, I will reveal unto you the Priesthood, by the hand of Elijah the prophet, before the coming of the great and dreadful day of the Lord.*

He also quoted the next verse differently: *And he shall plant in the hearts of the children the promises made to the fathers, and the hearts of the children shall turn to their fathers. If it were not so, the whole earth would be utterly wasted at his coming.*

In addition to these, he quoted the eleventh chapter of Isaiah, saying that it was about to be fulfilled. He quoted also the third chapter of Acts, twenty-second and twenty-third verses, precisely as they stand in our New Testament. He said that that prophet was Christ; but the day had not yet come when "they who would not hear his voice should be cut off from among the people," but soon would come.

He also quoted the second chapter of Joel, from the twenty-eighth verse to the last. He also said that this was not yet fulfilled, but was soon to be. And he further stated that the fulness of the Gentiles was soon to come in. He quoted many other passages of scripture, and offered many explanations which cannot be mentioned here.

Again, he told me, that when I got those plates of which he

9

had spoken—for the time that they should be obtained was not yet fulfilled—I should not show them to any person; neither the breastplate with the Urim and Thummim; only to those to whom I should be commanded to show them; if I did I should be destroyed. While he was conversing with me about the plates, the vision was opened to my mind that I could see the place where the plates were deposited, and that so clearly and distinctly that I knew the place again when I visited it.

After this communication, I saw the light in the room begin to gather immediately around the person of him who had been speaking to me, and it continued to do so until the room was again left dark, except just around him; when, instantly I saw, as it were, a conduit open right up into heaven, and he ascended till he entirely disappeared, and the room was left as it had been before this heavenly light had made its appearance.

I lay musing on the singularity of the scene, and marveling greatly at what had been told to me by this extraordinary messenger; when, in the midst of my meditation, I suddenly discovered that my room was again beginning to get lighted, and in an instant, as it were, the same heavenly messenger was again by my bedside.

He commenced, and again related the very same things which he had done at his first visit, without the least variation; which having done, he informed me of great judgments which were coming upon the earth, with great desolations by famine, sword, and pestilence; and that these grievous judgments would come on the earth in this generation. Having related these things, he again ascended as he had done before.

By this time, so deep were the impressions made on my mind, that sleep had fled from my eyes, and I lay overwhelmed in astonishment at what I had both seen and heard. But what was my surprise when again I beheld the same messenger at my bedside, and heard him rehearse or repeat over again to me the same things as before; and added a caution to me, telling me that Satan would

Your Online Bookstore

5750 Campbell Rd
Houston, TX, 77041, USA

acking slip for AmazonUS order 105-2144289-4184204 (this IS NOT a bill)

Order Date: Sep 26 2013
Shipping Service: expedited
Shipping To: DANIEL ROSENBAUM
                   129 PENN ST
                   MONTGOMERY, PA, 17752-1145

Product Details	Price
Title: Best-Loved Stories of the LDS People (Volume 1) **ISBN:** 1573452661 **SKU:** HDT3879AUJM08062013H2538B **Condition:** New - New **Quantity:** 1 **Comments:** Unbeatable customer service, and we usually ship the same or next day. Over one million satisfied customers!	$16.45

Subtotal: $16.45
Shipping & Handling: $6.99
Tax: $0.00
Total: $23.44

4038573PA; 0+0

hank you for your order! If you have any questions or concerns, please feel free to ontact us directly at customerservice@youronlinebookstore.com.

try to tempt me (in consequence of the indigent circumstances of my father's family), to get the plates for the purpose of getting rich. This he forbade me, saying that I must have no other object in view in getting the plates but to glorify God, and must not be influenced by any other motive than that of building his kingdom; otherwise I could not get them.

After this third visit, he again ascended into heaven as before, and I was again left to ponder on the strangeness of what I had just experienced; when almost immediately after the heavenly messenger had ascended from me for the third time, the cock crowed, and I found that day was approaching, so that our interviews must have occupied the whole of that night.

I shortly after arose from my bed, and, as usual, went to the necessary labors of the day; but, in attempting to work as at other times, I found my strength so exhausted as to render me entirely unable. My father, who was laboring along with me, discovered something to be wrong with me, and told me to go home. I started with the intention of going to the house; but, in attempting to cross the fence out of the field where we were, my strength entirely failed me, and I fell helpless on the ground, and for a time was quite unconscious of anything.

The first thing that I can recollect was a voice speaking unto me, calling me by name. I looked up, and beheld the same messenger standing over my head, surrounded by light as before. He then again related unto me all that he had related to me the previous night, and commanded me to go to my father and tell him of the vision and commandments which I had received.

I obeyed; I returned to my father in the field, and rehearsed the whole matter to him. He replied to me that it was of God, and told me to go and do as commanded by the messenger.

Joseph Smith–History 1:29–50.

"A MESSENGER FROM HEAVEN ORDAINED US"

JOSEPH SMITH

On the 5th day of April, 1829, Oliver Cowdery came to my house, until which time I had never seen him. He stated to me that having been teaching school in the neighborhood where my father resided, and my father being one of those who sent to the school, he went to board for a season at his house, and while there the family related to him the circumstances of my having received the plates, and accordingly he had come to make inquiries of me.

Two days after the arrival of Mr. Cowdery (being the 7th of April) I commenced to translate the Book of Mormon, and he began to write for me.

We still continued the work of translation, when, in the ensuing month (May, 1829), we on a certain day went into the woods to pray and inquire of the Lord respecting baptism for the remission of sins, that we found mentioned in the translation of the plates. While we were thus employed, praying and calling upon the Lord, a messenger from heaven descended in a cloud of light, and having laid his hands upon us, he ordained us, saying:

Upon you my fellow servants, in the name of Messiah, I confer the Priesthood of Aaron, which holds the keys of the ministering of angels, and of the gospel of repentance, and of baptism by immersion for the remission of sins; and this shall never be taken again from the earth until the sons of Levi do offer again an offering unto the Lord in righteousness.

He said this Aaronic Priesthood had not the power of laying

on hands for the gift of the Holy Ghost, but that this should be conferred on us hereafter; and he commanded us to go and be baptized, and gave us directions that I should baptize Oliver Cowdery, and that afterwards he should baptize me.

Accordingly we went and were baptized. I baptized him first, and afterwards he baptized me—after which I laid my hands upon his head and ordained him to the Aaronic Priesthood, and afterwards he laid his hands on me and ordained me to the same Priesthood—for so we were commanded.

The messenger who visited us on this occasion and conferred this Priesthood upon us, said that his name was John, the same that is called John the Baptist in the New Testament, and that he acted under the direction of Peter, James and John, who held the keys of the Priesthood of Melchizedek, which Priesthood, he said, would in due time be conferred on us, and that I should be called the first Elder of the Church, and he (Oliver Cowdery) the second. It was on the fifteenth day of May, 1829, that we were ordained under the hand of this messenger, and baptized.

Immediately on our coming up out of the water after we had been baptized, we experienced great and glorious blessings from our Heavenly Father. No sooner had I baptized Oliver Cowdery, than the Holy Ghost fell upon him, and he stood up and prophesied many things which should shortly come to pass. And again, so soon as I had been baptized by him, I also had the spirit of prophecy, when, standing up, I prophesied concerning the rise of this Church, and many other things connected with the Church, and this generation of the children of men. We were filled with the Holy Ghost, and rejoiced in the God of our salvation.

Joseph Smith–History 1:66–73.

The Golden Plates

JOSEPH SMITH

Convenient to the village of Manchester, Ontario county, New York, stands a hill of considerable size, and the most elevated of any in the neighborhood. On the west side of this hill, not far from the top, under a stone of considerable size, lay the plates, deposited in a stone box. This stone was thick and rounding in the middle on the upper side, and thinner towards the edges, so that the middle part of it was visible above the ground, but the edge all around was covered with earth.

Having removed the earth, I obtained a lever, which I got fixed under the edge of the stone, and with a little exertion raised it up. I looked in, and there indeed did I behold the plates, the Urim and Thummim, and the breastplate, as stated by the messenger. The box in which they lay was formed by laying stones together in some kind of cement. In the bottom of the box were laid two stones crossways of the box, and on these stones lay the plates and the other things with them.

I made an attempt to take them out, but was forbidden by the messenger, and was again informed that the time for bringing them forth had not yet arrived, neither would it, until four years from that time; but he told me that I should come to that place precisely in one year from that time, and that he would there meet with me, and that I should continue to do so until the time should come for obtaining the plates.

Accordingly, as I had been commanded, I went at the end of each year, and at each time I found the same messenger there, and received instruction and intelligence from him at each of our interviews, respecting what the Lord was going to do, and how and in what manner his kingdom was to be conducted in the last days. . . .

At length the time arrived for obtaining the plates, the Urim and Thummim, and the breastplate. On the twenty-second day of September, one thousand eight hundred and twenty-seven, having gone as usual at the end of another year to the place where they were deposited, the same heavenly messenger delivered them up to me with this charge: that I should be responsible for them; that if I should let them go carelessly, or through any neglect of mine, I should be cut off; but that if I would use all my endeavors to preserve them, until he, the messenger, should call for them, they should be protected.

Joseph Smith–History 1:51–54, 59.

JOSEPH PREVENTED FROM OBTAINING THE PLATES

OLIVER COWDERY

In 1823 . . . a man [Joseph Smith] with whom I have had the most intimate and personal acquaintance, for almost seven years, actually discovered by the vision of God, the plates from which the Book of Mormon, as much as it is disbelieved, was translated! Such is the case, though men rack their very brains to

15

invent falsehoods, and then waft them upon every breeze, to the contrary notwithstanding. . . .

[He arrived] at Cumorah, on the morning of the 22nd of September, 1823. . . .

After arriving at the repository, a little exertion in removing the soil from the edges of the top of the box, and a light pry, brought to his natural vision its contents. . . .

On attempting to take possession of the record, a shock was produced upon his system, by an invisible power, which deprived him, in a measure, of his natural strength. He desisted for an instant, and then made another attempt, but was more sensibly shocked than before. What was the occasion of this he knew not—there was a pure unsullied record, as has been described. . . . He therefore made a third attempt with an increased exertion, when his strength failed him more than at either of the former times, and without premeditating he exclaimed, "Why can I not obtain this book?"

"Because you have not kept the commandments of the Lord," answered a voice, within a seeming short distance. He looked and to his astonishment there stood the angel who had previously given him the directions concerning this matter. In an instant, all the former instructions, the great intelligence concerning Israel and the last days were brought to his mind; he thought of the time when his heart was fervently engaged in prayer to the Lord, when his spirit was contrite, and when this holy messenger from the skies unfolded the wonderful things connected with this record. He had come, to be sure, and found the word of the angel fulfilled concerning the reality of the record, but he had failed to remember the great end for which they had been kept, and in consequence could not have power to take them into his possession and bear them away.

At that instant he looked to the Lord in prayer, and as he prayed, darkness began to disperse from his mind and his soul was lit up as it was the evening before, and he was filled with the Holy

Spirit; and again did the Lord manifest His condescension and mercy; the heavens were opened and the glory of the Lord shone around about and rested upon him. While thus he stood gazing and admiring, the angel said, "Look!" and as he thus spake he beheld the prince of darkness, surrounded by his innumerable train of associates. All this passed before him, and the heavenly messenger said, "All this is shown, the good and the evil, the holy and the impure, the glory of God and the power of darkness, that ye may know hereafter the two powers and never be influenced or overcome by that wicked one. Behold, whatever entices and leads to good and to do good, is of God, and whatever does not is of that wicked one: it is he that fills the hearts of men with evil, to walk in darkness and blaspheme God; and you may learn from henceforth, that his ways are to destruction, but the way of holiness is peace and rest."

Francis W. Kirkham, *A New Witness for Christ in America,* 3rd ed. (Independence, Mo.: Zion's Printing and Publishing Co., 1951), pp. 95, 97–99.

"THE HILL OPENED"

BRIGHAM YOUNG

I lived right in the country where the plates were found from which the Book of Mormon was translated, and I know a great many things pertaining to that country. I believe I will take the liberty to tell you of another circumstance that will be as marvelous as anything can be. This is an incident in the life of Oliver Cowdery, but he did not take the liberty of telling such things in meeting as I take. I tell these things to you, and I have a motive for doing so. I want to carry them to the ears of my brethren and sisters, and to the children also, that they may grow to an understanding of some things that seem to be entirely hidden from the human family.

Oliver Cowdery went with the Prophet Joseph when he deposited these plates. Joseph did not translate all of the plates; there was a portion of them sealed, which you can learn from the Book of Doctrine and Covenants. When Joseph got the plates, the angel instructed him to carry them back to the hill Cumorah, which he did. Oliver says that when Joseph and Oliver went there, the hill opened, and they walked into a cave, in which there was a large and spacious room. He says he did not think, at the time, whether they had the light of the sun or artificial light; but that it was just as light as day. They laid the plates on a table; it was a large table that stood in the room. Under this table there was a pile of plates as much as two feet high, and there were altogether in this room more plates than probably many wagon loads; they were piled up in the corners and along the walls. The first time they went there the sword of Laban hung upon the wall; but when they went again it had been taken down and laid upon the table across the gold plates; it was unsheathed, and on it was written these words: "This sword will never be sheathed again until the kingdoms of this world become the kingdom of our God and his Christ." I tell you this as coming not only from Oliver Cowdery, but others who were familiar with it.

Journal of Discourses, 26 vols. (London: Latter-day Saints' Book Depot, 1854–86), 19:38.

"MINE EYES HAVE BEHELD"

JOSEPH SMITH

Not many days after the above commandment [Doctrine and Covenants section 17] was given, we four, viz., Martin Harris, David Whitmer, Oliver Cowdery and myself, agreed to retire into the woods, and try to obtain, by fervent and humble prayer, the fulfilment of the promises given in the above revelation—that they should have a view of the plates. We accordingly made choice of a piece of woods convenient to Mr. Whitmer's house, to which we retired, and having knelt down, we began to pray in much faith to Almighty God to bestow upon us a realization of these promises.

According to previous arrangement, I commenced by vocal prayer to our Heavenly Father, and was followed by each of the others in succession. We did not at the first trial, however, obtain any answer or manifestation of divine favor in our behalf. We again observed the same order of prayer, each calling on and praying fervently to God in rotation, but with the same result as before.

Upon this, our second failure, Martin Harris proposed that he should withdraw himself from us, believing, as he expressed himself, that his presence was the cause of our not obtaining what we wished for. He accordingly withdrew from us, and we knelt down again, and had not been many minutes engaged in prayer, when presently we beheld a light above us in the air, of exceeding brightness; and behold, an angel stood before us. In his hands he held the plates which we had been praying for these to have a view of. He turned over the leaves one by one, so that we could see them, and discern the engravings thereon distinctly. He then addressed himself to David Whitmer, and said, "David, blessed is the Lord, and he that keeps His commandments;" when, immediately afterwards, we heard a voice from out of the bright light above us, saying, "These plates have been revealed by the power of God, and they have been translated by the power of God. The translation of them which you have seen is correct, and I command you to bear record of what you now see and hear."

I now left David and Oliver, and went in pursuit of Martin Harris, whom I found at a considerable distance, fervently engaged in prayer. He soon told me, however, that he had not yet prevailed with the Lord, and earnestly requested me to join him in prayer, that he also might realize the same blessings which we had just received. We accordingly joined in prayer, and ultimately obtained our desires, for before we had yet finished, the same vision was opened to our view, at least it was again opened to me, and I once more beheld and heard the same things; whilst at the same moment, Martin Harris cried out, apparently in an ecstasy of joy, "'Tis enough; 'tis enough; mine eyes have beheld; mine eyes have beheld;" and jumping up, he shouted, "Hosanna," blessing God, and otherwise rejoiced exceedingly.

Joseph Smith, *History of The Church of Jesus Christ of Latter-day Saints,* 7 vols., 2d ed. rev., edited by B. H. Roberts (Salt Lake City: The Church of Jesus Christ of Latter-day Saints, 1932–51), 1:54–55.

"THE ANGEL
SHOWED US THE PLATES"

⌒

DAVID WHITMER

It was in June, 1829—the latter part of the month, and the eight witnesses saw them [the golden plates], I think, the next day or the day after (i.e., one or two days after). Joseph showed them the plates himself, but the angel showed us (the three witnesses) the plates, as I suppose to fulfill the words of the book itself. Martin Harris was not with us at this time; he obtained a view of them afterwards (the same day). Joseph, Oliver and myself were together when I saw them. We not only saw the plates of the Book of Mormon but also the brass plates, the plates of the Book of Ether, the plates containing the records of the wickedness and secret combinations of the people of the world down to the time of their being engraved, and many other plates. The fact is, it was just as though Joseph, Oliver and I were sitting just here on a log, when we were overshadowed by a light. It was not like the light of the sun nor like that of a fire, but more glorious and beautiful. It extended away round us, I cannot tell how far, but in the midst of this light about as far off as he sits (pointing to John C. Whitmer, sitting a few feet from him), there appeared as it were, a table with many records or plates upon it, besides the plates of the Book of Mormon, also the Sword of Laban, the Directors—i.e., the ball which Lehi had—and the Interpreters. I saw them just as plain as I see this bed (striking the bed beside him with his hand), and I heard the voice of the Lord, as distinctly as I ever heard anything in my life, declaring that the

records of the plates of the Book of Mormon were translated by
the gift and power of God.

Millennial Star 40:771–72.

GUARDING THE PLATES

LUCY MACK SMITH

My husband soon learned that ten or twelve men were
clubbed together, with one Willard Chase, a Methodist
class leader, at their head, and what was still more
ridiculous, they had sent sixty or seventy miles for a certain con-
jurer to come and divine the place where the plates were secreted.

We supposed that Joseph had taken the plates and hid them
somewhere, and we were apprehensive that our enemies might
discover their place of deposit. Accordingly, the next morning
after hearing of their plans, my husband concluded to go among
the neighbors to see what he could learn with regard to the plans
of the adverse party. The first house he came to he found the conjuror and Willard Chase, together with the rest of the clan.
Making an errand, he went in and sat down near the door, leaving it a little ajar in order to overhear their conversation. They
stood in the yard near the door and were devising plans to find
"Joe Smith's gold Bible," as they expressed themselves. The con-

juror seemed much animated although he had traveled sixty miles the day and night previous.

Presently the woman of the house, becoming uneasy at the exposures they were making, stepped through a back door into the yard and called to her husband, in a suppressed tone, but loud enough to be heard distinctly by Mr. Smith, "Sam, Sam, you are cutting your own throat." At this the conjuror bawled out at the top of his voice, "I am not afraid of anybody—we will have them plates in spite of Joe Smith or all the devils in hell."

When the woman came in again, Mr. Smith laid aside the newspaper he had been holding in his hand and remarked, "I believe I have not time to finish reading the paper now." He then left the house and returned home.

Mr. Smith, on returning home, asked Emma if she knew whether Joseph had taken the plates from their place of deposit, or if she was able to tell where they were. She said she could not tell where they were, or whether they were removed from their place. My husband then related what he had both seen and heard.

Upon this, Emma said that she did not know what to do, but she supposed if Joseph was to get the Record, he *would* get it and that they would not be able to prevent him.

"Yes," replied Mr. Smith, "he will, if he is watchful and obedient; but remember that for a small thing, Esau lost his birthright and his blessing. It may be so with Joseph."

"Well," said Emma, "if I had a horse I would go and see him."

Mr. Smith then said, "You shall have one in fifteen minutes, for although my team is gone, there is a stray on the place and I will send William to bring him immediately."

In a few minutes William brought up the horse with a large hickory withe around his neck (for it was according to law to put a withe around the neck of a stray before turning it into an enclosure), and Emma was soon under way for Macedon.

Joseph kept the Urim and Thummim constantly about his

person, by the use of which he could in a moment tell whether the plates were in any danger. Just before Emma rode up to Mr. Wells', Joseph, from an impression that he had had, came up out of the well in which he was laboring and met her not far from the house. Emma immediately informed him of what had transpired, whereupon he looked in the Urim and Thummim and saw that the Record was as yet safe; nevertheless, he concluded to return with his wife as something might take place that would render it necessary for him to be at home where he could take care of it.

He then told Mrs. Wells that business at home rendered it necessary for him to return. To this she did not agree at first, but finally consented. She then sent a boy for a horse, which Joseph mounted in his linen frock, and with his wife by his side on her horse decorated as before with a hickory withe around his neck, he rode through the village of Palmyra, which was on the way home.

On arriving at home he found his father pacing the ground near his door in great anxiety of mind. Joseph spoke to him, saying, "Father, there is no danger—all is perfectly safe—there is no cause of alarm."

When he had taken a little refreshment, he sent Carlos, my youngest son, to his brother Hyrum's, to have him come up immediately as he desired to see him. When he came, Joseph requested him to get a chest, having a good lock and key, and to have it there by the time he (Joseph) should return. And after giving these instructions, Joseph started for the plates.

The plates were secreted about three miles from home, in the following manner: Finding an old birch log much decayed, excepting the bark, which was in a measure sound, he took his pocket knife and cut the bark with some care, then turned it back and made a hole of sufficient size to receive the plates, and, laying them in the cavity thus formed, he replaced the bark; after which he laid across the log, in several places, some old stuff that happened to lay near, in order to conceal as much as possible the place in which they were deposited.

Joseph, on coming to them, took them from their secret place, and, wrapping them in his linen frock, placed them under his arm and started for home.

After proceeding a short distance, he thought it would be more safe to leave the road and go through the woods. Traveling some distance after he left the road, he came to a large windfall, and as he was jumping over a log, a man sprang up from behind it and gave him a heavy blow with a gun. Joseph turned around and knocked him down, then ran at the top of his speed. About half a mile farther he was attacked again in the same manner as before; he knocked this man down in like manner as the former and ran on again; and before he reached home he was assaulted the third time. In striking the last one, he dislocated his thumb, which, however, he did not notice until he came within sight of the house, when he threw himself down in the corner of the fence in order to recover his breath. As soon as he was able, he arose and came to the house. He was still altogether speechless from fright and the fatigue of running.

After resting a few moments, he desired me to send Carlos for my husband, Mr. Knight, and his friend Stoal, and have them go immediately and see if they could find the men who had been pursuing him. And after Carlos had done this, he wished to have him sent to Hyrum's, to tell him to bring the chest.

I did as I was requested, and when Carlos arrived at Hyrum's, he found him at tea with two of his wife's sisters. Just as Hyrum was raising a cup to his mouth, Carlos touched his shoulder. Without waiting to hear one word from the child, he dropped the cup, sprang from the table, caught the chest, turned it upside down, and emptying its contents on the floor, left the house instantly with the chest on his shoulder.

The young ladies were greatly astonished at his singular

behavior and declared to his wife—who was then confined to her bed, her eldest daughter, Lovina, being but four days old—that he was certainly crazy.

His wife laughed heartily and replied, "Oh, not in the least; he has just thought of something which he has neglected; and it is just like him to fly off on a tangent when he thinks of anything in that way."

When the chest came, Joseph locked up the Record, then threw himself upon the bed and after resting a little, so that he could converse freely, he arose and went into the kitchen, where he related his recent adventure to his father, Mr. Knight, and Mr. Stoal, besides many others who had by this time collected, with the view of hearing something in regard to the strange circumstance which had taken place. He showed them his thumb, saying, "I must stop talking, father, and get you to put my thumb in place, for it is very painful."

I will here mention that my husband, Mr. Knight, and Mr. Stoal went in pursuit of those villains who had attempted Joseph's life, but were not able to find them.

Lucy Mack Smith, *History of Joseph Smith,* edited by Preston Nibley (Salt Lake City: Bookcraft, 1958), pp. 105–9.

A BARREL OF BEANS

PARLEY P. PRATT

The inhabitants of that vicinity [Palmyra, New York], having been informed that Mr. Smith had seen heavenly visions, and that he had discovered sacred records, began to ridicule and mock at those things. And after having obtained those sacred things, while proceeding home through the wilderness and fields, he was waylaid by two ruffians, who had secreted themselves for the purpose of robbing him of the records. One of them struck him with a club before he perceived them; but being a strong man, and large in stature, with great exertion he cleared himself from them, and ran towards home, being closely pursued until he came near his father's house, when his pursuers, for fear of being detected, turned and fled the other way.

Soon the news of his discoveries spread abroad throughout all those parts. False reports, misrepresentations, and base slanders flew as if upon the wings of the wind in every direction. The house was frequently beset by mobs and evil designing persons. Several times he was shot at and very narrowly escaped. Every device was used to get the plates away from him. And being continually in danger of his life, from a gang of abandoned wretches, he at length concluded to leave the place, and go to Pennsylvania and accordingly packed up his goods; putting the plates into a barrel of beans, and proceeded upon his journey.

He had not gone far before he was overtaken by an officer with a search warrant, who flattered himself with the idea that he should surely obtain the plates; after searching very diligently, he was sadly disappointed at not finding them. Mr. Smith then drove on; but before he got to his journey's end, he was again overtaken by an officer on the same business, and, after ransacking the wagon very carefully he went his way, as much chagrined as the first at not being able to discover the object of his search. Without any further molestation he pursued his journey until he came into the northern part of Pennsylvania, near the Susquehanna river, in which part his father-in-law resided.

Parley P. Pratt, *Key to the Science of Theology/A Voice of Warning,* Classics in Mormon Literature ed. (Salt Lake City: Deseret Book Co., 1978), p. 65.

"I CANNOT READ A SEALED BOOK"

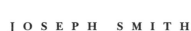

JOSEPH SMITH

Sometime in this month of February, the aforementioned Mr. Martin Harris came to our place, got the characters which I had drawn off the plates, and started with them to the city of New York. For what took place relative to him and the characters, I refer to his own account of the circumstances, as he related them to me after his return, which was as follows:

"I went to the city of New York, and presented the characters which had been translated, with the translation thereof, to Professor Charles Anthon, a gentleman celebrated for his literary attainments. Professor Anthon stated that the translation was correct, more so than any he had before seen translated from the Egyptian. I then showed him those which were not yet translated, and he said that they were Egyptian, Chaldaic, Assyriac, and Arabic; and he said they were true characters. He gave me a certificate, certifying to the people of Palmyra that they were true characters, and that the translation of such of them as had been translated was also correct. I took the certificate and put it into my pocket, and was just leaving the house, when Mr. Anthon called me back, and asked me how the young man found out that there were gold plates in the place where he found them. I answered that an angel of God had revealed it unto him.

"He then said to me, 'Let me see that certificate.' I accordingly took it out of my pocket and gave it to him, when he took it and tore it to pieces, saying that there was no such thing now as ministering of angels, and that if I would bring the plates to him he would translate them. I informed him that part of the plates were sealed, and that I was forbidden to bring them. He replied, 'I cannot read a sealed book.' I left him and went to Dr. Mitchell, who sanctioned what Professor Anthon had said respecting both the characters and the translation."

Joseph Smith–History 1:63–65.

THE LOST MANUSCRIPT

LUCY MACK SMITH

Martin Harris, having written some one hundred and sixteen pages for Joseph, asked permission of my son to carry the manuscript home with him, in order to let his wife read it, as he hoped it might have a salutary effect upon her feelings.

Joseph was willing to gratify his friend as far as he could consistently, and he inquired of the Lord to know if he might do as Martin Harris had requested, but was refused. With this, Mr. Harris was not altogether satisfied, and, at his urgent request, Joseph inquired again, but received a second refusal. Still, Martin Harris persisted as before, and Joseph applied again, but the last answer was not like the two former ones. In this, the Lord permitted Martin Harris to take the manuscript home with him, on condition that he would exhibit it to none, save five individuals whom he had mentioned, and who belonged to his own family.

Mr. Harris was delighted with this, and bound himself in a written covenant of the most solemn nature, that he would strictly comply with the injunctions which he had received. Which being done, he took the manuscript and went home.

Joseph did not suspect but that his friend would keep his faith, consequently, he gave himself no uneasiness with regard to the matter.

Shortly after Mr. Harris left, Joseph's wife became the mother of a son, which, however, remained with her but a short time before it was snatched from her arms by the hand of death. And the mother seemed, for some time, more like sinking with her

infant into the mansion of the dead, than remaining with her husband among the living. Her situation was such for two weeks, that
Joseph slept not an hour in undisturbed quiet. At the expiration
of this time she began to recover, but as Joseph's anxiety about her
began to subside, another cause of trouble forced itself upon his
mind. Mr. Harris had been absent nearly three weeks, and Joseph
had received no intelligence whatever from him, which was altogether aside of the arrangement when they separated. But Joseph
kept his feelings from his wife, fearing that if she became
acquainted with them it might agitate her too much.

In a few days, however, she mentioned the subject herself, and
desired her husband to go and get her mother to stay with her,
while he should repair to Palmyra, for the purpose of learning the
cause of Mr. Harris' absence as well as silence. At first Joseph
objected, but seeing her so cheerful, and so willing to have him
leave home, he finally consented.

He set out in the first stage that passed for Palmyra, and, when
he was left to himself, he began to contemplate the course which
Martin had taken, and the risk which he (Joseph) had run in letting the manuscript go out of his hands—for it could not be
obtained again, in case Martin had lost it through transgression,
except by the power of God, which was something Joseph could
hardly hope for—and that, by persisting in his entreaties to the
Lord, he had perhaps fallen into transgression, and thereby lost
the manuscript. When, I say, he began to contemplate these
things, they troubled his spirit, and his soul was moved with fearful
apprehensions. And, although he was now nearly worn out, sleep
fled from his eyes, neither had he any desire for food, for he felt
that he had done wrong, and how great his condemnation was he
did not know.

Only one passenger was in the stage besides himself: this man
observing Joseph's gloomy appearance, inquired the cause of
his affliction, and offered to assist him if his services would be

acceptable. Joseph thanked him for his kindness, and mentioned that he had been watching some time with a sick wife and child, that the child had died, and that his wife was still very low; but refrained from giving any further explanation. Nothing more passed between them upon this subject, until Joseph was about leaving the stage; at which time he remarked, that he still had twenty miles further to travel on foot that night, it being then about ten o'clock. To this the stranger objected, saying, "I have watched you since you first entered the stage, and I know that you have neither slept nor eaten since that time, and you shall not go on foot twenty miles alone this night; for, if you must go, I will be your company. Now tell me what can be the trouble that makes you thus dispirited?"

Joseph replied, about as before—that he had left his wife in so low a state of health, that he feared he should not find her alive when he returned; besides, he had buried his first and only child but a few days previous. This was true, though there was another trouble lying at his heart, which he dared not to mention.

The stranger then observed, "I feel to sympathize with you, and I fear that your constitution, which is evidently not strong, will be inadequate to support you. You will be in danger of falling asleep in the forrest, and of meeting with some awful disaster."

Joseph again thanked the gentleman for his kindness, and, leaving the stage, they proceeded together. When they reached our house it was nearly daylight. The stranger said he was under the necessity of leading Joseph the last four miles by the arm; for nature was too much exhausted to support him any longer, and he would fall asleep as he was walking along, every few minutes, towards the last of this distance.

On entering our house, the stranger remarked that he had brought our son through the forest, because he had insisted on coming, that he was sick, and needed rest, as well as refreshment, and that he ought to have some pepper tea to warm his stomach.

After thus directing us, relative to our son, he said, that when we had attended to Joseph he would thank us for a little breakfast for himself, as he was in a haste to be on his journey again.

When Joseph had taken a little nourishment, according to the directions of the stranger, he requested us to send immediately for Mr. Harris. This we did without delay. And when we had given the stranger his breakfast, we commenced preparing breakfast for the family; and we supposed that Mr. Harris would be there, as soon as it was ready, to eat with us, for he generally came in such haste when he was sent for. At eight o'clock we set the victuals on the table, as we were expecting him every moment. We waited till nine, and he came not—till ten, and he was not there—till eleven, still he did not make his appearance. But at half past twelve we saw him walking with a slow and measured tread towards the house, his eyes fixed thoughtfully upon the ground. On coming to the gate, he stopped, instead of passing through, and got upon the fence, and sat there some time with his hat drawn over his eyes. At length he entered the house. Soon after which we sat down to the table, Mr. Harris with the rest. He took up his knife and fork as if he were going to use them, but immediately dropped them. Hyrum, observing this, said "Martin, why do you not eat; are you sick?" Upon which Mr. Harris pressed his hands upon his temples, and cried out in a tone of deep anguish, "Oh, I have lost my soul! I have lost my soul!"

Joseph who had not expressed his fears till now, sprang from the table, exclaiming, "Martin, have you lost that manuscript? Have you broken your oath, and brought down condemnation upon my head as well as your own?"

"Yes; it is gone," replied Martin, "and I know not where."

"Oh, my God!" said Joseph, clinching his hands. "All is lost! all is lost! What shall I do? I have sinned—it is I who tempted the wrath of God. I should have been satisfied with the first answer which I received from the Lord; for he told me that it was not safe

33

to let the writing go out of my possession." He wept and groaned, and walked the floor continually.

At length he told Martin to go back and search again.

"No," said Martin, "it is all in vain; for I have ripped open beds and pillows; and I know it is not there."

"Then must I," said Joseph, "return with such a tale as this? I dare not do it. And how shall I appear before the Lord? Of what rebuke am I not worthy from the angel of the Most High?"

I besought him not to mourn so, for perhaps the Lord would forgive him, after a short season of humiliation and repentance. But what could I do to comfort him, when he saw all the family in the same situation of mind as himself; for sobs and groans, and the most bitter lamentations filled the house. However, Joseph was more distressed than the rest, as he better understood the consequences of disobedience. And he continued pacing back and forth, meantime weeping and grieving, until about sunset, when, by persuasion, he took a little nourishment.

The next morning, he set out for home. We parted with heavy hearts, for it now appeared that all which we had so fondly anticipated, and which had been the source of so much secret gratification, had in a moment fled, and fled forever.

Lucy Mack Smith, *History of Joseph Smith,* edited by Preston Nibley (Salt Lake City: Bookcraft, 1958), pp. 124–29.

"HE ASKED EMMA'S FORGIVENESS"

DAVID WHITMER

Joseph Smith] was a religious and straightforward man. He had to be; for he was illiterate and he could do nothing himself. He had to trust in God. He could not translate unless he was humble and possessed the right feelings towards everyone. To illustrate so you can see: One morning when he was getting ready to continue the translation, something went wrong about the house and he was put out about it. Something that Emma, his wife, had done. Oliver and I went upstairs and Joseph came up soon after to continue the translation but he could not do anything. He could not translate a single syllable. He went downstairs, out into the orchard, and made supplication to the Lord; was gone about an hour—came back to the house, and asked Emma's forgiveness and then came upstairs where we were and then the translation went on all right. He could do nothing save he was humble and faithful.

B. H. Roberts, *A Comprehensive History of The Church of Jesus Christ of Latter-day Saints,* 6 vols. (Salt Lake City: The Church of Jesus Christ of Latter-day Saints, 1930), 1:131.

"THEY SAW THREE
MEN AT WORK IN THE FIELD"

~~~

LUCY MACK SMITH

As Joseph was translating by means of the Urim and Thummim, he received instead of the words of the Book, a commandment to write a letter to a man by the name of David Whitmer, who lived in Waterloo, requesting him to come immediately with his team, and convey himself and Oliver to his own residence, as an evil-designing people were seeking to take away his (Joseph's) life, in order to prevent the work of God from going forth to the world. The letter was written and delivered, and was shown by Mr. Whitmer to his father, mother, brothers, and sisters, and their advice was asked in regard to the best course for him to take in relation to the matter.

His father reminded him that he had as much wheat sown upon the ground as he could harrow in two days, at least; besides this, he had a quantity of plaster of paris to spread, which must be done immediately, consequently he could not go, unless he could get a witness from God that it was absolutely necessary.

This suggestion pleased David, and he asked the Lord for a testimony concerning his going for Joseph, and was told by the voice of the Spirit to go as soon as his wheat was harrowed in. The next morning, David went to the field, and found that he had two heavy days' work before him. He then said to himself that, if he should be enabled, by any means, to do this work sooner than the same had ever been done on the farm before, he would receive it as an evidence, that it was the will of God, that he should do all in his power to assist Joseph Smith in the work in which he was engaged. He then fastened his horses to the harrow, and instead of dividing the field into what is, by farmers, usually termed lands, drove around the whole of it, continuing thus till noon, when, on stopping for dinner, he looked around, and discovered to his surprise, that he had harrowed in full half the wheat. After dinner he went on as before, and by evening he finished the whole two days' work.

His father, on going into the field the same evening, saw what had been done, and he exclaimed, "There must be an overruling hand in this, and I think you would better go down to Pennsylvania as soon as your plaster of paris is sown."

The next morning, David took a wooden measure under his arm and went out to sow the plaster, which he had left, two days previous, in heaps near his sister's house, but, on coming to the place, he discovered that it was gone! He then ran to his sister, and inquired of her if she knew what had become of it. Being surprised she said, "Why do you ask me? was it not all sown yesterday?"

"Not to my knowledge," answered David.

"I am astonished at that," replied his sister, "for the children came to me in the forenoon, and begged of me to go out and see the men sow plaster in the field, saying, that they never saw anybody sow plaster so fast in their lives. I accordingly went, and saw three men at work in the field, as the children said, but, supposing that you had hired some help, on account of your hurry, I went immediately into the house, and gave the subject no further attention."

David made considerable inquiry in regard to the matter, both among his relatives and neighbors, but was not able to learn who had done it. However, the family were convinced that there was an exertion of supernatural power connected with this strange occurrence.

Lucy Mack Smith, *History of Joseph Smith,* edited by Preston Nibley (Salt Lake City: Bookcraft, 1958), pp. 147–49.

"THE OLD MAN INSTANTLY DISAPPEARED"

⌒∼

DAVID WHITMER

I did not know what to do, I was pressed with my work. I had some twenty acres to plow, so I concluded I would finish plowing and then go [to assist Joseph Smith in the translation of the Book of Mormon]. I got up one morning to go to work as usual, and on going to the field, found between five and seven acres of my ground had been plowed during the night. I don't know who did it; but it was done just as I would have done it myself, and the plow was left standing in the furrow. This enabled me to start sooner.

When I arrived at Harmony, Joseph and Oliver were coming toward me, and met me some distance from the house. Oliver told me that Joseph had informed him when I started from home, where I had stopped the first night, how I read the sign at the tavern, where I stopped the next night, etc., and that I would be there that day before dinner, and this was why they had come out to meet me; all of which was exactly as Joseph had told Oliver, at which I was greatly astonished. When I was returning to Fayette, with Joseph and Oliver, all of us riding in the wagon, Oliver and I on an old-fashioned wooden spring seat and Joseph behind us—when traveling along in a clear open place, a very pleasant, nice-looking old man suddenly appeared by the side of our wagon and saluted us with, "good morning, it is very warm," at the same time wiping his face or forehead with his hand. We returned the salutation, and, by a sign from Joseph, I invited him to ride if he was going our way. But he said very pleasantly, "No, I am going to Cumorah." This name was something new to me, I did not know what Cumorah meant. We all gazed at him and at each other, and as I looked around enquiringly of Joseph, the old man instantly disappeared, so that I did not see him again. . . . He was, I should think, about five feet eight or nine inches tall and heavy set. . . . He was dressed in a suit of brown woolen clothes, his hair and beard were white. . . . I also remember that he had on his back a sort of knapsack with something in, shaped like a book. It was the messenger who had the plates, who had taken them from Joseph just prior to our starting from Harmony.

Soon after our arrival home, I saw something which led me to the belief that the plates were placed or concealed in my father's barn. I frankly asked Joseph if my supposition was right, and he told me it was. Some time after this, my mother was going to milk the cows, when she was met out near the yard by the same old man (judging by her description of him), who said to her: "You have been very faithful and diligent in your labors, but you are tired because of the increase in your toil; it is proper, therefore, that you should receive a witness that your faith may be strengthened." Thereupon he showed her the plates. My father and mother had a large family of their own, the addition to it therefore, of Joseph, his wife Emma and Oliver very greatly increased the toil and anxiety of my mother.

And although she had never complained she had sometimes felt that her labor was too much, or at least she was perhaps beginning to feel so. This circumstance, however, completely removed all such feelings and nerved her up for her increased responsibilities.

Andrew Jenson, *Latter-day Saint Biographical Encyclopedia*, 4 vols. (Salt Lake City: Andrew Jenson History Co., 1901), 1:267.

THE CONVERSION
OF PARLEY P. PRATT

PARLEY P. PRATT

My brother William, who journeyed to the West with me in my seventeenth year, had now been missing to the family for five years, and was supposed to be dead. About the time he disappeared and was lost sight of, he was known to leave the city of New York, where he had been employed, and to pass up the Hudson on a steamer. He was heard of no more; and, as a notice appeared in the papers of the same date that a young gentleman by the name of William Pratt was drowned in the Hudson, on his way up the river, our parents and the family had given him up for lost.

One morning, as I was absent from home on business, about two miles distant, I heard of him; and that he was then residing about ten miles from me. On hearing this I ran nearly the whole distance on foot, and in about two hours had him by the hand. He was much surprised, although he had heard of a man of my name living in the neighborhood; but could not believe it was me. We had each of us taken our chance amid the hardships and toils of a new country for years, and at last found ourselves together about six hundred miles from our starting point.

This was a joyful and unexpected meeting of two brothers. He immediately accompanied me home, and was introduced to my wife and our little farm in the wilderness, where we spent some days together. He admired my wife; but above all my farm. "Brother Parley," said he, "how have you done all this? When we

40

were last together you had no wife, no farm, no house, no orchard, and now you are here with everything smiling around you." I replied that hard work had accomplished it all. And, continued I, we are now about to leave this quiet home which we have toiled so hard to make, and perhaps, never see it again. "How so?" said he, with much surprise, and somewhat of disappointment. I then unfolded to him the gospel and prophecies as they had been opened to me, and told him that the spirit of these things had wrought so powerfully on my mind of late that I could not rest; that I could no longer be contented to dwell in quiet and retirement on my farm, while I had light to impart to mankind, of which I knew they were in a great measure ignorant. "But," said he, "if I had fifty acres of land, a comfortable house, a fine orchard, a beautiful garden, with meadow land, grain, and above all, such beautiful flowers and so valuable a housekeeper as you have, and all these things the work of our own hands, I am sure I would stay and enjoy the same while I lived; and the world might go on its own jog, and its own way, for all me. Besides, how are you to get your living? This is your all; you have toiled for years to obtain it, and why not now continue to enjoy it?" "William," said I, "I see plainly you know but little of my circumstances—of the changes which have taken place with me since we parted five years ago, nor how vastly wealthy I have become within that time. Why, sir, I have bank bills enough, on the very best institutions in the world, to sustain myself and family while we live."

"Indeed," said he, "well, I should like to see some of them; I hope they are genuine." "Certainly," I replied, "there is no doubt of that. They are true bills and founded on capital that will never fail, though heaven and earth should pass away. Of this I will convince you in a moment."

I then unlocked my treasury and drew from thence a large pocket book, full of promissory notes like the following: *"Whoever shall forsake father or mother, brethren or sisters, houses or lands, wife or children, for my sake and the gospel's, shall receive an hundred fold in this life, and in the world to come life everlasting." "If ye abide in me, and my words abide in you, you shall ask what you will in my name and I will give it you." "All things are possible to him that believeth."*

"Now, William," said I, "are these the words of Jesus Christ, or are they not?" "They certainly are," said he, "I always believed the New Testament."

"Then you admit they are genuine bills?"

"I do."

"Is the signer able to meet his engagements?"

"He certainly is."

"Is he willing?"

"He is."

"Well, then, I am going to fulfil the conditions to the letter on my part. I feel called upon by the Holy Ghost to forsake my house and home for the gospel's sake; and I will do it, placing both feet firm on these promises with nothing else to rely upon."

"If I sink, they are false."

"If I am sustained, they are true. I will put them to the test. Experiment shall now establish the truth of Christ's promises, or the truth of infidelity."

"Well," said he, "try it, if you will; but, for my part, although I always believed the Bible, I would not dare believe it *literally*, and really stand upon its promises, with no other prop."

We parted. He to his business, I to my preparations for a mission which should only end with my life.

In August, 1830, I had closed my business, completed my arrangements, and we bid adieu to our wilderness home and never saw it afterwards.

On settling up, at a great sacrifice of property, we had about ten dollars left in cash. With this small sum, we launched forth into the wide world, determining first to visit our native place, on our mission, and then such other places as I might be led to by the Holy Spirit. . . .

Arriving at Rochester, I informed my wife that, notwithstanding our [canal boat] passage being paid through the whole distance [to Albany, New York], yet I must leave the boat and her to pursue her passage to our friends; while I would stop awhile in this region. Why, I did not know; but so it was plainly manifest by the Spirit to me. I said to her, "we part for a season; go and visit our friends in our native place; I will come soon, but how soon I know not; for I have a work to do in this region of country, and what it is, or how long it will take to perform it, I know not; but I will come when it is performed."

My wife would have objected to this; but she had seen the hand of God so plainly manifest in His dealings with me many times, that she dare not oppose the things manifest to me by His spirit. She, therefore, consented; and I accompanied her as far as Newark, a small town upwards of 100 miles from Buffalo, and then took leave of her, and of the boat.

It was early in the morning, just at the dawn of day, I walked ten miles into the country, and stopped to breakfast with a Mr. Wells. I proposed to preach in the evening. Mr. Wells readily accompanied me through the neighborhood to visit the people, and circulate the appointment.

We visited an old Baptist deacon by the name of Hamlin. After hearing of our appointment for evening, he began to tell of a *book*, a STRANGE BOOK, a VERY STRANGE BOOK! in his possession, which had been just published. This book, he said, purported to have been originally written on plates either of gold or brass, by a branch of the tribes of Israel; and to have been discovered and translated by a young man near Palmyra, in the State of New York, by the aid of visions, or the ministry of angels. I inquired of him how or where the book was to be obtained. He promised me the perusal of it, at his house the next day, if I would call. I felt a strange interest in the book. . . . Next morning I called at his house, where, for the first time, my eyes beheld the "BOOK OF MORMON"—that book of books—that record which reveals the antiquities of the *"New World"* back to the remotest ages, and which unfolds the destiny of its people and the world for all time to come; that Book which contains the fulness of the gospel of a crucified and risen Redeemer;—that Book which reveals a lost remnant of Joseph, and which was the principal means, in the hands of God, of directing the entire course of my future life.

I opened it with eagerness, and read its title page. I then read the testimony of several witnesses in relation to the manner of its being found and translated. After this I commenced its contents by course. I read all day; eating was a burden, I had no desire for food; sleep was a burden when the night came, for I preferred reading to sleep.

As I read, the spirit of the Lord was upon me, and I knew and comprehended that the book was true, as plainly and manifestly as a man comprehends and knows that he exists. My joy was now full, as it were, and I rejoiced sufficiently to more than pay me for all the sorrows, sacrifices and toils of my life. I soon determined to see the young man who had been the instrument of its discovery and translation.

I accordingly visited the village of Palmyra, and inquired for the residence of Mr. Joseph Smith. I found it some two or three miles from the village. As I approached the house at the close of the day I overtook a man who was driving some cows, and inquired of him for Mr. Joseph Smith, the translator of the *"Book of Mormon."* He informed me that he now resided in Pennsylvania; some one hundred miles distant. I inquired for his father, or for any of the family. He told me that his father had gone [on] a journey; but that his residence was a small house just before me; and, said he, I am his brother. It was Mr. Hyrum Smith. I informed him of the interest I felt in the Book, and of my desire to learn more about it. He welcomed me to his house, and we spent the night together; for neither of us felt disposed to sleep. We conversed most of the night, during which I unfolded to him much of my experience in my search after truth, and my success so far; together with that which I felt was lacking, viz: a commissioned priesthood, or apostleship to minister in the ordinances of God.

He also unfolded to me the particulars of the discovery of the Book; its translation; the rise of the Church of Latter-day Saints, and the commission of his brother Joseph, and others, by revelation and the ministering of angels, by which the apostleship and authority had been again restored to the earth. After duly weighing the whole matter in my mind I saw clearly that these things were true; and that myself and the whole world were without baptism, and without the ministry and ordinances of God; and that the whole world had been in this condition since the days that inspiration and revelation had ceased—in short, that this was a *new dispensation* or *commission,* in fulfillment of prophecy, and for the restoration of Israel, and to prepare the way before the second coming of the Lord.

In the morning I was compelled to take leave of this worthy man and his family—as I had to hasten back a distance of thirty miles, on foot, to fulfil an appointment in the evening. As we parted he kindly presented me with a copy of the Book of Mormon. I had not yet completed its perusal, and was glad indeed to possess a copy of my own. I travelled on a few miles, and, stopping to rest, I commenced again to read the book. To my great joy I found that Jesus Christ, in his glorified resurrected body, had appeared to the remnant of Joseph on the continent of America, soon after his resurrection and ascension into heaven; and that he also administered, in person, to the ten lost tribes; and that through his personal ministry in these countries his gospel was revealed and written in countries and among nations entirely unknown to the Jewish apostles.

Thus revealed, written, handed down and preserved, till revealed in this age by the angels of God, it had, of course, escaped the corruptions of the great and abominable church; and been preserved in purity.

This discovery greatly enlarged my heart, and filled my soul with joy and gladness. I esteemed the Book, or the information contained in it, more than all the riches of the world. Yes; I verily believe that I would not at that time have exchanged the knowledge I then possessed, for a legal title to all the beautiful farms, houses, villages and property which passed in review before me, on my journey through one of the most flourishing settlements of western New York.

Parley P. Pratt, *Autobiography of Parley P. Pratt,* edited by Parley P. Pratt Jr., Classics in Mormon Literature ed. (Salt Lake City: Deseret Book Co., 1985), pp. 16–22.

A MOB TRIED
TO PREVENT THEIR BAPTISMS

JOSEPH SMITH

Immediately after conference I returned to my own house, and from thence, accompanied by my wife, Oliver Cowdery, John Whitmer and David Whitmer, went again on a visit to Mr. Knight, of Colesville, Broome county. We found a number in the neighborhood still believing, and now anxious to be baptized. We appointed a meeting for the Sabbath, and on the afternoon of Saturday we erected a dam across a stream of water, which was convenient, for the purpose of there attending to the ordinance of baptism; but during the night a mob collected and tore down our dam, which hindered us from attending to the baptism on the Sabbath. We afterward found out that this mob had been instigated to this act of molestation by certain sectarian priests of the neighborhood, who began to consider their craft in danger, and took this plan to stop the progress of the truth; and the sequel will show how determinedly they prosecuted their opposition, as well as to how little purpose in the end. The Sabbath arrived, and we held our meeting. Oliver Cowdery preached, and others of us bore testimony to the truth of the Book of Mormon, the doctrine of repentance, baptism for the remission of sins, and laying on of hands for the gift of the Holy Ghost, etc. Amongst our audience were those who had torn down our dam, and who seemed desirous to give us trouble, but did not until after the meeting was dismissed, when they immediately commenced talking to those whom they considered our friends, and tried to turn them against us and our doctrines.

Joseph Smith, *History of The Church of Jesus Christ of Latter-day Saints,* 7 vols., 2d ed. rev., edited by B. H. Roberts (Salt Lake City: The Church of Jesus Christ of Latter-day Saints, 1932–51), 1:86–87.

TARRED AND FEATHERED

JOSEPH SMITH

On the 24th of March [1832], the twins . . . which had been sick of the measles for some time, caused us to be broken of our rest in taking care of them, especially my wife. In the evening I told her she had better retire to rest with one of the children, and I would watch with the sicker child. In the night she told me I had better lie down on the trundle bed, and I did so, and was soon after awakened by her screaming murder, when I found myself going out of the door, in the hands of about a dozen men; some of whose hands were in my hair, and some had hold of my shirt, drawers and limbs. The foot of the trundle bed was towards the door, leaving only room enough for the door to swing open. My wife heard a gentle tapping on the windows which she then took no particular notice of (but which was unquestionably designed for ascertaining whether or not we were all asleep), and soon after the mob burst open the door and surrounded the bed in an instant, and, as I said, the first I knew I was going out of the door in the hands of an infuriated mob. I made a desperate struggle, as I was forced out, to extricate myself, but only cleared one leg, with which I made a pass at one man, and he fell on the door steps. I was immediately overpowered again; and they swore by G—, they would kill me if I did not be still, which quieted me. As they passed around the house with me, the fellow that I kicked came to me and thrust his hand, all covered with blood, into my face and with an exulting hoarse laugh, muttered: "*Ge, gee, G—d—ye, I'll fix ye.*"

They then seized me by the throat and held on till I lost my breath. After I came to, as they passed along with me, about thirty rods from the house, I saw Elder Rigdon stretched out on the ground, whither they had dragged him by his heels. I supposed he was dead. I began to plead with them, saying, "You will have mercy and spare my life, I hope." To which they replied, "G—d—ye, call on yer God for help, we'll show ye no mercy;" and the people began to show themselves in every direction; one coming from the orchard had a plank; and I expected they would kill me, and carry me off on the plank. They then turned to the right, and went on about thirty rods further; about sixty rods from the house, and thirty from where I saw Elder Rigdon, into the meadow, where they stopped, and one said, "Simonds, Simonds," (meaning, I supposed, Simonds Ryder,) "pull up his drawers, pull up his drawers, he will take cold." Another replied: "*Ain't ye going to kill 'im? ain't ye going to kill 'im?*" when a group of mobbers collected a little way off, and said: "Simonds, Simonds, come here;" and "Simonds" charged those who had hold of me to keep me from touching the ground (as they had done all the time), lest I should get a spring upon them. They held a council, and as I could occasionally over-hear a word, I supposed it was to know whether or not it was best to kill me. They returned after a while, when I learned that they had concluded not to kill me, but to beat and scratch me well, tear off my shirt and drawers, and leave me naked. One cried, "Simonds, Simonds, *where's the tar bucket?*" "I don't know," answered one, "*where 'tis, Eli's left it.*" They ran back and fetched the bucket of tar, when one exclaimed, with an oath, "*Let us tar up his mouth;*" and they tried to force the tar-paddle into my mouth; I twisted my head around, so that they could not; and they cried out, "*G—d—ye, hold up yer head and let us giv ye some tar.*" They then tried to force a vial into my mouth, and broke it in my teeth. All my clothes were torn off me except my shirt collar; and one man fell on me and scratched my body with his nails like a mad cat, and then muttered out: "*G—d—ye, that's the way the Holy Ghost falls on folks!*"

They then left me, and I attempted to rise, but fell again; I pulled the tar away from my lips, so that I could breathe more freely, and after a while I began to recover, and raised myself up, whereupon I saw two lights. I made my way towards one of them, and found it was Father Johnson's. When I came to the door I was naked, and the tar made me look as if I were covered with blood, and when my wife saw me she thought I was all crushed to pieces, and fainted. During the affray abroad, the sisters of the neighborhood had collected at my room. I called for a blanket, they threw me one and shut the door; I wrapped it around me and went in. . . .

My friends spent the night in scraping and removing the tar, and washing and cleansing my body; so that by morning I was ready to be clothed again. This being the Sabbath morning, the people assembled for meeting at the usual hour of worship, and among them came also the mobbers; viz.: Simonds Ryder, a Campbellite preacher and leader of the mob; one McClentic, who had his hands in my hair; one Streeter, son of a Campbellite minister; and Felatiah Allen, Esq., who gave the mob a barrel of whiskey to raise their spirits. Besides these named, there were many others in the mob. With my flesh all scarified and defaced, I preached to the congregation as usual, and in the afternoon of the same day baptized three individuals.

The next morning I went to see Elder Rigdon, and found him crazy, and his head highly inflamed, for they had dragged him by his heels, and those, too, so high from the ground that he could not raise his head from the rough, frozen surface, which lacerated it exceedingly; . . . he continued delirious some days. The feathers which were used with the tar on this occasion, the mob took out of Elder Rigdon's house. After they had seized him, and dragged him out, one of the banditti returned to get some pillows; when the women shut him in and kept him a prisoner some time.

During the mobbing one of the twins contracted a severe cold, continued to grow worse until Friday, and then died.

Joseph Smith, *History of The Church of Jesus Christ of Latter-day Saints,* 7 vols., 2d ed. rev., edited by B. H. Roberts (Salt Lake City: The Church of Jesus Christ of Latter-day Saints, 1932–51), 1:261–65.

WORD OF WISDOM RECEIVED

BRIGHAM YOUNG

I think I am as well acquainted with the circumstances which led to the giving of the Word of Wisdom as any man in the Church, although I was not present at the time to witness them. The first school of the prophets was held in a small room situated over the Prophet Joseph's kitchen, in a house which belonged to Bishop Whitney, and which was attached to his store, which store probably might be about fifteen feet square. In the rear of this building was a kitchen, probably ten by fourteen feet, containing rooms and pantries. Over this kitchen was situated the room in which the Prophet received revelations and in which he instructed his brethren. The brethren came to that place for hundreds of miles to attend school in a little room probably no larger than eleven by fourteen. When they assembled together in this room after breakfast, the first they did was to light their pipes, and, while smoking, talk about the great things of the kingdom, and spit all over the room, and as soon as the pipe was out of their mouths a large chew of tobacco would then be taken. Often when the Prophet entered the room to give the school instructions he would find himself in a cloud of tobacco smoke. This, and the complaints of his wife at having to clean so filthy a floor, made the Prophet think upon the matter, and he inquired of the Lord relating to the conduct of the Elders in using tobacco, and the revelation known as the Word of Wisdom was the result of his inquiry.

Journal of Discourses, 26 vols. (London: Latter-day Saints' Book Depot, 1854–86), 12:158.

"The Heavens
Were Opened upon Us"

JOSEPH SMITH

About three o'clock, P.M., I dismissed the school, and the Presidency retired to the attic story of the printing office, where we attended the ordinance of washing our bodies in pure water. We also perfumed our bodies and our heads in the name of the Lord.

At early candle-light I met with the Presidency at the west school room, in the Temple, to attend to the ordinance of anointing our heads with holy oil; also the Councils of Kirtland and Zion met in the two adjoining rooms, and waited in prayer while we attended to the ordinance.

I took the oil in my left hand, Father Smith being seated before me, and the remainder of the Presidency encircled him round about. We then stretched our right hands towards heaven, and blessed the oil, and consecrated it in the name of Jesus Christ.

We then laid our hands upon our aged Father Smith, and invoked the blessings of heaven. I then anointed his head with the consecrated oil, and sealed many blessings upon him. The Presidency then in turn laid their hands upon his head, beginning at the oldest, until they had all laid their hands upon him, and pronounced such blessings upon his head, as the Lord put into their hearts, all blessing him to be our Patriarch, to anoint our heads, and attend to all duties that pertain to that office. The Presidency then took the seat in their turn, according to their age, beginning at the oldest, and received their anointing and blessing under the hands of Father Smith. And in my turn, my father anointed my head, and sealed upon me the blessings of Moses, to lead Israel in the latter days, even as Moses led him in days of old; also the blessings of Abraham, Isaac and Jacob. All of the Presidency laid their hands upon me, and pronounced upon my head many prophecies and blessings, many of which I shall not notice at this time. But as Paul said, so say I, let us come to visions and revelations.

The heavens were opened upon us, and I beheld the celestial kingdom of God, and the glory thereof, whether in the body or out I cannot tell. I saw the transcendent beauty of the gate through which the heirs of that kingdom will enter, which was like unto circling flames of fire; also the blazing throne of God, whereon was seated the Father and the Son. I saw the beautiful streets of that kingdom, which had the appearance of being paved with gold. I saw Fathers Adam and Abraham, and my father and mother, my brother, Alvin, that has long since slept, and marvelled how it was that he had obtained an inheritance in that kingdom, seeing that he had departed this life before the Lord had set His hand to gather Israel the second time, and had not been baptized for the remission of sins.

Joseph Smith, *History of The Church of Jesus Christ of Latter-day Saints,* 7 vols., 2d ed. rev., edited by B. H. Roberts (Salt Lake City: The Church of Jesus Christ of Latter-day Saints, 1932–51), 2:379–80.

"THE ADVERSARY
OF SOULS BEGAN TO RAGE"

ORSON F. WHITNEY

Saturday evening," says Heber C. Kimball, "it was agreed that I should go forward and baptize, the next morning, in the river Ribble, which runs through Preston.

"By this time the adversary of souls began to rage, and he felt determined to destroy us before we had fully established the kingdom of God in that land, and the next morning I witnessed a scene of satanic power and influence which I shall never forget.

"Sunday, July 30th (1837), about daybreak, Elder Isaac Russell (who had been appointed to preach on the obelisk in Preston Square, that day), who slept with Elder Richards in Wilfred Street, came up to the third story, where Elder Hyde and myself were sleeping, and called out, 'Brother Kimball, I want you should get up and pray for me that I may be delivered from the evil spirits that are tormenting me to such a degree that I feel I cannot live long, unless I obtain relief.'

"I had been sleeping on the back of the bed. I immediately arose, slipped off at the foot of the bed, and passed around to where he was. Elder Hyde threw his feet out, and sat up in the bed, and we laid hands on him, I being mouth, and prayed that the Lord would have mercy on him, and rebuked the devil.

"While thus engaged, I was struck with great force by some invisible power, and fell senseless on the floor. The first thing I recollected was being supported by Elders Hyde and Richards, who were praying for me; Elder Richards having followed Russell up to my room. Elder Hyde and Richards then assisted me to get on the bed, but my agony was so great I could not endure it, and I arose, bowed my knees and prayed. I then arose and sat up on the bed, when a vision was opened to our minds, and we could distinctly see the evil spirits, who foamed and gnashed their teeth at us. We gazed upon them about an hour and a half (by Willard's watch). We were not looking towards the window, but towards the wall. Space appeared before us, and we saw the devils coming in legions, with their leaders, who came within a few feet of us. They came towards us like armies rushing to battle. They appeared to be men of full stature, possessing every form and feature of men in the flesh, who were angry and desperate; and I shall never forget the vindictive malignity depicted on their countenances as they looked me in the eye; and any attempt to paint the scene which then presented itself, or portray their malice and enmity, would be vain. I perspired exceedingly, my clothes becoming as wet as if I had been taken out of the river. I felt excessive pain, and was in the greatest distress for some time. I cannot even look back on the scene without feelings of horror; yet by it I learned the power of the adversary, his enmity against the servants of God, and got some understanding of the invisible world. We distinctly heard those spirits talk and express their wrath and hellish designs against us. However, the Lord delivered us from them, and blessed us exceedingly that day."

Elder Hyde's supplemental description of that fearful scene is as follows, taken from a letter addressed to President Kimball:

"Every circumstance that occurred at that scene of devils is just as fresh in my recollection at this moment as it was at the moment of its occurrence, and will ever remain so. After you were overcome by them and had fallen, their awful rush upon me with knives, threats, imprecations and hellish grins, amply convinced me that they were no friends of mine. While you were apparently senseless and lifeless on the floor and upon the bed (after we had laid you there), I stood between you and the devils and fought them and contended with them face to face, until they began to diminish in number and to retreat from the room. The last imp that left turned round to me as he was going out and said, as if to apologize, and appease my determined opposition to them, 'I never said anything against you!' I replied to him thus: 'It matters not to me whether you have or have not; you are a liar from the beginning! In the name of Jesus Christ, depart!' He immediately left, and the room was clear. That closed the scene of devils for that time."

Years later, narrating the experience of that awful morning to the Prophet Joseph, Heber asked him what it all meant, and whether there was anything wrong with him that he should have such a manifestation.

"No, Brother Heber," he replied, "at that time you were nigh unto the Lord; there was only a veil between you and Him, but you could not see Him. When I heard of it, it gave me great joy, for I then knew that the work of God had taken root in that land. It was this that caused the devil to make a struggle to kill you."

Orson F. Whitney, *Life of Heber C. Kimball*, 2d ed. (Salt Lake City: Stevens & Wallis, 1945), pp. 129–32.

BUILDING THE KIRTLAND TEMPLE

HEBER C. KIMBALL

Our women were engaged in knitting and spinning, in order to clothe those who were laboring at the building; and the Lord only knows the scenes of poverty, tribulation and distress which we passed through to accomplish it. My wife had toiled all summer in lending her aid towards its accomplishment. She took a hundred pounds of wool to spin on shares, which, with the assistance of a girl, she spun, in order to furnish clothing for those engaged in building the temple; and although she had the privilege of keeping half the quantity of wool for herself, as a recompense for her labor, she did not reserve even so much as would make a pair of stockings, but gave it for those who were laboring at the house of the Lord. She spun and wove, and got the cloth dressed and cut and made up into garments, and gave them to the laborers on the temple. Almost all the sisters in Kirtland labored in knitting, sewing, spinning, etc., for the same purpose; while we went up to Missouri to endeavor to reinstate our brethren on the lands from which they had been driven.

Elder Rigdon, when addressing the brethren upon the importance of building this house, spake to this effect: That we should use every effort to accomplish this building by the time appointed; if we did the Lord would accept it at our hands; and on it depends the salvation of the Church, and also of the world.

Looking at the sufferings and poverty of the Church, he frequently went upon the walls of the building, both by night and day, and wept, crying aloud to the Almighty to send means whereby we might accomplish the building.

. . . The whole Church united in this great undertaking, and every man lent a helping hand. Those who had not teams went to work in the stone quarry and prepared the stones for drawing to the house.

The Prophet, being our foreman, would put on his tow frock and tow pantaloons and go into the quarry. The Presidency, High Priests, and Elders all alike assisting. Those who had teams assisted in drawing the stone to the house. These all laboring one day in the week, brought as many stones to the house as supplied the masons through the whole week. We continued in this manner until the walls of the house were reared. The committee who were appointed by revelation to superintend the building were Hyrum Smith, Reynolds Cahoon and Jared Carter. They used every exertion in their power to forward the work.

Orson F. Whitney, *Life of Heber C. Kimball,* 2d ed. (Salt Lake City: Stevens & Wallis, 1945), pp. 67–69.

PRAYER OF A PROPHET

DANIEL TYLER

At the time William Smith and others rebelled against the Prophet, as recorded in his history, when the walls of the Kirtland Temple were raised but a few feet above the ground. I attended a meeting "on the flats," where "Joseph" presided. Entering the school-house a little before meeting opened, and gazing upon the man of God, I perceived sadness in his countenance and tears trickling down his cheeks. I naturally supposed the all-absorbing topic of the difficulty must be the cause. I was not mistaken. A few moments later a hymn was sung and he opened the meeting by prayer. Instead, however, of facing the audience, he turned his back and bowed upon his knees, facing the wall. This, I suppose, was done to hide his sorrow and tears.

I had heard men and women pray—especially the former—from the most ignorant, both as to letters and intellect, to the most learned and eloquent, but never until then had I heard a man address his Maker as though He was present listening as a kind father would listen to the sorrows of a dutiful child. Joseph was at that time unlearned, but that prayer, which was to a considerable extent in behalf of those who accused him of having gone astray and fallen into sin, that the Lord would forgive them and open their eyes that they might see aright—that prayer, I say, to my humble mind, partook of the learning and eloquence of heaven. There was no ostentation, no raising of the voice as by enthusiasm, but a plain conversational tone, as a man would address a present friend. It appeared to me as though, in case the veil were taken away, I could see the Lord standing facing His humblest of all servants I had ever seen. Whether this was really the case I cannot say; but one thing I can say, it was the crowning, so to speak, of all the prayers I ever heard.

Juvenile Instructor 27:127–28.

A DAY OF PENTECOST

JOSEPH SMITH

*S*unday, *March 27.*—The congregation began to assemble at the Temple, at about seven o'clock, an hour earlier than the doors were to be opened. Many brethren had come in from the regions round about, to witness the dedication of the Lord's House and share in His blessings; and such was the anxiety on this occasion that some hundreds (probably five or six) assembled before the doors were opened. The presidents entered with the doorkeepers, and stationed the latter at the inner and outer doors; also placed our stewards to receive donations from those who should feel disposed to contribute something to defray the expense of building the House of the Lord. We also dedicated the pulpits, and consecrated them to the Lord.

The doors were then opened. Presidents Rigdon, Cowdery and myself seated the congregation as they came in, and, according to the best calculation we could make, we received between nine and ten hundred, which were as many as could be comfortably seated. We then informed the doorkeepers that we could receive no more, and a multitude were deprived of the benefits of the meeting on account of the house not being sufficiently capacious to receive them; and I felt to regret that any of my brethren and sisters should be deprived of the meeting, and I recommended them to repair to the schoolhouse and hold a meeting, which they did, and filled that house also, and yet many were left out. . . .

President Rigdon . . . spoke two hours and a half in his usual logical manner. His prayer and address were very forcible and sublime, and well adapted to the occasion. At one time, in the course of his remarks, he was rather pathetic, and drew tears from many eyes. . . .

[After singing hymns and the sustaining of officers, the dedicatory prayer was offered, followed by the hymn "The Spirit of God Like a Fire Is Burning," the sacrament of the Lord's Supper, and the bearing of testimonies.]

President Frederick G. Williams arose and testified that while President Rigdon was making his first prayer, an angel entered the window and took his seat between Father Smith and himself, and remained there during the prayer.

President David Whitmer also saw angels in the house. . . .

President Rigdon then made a few appropriate closing remarks, and a short prayer, at the close of which we sealed the proceedings of the day by shouting hosanna, hosanna, hosanna to God and the Lamb, three times, sealing it each time with amen, amen, and amen.

President Brigham Young gave a short address in tongues, and David W. Patten interpreted, and gave a short exhortation in tongues himself, after which I blessed the congregation in the name of the Lord, and the assembly dispersed a little past four o'clock, having manifested the most quiet demeanor during the whole exercise.

I met the quorums in the evening and instructed them respecting the ordinance of washing of feet, which they were to attend to on Wednesday following; and gave them instructions in relation to the spirit of prophecy, and called upon the congregation to speak, and not to fear to prophesy good concerning the Saints, for if you prophesy the falling of these hills and the rising of the valleys, the downfall of the enemies of Zion and the rising of the kingdom of God, it shall come to pass. Do not quench the Spirit, for the first one that opens his mouth shall receive the Spirit of prophecy.

Brother George A. Smith arose and began to prophesy, when a noise was heard like the sound of a rushing mighty wind, which filled the Temple, and all the congregation simultaneously arose, being moved upon by an invisible power; many began to speak in tongues and prophesy; others saw glorious visions; and I beheld the Temple was filled with angels, which fact I declared to the congregation. The people of the neighborhood came running together (hearing an unusual sound within, and seeing a bright light like a pillar of fire resting upon the Temple), and were astonished at what was taking place. This continued until the meeting closed at eleven P.M.

The number of official members present on this occasion was four hundred and sixteen, being a greater number than ever assembled on any former occasion.

[The following Tuesday], at eleven o'clock, A.M., Presidents Joseph Smith, Jun., Frederick G. Williams, Sidney Rigdon, Hyrum Smith, and Oliver Cowdery, met in the most holy place in the Lord's House, and sought for a revelation from Him concerning the authorities of the Church going to Zion, and other important matters. After uniting in prayer, the voice of the Spirit was that we should come into this place three times, and also call the other presidents, the two Bishops and their counselors, each to stand in his place, and fast through the day and also the night, and that during this, if we would humble ourselves, we should receive further communications from Him. After this word was received we immediately sent for the other brethren, who came. . . .

Soon after this, the word of the Lord came, through President Joseph Smith, Jun., that those who had entered the holy place, must not leave the house until morning, but send for such things as were necessary, and, also, during our stay, we must cleanse our feet and partake of the Sacrament that we might be made holy before Him, and thereby be qualified to officiate in our calling, upon the morrow, in washing the feet of the Elders.

... The Holy Spirit rested down upon us, and we continued in the Lord's House all night, prophesying and giving glory to God.

Joseph Smith, *History of The Church of Jesus Christ of Latter-day Saints,* 7 vols., 2d ed. rev., edited by B. H. Roberts (Salt Lake City: The Church of Jesus Christ of Latter-day Saints, 1932–51), 2:410–11, 413–14, 427, 429–30.

"THE PROPHET CAME TO THE DOOR"

WILLIAM F. CAHOON

I was called and ordained to act as a [ward] teacher to visit the families of the Saints. I got along very well until I was obliged to pay a visit to the Prophet [Joseph Smith]. Being young, only seventeen years of age, I felt my weakness in visiting the Prophet and his family in the capacity of a teacher. I almost felt like shrinking from my duty.

Finally, I went to the door and knocked, and in a minute the Prophet came to the door. I stood there trembling and said to him:

"Brother Joseph, I have come to visit you in the capacity of a [ward] teacher, if it is convenient for you."

He said, "Brother William, come right in. I am glad to see you; sit down in that chair there and I will go and call my family in."

They soon came in and took seats. He then said, "Brother

William, I submit myself and family into your hands," and took his seat. "Now, Brother William," said he, "Ask all the questions you feel like."

By this time, my fears and trembling had ceased, and I said, "Brother Joseph, are you trying to live your religion?"

He answered, "Yes."

I then said, "Do you pray in your family?"

He answered "Yes."

"Do you teach your family the principles of the gospel?"

He replied, "Yes, I am trying to do it."

"Do you ask a blessing on your food?"

He answered "Yes."

"Are you trying to live in peace and harmony with all your family?"

He said that he was.

I then turned to Sister Emma, his wife, and said, "Sister Emma, are you trying to live your religion? Do you teach your children to obey their parents? Do you try to teach them to pray?"

To all these questions she answered, "Yes, I am trying to do so."

I then turned to Joseph and said, "I am now through with my questions as a teacher; and now if you have any instructions to give, I shall be happy to receive them."

He said, "God bless you, Brother William; and if you are humble and faithful, you shall have power to settle all difficulties that may come before you in the capacity of a teacher."

I then left my parting blessing upon him and his family, as a teacher, and took my departure.

Juvenile Instructor 27:492–93.

EXODUS FROM JACKSON COUNTY

⌒

PARLEY P. PRATT

Thursday, November 7. The shore began to be lined on both sides of the ferry with men, women and children; goods, wagons, boxes, provisions, etc., while the ferry was constantly employed; and when night again closed upon us the cottonwood bottom had much the appearance of a camp meeting. Hundreds of people were seen in every direction, some in tents and some in the open air around their fires, while the rain descended in torrents. Husbands were inquiring for their wives, wives for their husbands; parents for children, and children for parents. Some had the good fortune to escape with their families, household goods, and some provisions; while others knew not the fate of their friends, and had lost all their goods. The scene was indescribable, and, I am sure, would have melted the hearts of any people on the earth, except our blind oppressors, and a blind and ignorant community.

Next day our company still increased, and we were principally engaged in felling cottonwood trees and erecting them into small cabins. The next night being clear, we began to enjoy some degree of comfort.

About two o'clock the next morning we were called up by the cry of signs in the heavens. We arose, and to our great astonishment all the firmament seemed enveloped in splendid fireworks, as if every star in the broad expanse had been hurled from its course, and sent lawless through the wilds of ether. Thousands of bright meteors were shooting through space in every direction, with long trains of light following in their course. This lasted for several hours, and was only closed by the dawn of the rising sun. Every heart was filled with joy at this majestic display of signs and wonders, showing the near approach of the coming of the Son of God.

All our goods, were left behind; but I obtained some of them afterwards at the risk of my life. But all my provisions for the winter were destroyed or stolen, and my grain left growing on the ground for my enemies to harvest. My house was afterwards burned, and my fruit trees and improvements destroyed or plundered. In short, every member of the society was driven from the county, and fields of corn were ravaged and destroyed; stacks of wheat burned, household goods plundered, and improvements and every kind of property destroyed. One of this banditti afterwards boasted to one of the brethren that, according to their own account of the matter, the number of houses burned was two hundred and three.

Parley P. Pratt, *Autobiography of Parley P. Pratt,* edited by Parley P. Pratt Jr., Classics in Mormon Literature ed. (Salt Lake City: Deseret Book Co., 1985), pp. 82–84.

A PINT OF STRIPPINGS

GEORGE A. SMITH

While the Saints were living in Far West, there were two sisters wishing to make cheese, and, neither of them possessing the requisite number of cows, they agreed to exchange milk.

The wife of Thomas B. Marsh, who was then President of the Twelve Apostles, and sister Harris concluded they would exchange milk, in order to make a little larger cheese than they otherwise could. To be sure to have justice done, it was agreed that they should not save the strippings [the last, extra-rich milk pressed from the cow when milking], but that the milk and strippings should all go together. Small matters to talk about here, to be sure, two women's exchanging milk to make cheese.

Mrs. Harris, it appeared, was faithful to the agreement and carried to Mrs. Marsh the milk and strippings, but Mrs. Marsh, wishing to make some extra good cheese, saved a pint of strippings from each cow and sent Mrs. Harris the milk without the strippings.

Finally it leaked out that Mrs. Marsh had saved strippings, and it became a matter to be settled by the Teachers. They began to examine the matter, and it was proved that Mrs. Marsh had saved the strippings, and consequently had wronged Mrs. Harris out of that amount.

An appeal was taken from the Teacher[s] to the Bishop, and a regular Church trial was had. President Marsh did not consider that the Bishop had done him and his lady justice, for they decided that the strippings were wrongfully saved, and that the woman had violated her covenant.

Marsh immediately took an appeal to the High Council, who investigated the question with much patience, and I assure you they were a grave body. Marsh being extremely anxious to maintain the character of his wife, as he was the President of the Twelve Apostles, and a great man in Israel, made a desperate defence, but the High Council finally confirmed the Bishop's decision.

Marsh, not being satisfied, took an appeal to the First Presidency of the Church, and Joseph and his Counsellors had to sit upon the case, and they approved the decision of the High Council.

This little affair, you will observe, kicked up a considerable breeze, and Thomas B. Marsh then declared that he would sustain the character of his wife, even if he had to go to hell for it.

The then President of the Twelve Apostles, the man who should have been the first to do justice and cause reparation to be made for wrong, committed by any member of his family, took that position, and what next? He went before a magistrate and swore that the "Mormons" were hostile towards the State of Missouri.

That affidavit brought from the government of Missouri an exterminating order, which drove some 15,000 Saints from their homes and habitations, and some thousands perished through suffering the exposure consequent on this state of affairs.

Do you understand what trouble was consequent to the dispute about a pint of strippings? Do you understand that the want of fences around gardens, fields, and yards, in town and country, allowing cattle to get into mischief and into the stray pen, may end in some serious result? That the corroding influence of such circumstances may be brought to bear upon us, in such a way that we may lose the Spirit of the Almighty and become hostile to the people? And if we should not bring about as mighty results as the

pint of strippings, yet we might bring entire destruction to ourselves. If you wish to enjoy your religion and the Spirit of the
Almighty, you must make your calculations to avoid annoyances,
as much as possible.

Journal of Discourses, 26 vols. (London: Latter-day Saints' Book Depot, 1854–86), 3:283–94.

BEGINNINGS OF
THE RELIEF SOCIETY

I V A N   J .   B A R R E T T

Early in 1842 Sarah M. Kimball [wife of Hiram Kimball]
offered to furnish material if Miss Cook, her seamstress,
would make shirts for the workmen on the Nauvoo
Temple. Other women became interested in the project and suggested a society be organized for that purpose. At the home of
Sarah Kimball, Eliza R. Snow was asked to draw up a constitution
and by-laws to be submitted to the Prophet Joseph Smith for his
approval.

Joseph read Sister Snow's composition and said it was the best
he had ever seen. "But," said he, "this is not what you want. Tell
the sisters their offering is accepted of the Lord, and He has something better for them than a written constitution. Invite them all
to meet me and a few of the brethren in the Masonic Hall over at
my store next Thursday afternoon, and I will organize the sisters

under the priesthood after the pattern of the priesthood. This church will never be perfectly organized until the women are thus organized."

Accordingly, the next Thursday, March 17, 1842, the Prophet . . . organized the women of Nauvoo into an association known today as the Relief Society. . . .

There were seventeen meetings held by the Relief Society during the first year of its existence. The last meeting, on September 28, 1842, was held in the grove. The room above Joseph's store had long since become too small, for the membership had grown from 18 to 1,189. At some of these meetings Joseph met with and counseled the sisters. On April 28, 1842, he said:

"Let this Society teach women how to behave towards their husbands, to treat them with mildness and affection. When a man is borne down with trouble, when he is perplexed with care and difficulty, if he can meet a smile instead of an argument or murmur—if he can meet with mildness, it will calm down his soul and soothe his feelings; when a mind is going to despair, it needs a solace of affection and kindness. You will receive instructions through the order of the Priesthood which God has established through the medium of those appointed to lead, guide and direct the affairs of the Church in this last dispensation; and I now turn the key in your behalf in the name of the Lord, and this Society shall rejoice, and knowledge and intelligence shall flow down from this time henceforth; this is the beginning of better days to the poor and needy, who shall be made to rejoice and pour forth blessings on your heads."

Ivan J. Barrett, *Joseph Smith and the Restoration* (Provo: Brigham Young University Press, 1970), pp. 504–7.

"You Shall Witness Blood to Your Entire Satisfaction"

GEORGE Q. CANNON

When the morning came on the 25th of June, 1844, Joseph and his brethren voluntarily presented themselves to Constable Bettisworth, who had held the original writ against them. They sought and had an interview with the governor at his headquarters; and he then and there pledged his own faith and that of the state of Illinois that Joseph and Hyrum and the other prisoners should be protected from personal violence and should have a fair and impartial trial.

A few moments after 8 o'clock A.M., Joseph and Hyrum were arrested upon warrants issued by Justice Robert F. Smith, of Carthage, charging them with treason, upon the affidavits of Augustus Spencer and Henry O. Norton.

After making an inflammable speech to the rabble army, the governor led the brothers before the troops, as the mob had requested to have a clear view of Joseph and Hyrum. As they passed in front of the lines, Ford introduced the Prophet and Patriarch as Generals Joseph and Hyrum Smith. The Carthage Greys refused to receive them by that introduction, and some of the officers threw up their hats, drew their swords and said: "We will introduce ourselves to the damned Mormons in a different style." The Governor quieted them by saying:

You shall have full satisfaction.

An hour later the Carthage Greys revolted and were put under guard; they could not be content to wait another hour for the murder. But they were soon released.

Joseph had asked a private interview with Ford, but it had been refused. In declining, the governor looked down with shame.

In the afternoon several officers of the mob militia called upon Joseph at the tavern. They gazed upon him with much curiosity, and he asked them if he appeared like a desperate character. They replied that his outward appearance seemed to indicate exactly the opposite, but they could not tell what was in his heart. To this Joseph responded:

Very true, gentlemen, you cannot see what is in my heart, and you are therefore unable to judge me or my intentions; but I can see what is in your hearts, and will tell you what I see. I can see you thirst for blood, and nothing but my blood will satisfy you. It is not for a crime of any description that I and my brethren are thus continually persecuted and harassed by our enemies, but there are other motives, and some of them I have expressed, so far as relates to myself; and inasmuch as you and the people thirst for blood, I prophesy, in the name of the Lord, that you shall witness scenes of blood and sorrow to your entire satisfaction. Your souls shall be perfectly satiated with blood, and many of you who are now present shall have an opportunity to face the cannon's mouth from sources you think not of; and those people that desire this great evil upon me and my brethren, shall be filled with regret and sorrow because of the scenes of desolation and distress that await them. They shall seek for peace, and shall not be able to find it. Gentlemen, you will find what I have told you to be true.

George Q. Cannon, *Life of the Prophet Joseph Smith* (Salt Lake City: Deseret Book Co., 1986), pp. 508–9.

"ARE YOU AFRAID TO DIE?"

⌒‿‿⌒

FROM *HISTORY OF THE CHURCH*

During the evening the Patriarch Hyrum Smith read and commented upon extracts from the Book of Mormon, on the imprisonments and deliverance of the servants of God for the Gospel's sake. Joseph bore a powerful testimony to the guards of the divine authenticity of the Book of Mormon, the restoration of the Gospel, the administration of angels, and that the kingdom of God was again established upon the earth, for the sake of which he was then incarcerated in that prison, and not because he had violated any law of God or man.

They retired to rest late. Joseph and Hyrum occupied the only bedstead in the room, while their friends lay side by side on the matresses on the floor. Dr. Richards sat up writing until his last candle left him in the dark. The report of a gun fired close by caused Joseph to arise, leave the bed, and lay himself on the floor, having Dan Jones on his left, and John S. Fullmer on his right.

Joseph laid out his right arm, and said to John S. Fullmer, "Lay your head on my arm for a pillow Brother John;" and when all were quiet they conversed in a low tone about the prospects of their deliverance. Joseph gave expression to several presentiments that he had to die, and said "I would like to see my family again." and "I would to God that I could preach to the Saints in Nauvoo once more." Fullmer tried to rally his spirits, saying he thought he would often have that privilege, when Joseph thanked him for the remarks and good feelings expressed to him.

Soon after Dr. Richards retired to the bed which Joseph had left, and when all were apparently fast asleep, Joseph whispered to

Dan Jones, "are you afraid to die?" Dan said, "Has that time come, think you? Engaged in such a cause I do not think that death would have many terrors." Joseph replied, "You will yet see Wales, and fulfill the mission appointed you before you die."

Joseph Smith, *History of The Church of Jesus Christ of Latter-day Saints,* 7 vols., 2d ed. rev., edited by B. H. Roberts (Salt Lake City: The Church of Jesus Christ of Latter-day Saints, 1932–51), 6:600–601.

THE MARTYRDOM

WILLARD RICHARDS

P ossibly the following events occupied near three minutes, but I think only about two, and have penned them for the gratification of many friends.

CARTHAGE, June 27, 1844.

A shower of musket balls were thrown up the stairway against the door of the prison in the second story, followed by many rapid footsteps.

While Generals Joseph and Hyrum Smith, Mr. Taylor, and myself, who were in the front chamber, closed the door of our room against the entry at the head of the stairs, and placed ourselves against it, there being no lock on the door, and no catch that was usable.

The door is a common panel, and as soon as we heard the feet at the stairs head, a ball was sent through the door, which passed between us, and showed that our enemies were desperadoes, and we must change our position.

General Joseph Smith, Mr. Taylor and myself sprang back to the front part of the room, and General Hyrum Smith retreated two-thirds across the chamber directly in front of and facing the door.

A ball was sent through the door which hit Hyrum on the side of his nose, when he fell backwards, extended at length, without moving his feet.

From the holes in his vest (the day was warm, and no one had his coat on but myself), pantaloons, drawers, and shirt, it appears evident that a ball must have been thrown from without, through the window, which entered his back on the right side, and passing through, lodged against his watch, which was in his right vest pocket, completely pulverizing the crystal and face, tearing off the hands and mashing the whole body of the watch. At the same instant the ball from the door entered his nose.

As he struck the floor he exclaimed emphatically, "I am a dead man." Joseph looked towards him and responded, "Oh, dear brother Hyrum!" and opening the door two or three inches with his left hand, discharged one barrel of a six shooter (pistol) at random in the entry, from whence a ball grazed Hyrum's breast, and entering his throat passed into his head, while other muskets were aimed at him and some balls hit him.

Joseph continued snapping his revolver round the casing of the door into the space as before, three barrels of which missed fire, while Mr. Taylor with a walking stick stood by his side and knocked down the bayonets and muskets which were constantly discharging through the doorway, while I stood by him, ready to lend any assistance, with another stick, but could not come within striking distance without going directly before the muzzle of the guns.

When the revolver failed, we had no more firearms, and

expected an immediate rush of the mob, and the doorway full of muskets, half way in the room, and no hope but instant death from within.

Mr. Taylor rushed into the window, which is some fifteen or twenty feet from the ground. When his body was nearly on a balance, a ball from the door within entered his leg, and a ball from without struck his watch, a patent lever, in his vest pocket near the left breast, and smashed it into "pie," leaving the hands standing at 5 o'clock, 16 minutes, and 26 seconds, the force of which ball threw him back on the floor, and he rolled under the bed which stood by his side, where he lay motionless, the mob from the door continuing to fire upon him, cutting away a piece of flesh from his left hip as large as a man's hand, and were hindered only by my knocking down their muzzles with a stick; while they continued to reach their guns into the room, probably left handed, and aimed their discharge so far round as almost to reach us in the corner of the room to where we retreated and dodged, and then I recommenced the attack with my stick.

Joseph attempted, as the last resort, to leap the same window from whence Mr. Taylor fell, when two balls pierced him from the door, and one entered his right breast from without, and he fell outward, exclaiming, "Oh Lord, my God!" As his feet went out of the window my head went in, the balls whistling all around. He fell on his left side a dead man.

At this instant the cry was raised, "He's leaped the window!" and the mob on the stairs and in the entry ran out.

I withdrew from the window, thinking it of no use to leap out on a hundred bayonets, then around General Joseph Smith's body.

Not satisfied with this I again reached my head out of the window, and watched some seconds to see if there were any signs of life, regardless of my own, determined to see the end of him I loved. Being fully satisfied that he was dead, with a hundred men near the body and more coming round the corner of the jail, and expecting a return to our room, I rushed towards the prison door, at the head of the stairs, and through the entry from whence the firing had proceeded, to learn if the doors into the prison were open.

When near the entry, Mr. Taylor called out, "Take me." I pressed my way until I found all doors unbarred, returning instantly, caught Mr. Taylor under my arm and rushed by the stairs into the dungeon, or inner prison, stretched him on the floor and covered him with a bed in such a manner as not likely to be perceived, expecting an immediate return of the mob.

I said to Mr. Taylor, "This is a hard case to lay you on the floor, but if your wounds are not fatal, I want you to live to tell the story."

I expected to be shot the next moment, and stood before the door awaiting the onset.

Joseph Smith, *History of The Church of Jesus Christ of Latter-day Saints*, 7 vols., 2d ed. rev., edited by B. H. Roberts (Salt Lake City: The Church of Jesus Christ of Latter-day Saints, 1932–51), 6:619–21.

PIONEERS

NAUVOO DESERTED

⌒

THOMAS L. KANE

I was descending the last hillside upon my journey when a
landscape in delightful contrast broke upon my view. Half
encircled by a bend in the river, a beautiful city lay glittering
in the fresh morning sun. Its bright new dwellings, [were] set in
cool green gardens, ranging up around a stately domed-shaped
hill, which was crowned by a noble marble edifice, whose high
tapering spire was radiant with white and gold. The city appeared
to cover several miles, and beyond it, in the background, there
rolled off a fair country, checquered by the careful lines of fruitful
husbandry. The unmistakable marks of industry, enterprise and
educated wealth, everywhere, made the scene one of singular and
most striking beauty.

It was a natural impulse to visit this inviting region. I procured
a skiff, and rowing across the river, landed at the chief wharf of the
city. No one met me there. I looked and saw no one. I could hear
no one move, though the quiet everywhere was such that I heard
the flies buzz, and the water-ripples break against the shallow
beach. I walked through the solitary streets. The town lay as in a
dream, under some deadening spell of loneliness, from which I
almost feared to wake it. For plainly it had not slept long. There
was no grass growing up in the paved ways. Rains had not entirely
washed away the prints of dusty footsteps. Yet I went about
unchecked. I went into empty workshops, ropewalks and smithies.
The spinner's wheel was idle; the carpenter had gone from his
work-bench and shavings, his unfinished sash and casings. Fresh
bark was in the tanner's vat, and fresh-chopped light-wood stood

piled against the baker's oven. The blacksmith's shop was cold; but his coal heap and ladling pool and crooked water horn were all there, as if he had just gone for a holiday. No work people anywhere looked to know my errand. If I went into the gardens clinking the wicket-latch loudly after me, to pull the marigolds, heart's-ease, and lady-slippers, and draw a drink with the water sodden well-bucket and its noisy chain, or, knocking off with my stick the tall, heavy-headed dahlias and sunflowers, hunted over the beds for cucumbers and love-apples, no one called out to me from any opened window, or dog sprang forward to bark an alarm. I could have supposed the people hidden in the houses, but the doors were unfastened, and when at last I timidly entered them, I found dead ashes white upon the hearths, and I had to tread a tiptoe, as if walking down the aisle of a country church, to avoid arousing irreverent echoes from the naked floors.

On the outskirts of the town was the city graveyard. But there was no record of Plague there, nor did it in anywise differ much from other Protestant American cemeteries. Some of the mounds were not long sodded; some of the stones were newly set, their dates recent, and their black inscriptions glossy in the mason's hardly dried lettering ink. Beyond the graveyard, out in the fields, I saw, in one spot hard-by where the fruited bough of a young orchard had been roughly torn down, the still smouldering embers of a barbecue fire that had been constructed of rails from the fencing around it. It was the latest signs of life there. Fields upon fields of heavy-headed yellow grain lay rotting ungathered upon the ground. No one was at hand to take in their rich harvest. As far as the eye could reach they stretched away—they, sleeping too in the hazy air of autumn.

Only two portions of the city seemed to suggest the import of this mysterious solitude. On the southern suburb, the houses looking out upon the country showed, by their splintered woodwork and walls battered to the foundation, that there had lately been a mark of destructive cannonade. And in and around the splendid Temple, which had been the chief object of my admiration, armed men were barracked, surrounded by their stacks of musketry and pieces of heavy ordinance. These challenged me to render an account of myself, and why I had had the temerity to cross the water without a written permit from the leader of their band.

Though these men were more or less under the influence of ardent spirits, after I had explained myself as a passing stranger, they seemed anxious to gain my good opinion. They told the story of the Dead City: that it had been a notable manufacturing and commercial mart, sheltering over 20,000 persons, that they had waged war with its inhabitants for several years, and had been finally successful only a few days before my visit, in an action fought in front of the ruined suburb; after which, they had driven them forth at the point of the sword. The defence, they said, had been obstinate, but gave way on the third day's bombardment. They boasted greatly of their prowess, especially in this Battle, as they called it. But I discovered they were not of one mind as to certain of the exploits that had distinguished it; one of which, as I remember, was, that they had slain a father and his son, a boy of fifteen, not long a resident of the fated city, whom they admitted to have borne a character without reproach.

They also conducted me inside the massive sculptured walls of the curious Temple, in which they said, the banished inhabitants were accustomed to celebrate the mystic rites of an unhallowed worship. They particularly pointed out to me certain features of the building, which, having been the peculiar objects of a former superstitious regard, they had as a matter of duty sedulously defiled and defaced. The reputed sites of certain shrines they had thus particularly noticed, and various sheltered chambers, in one of which was a deep well, constructed they believed with a dreadful design. Besides these, they led me to see a large and deep chiseled marble vase or basin, supported upon twelve oxen, also of marble, and of the size of life, of which they told some romantic stories. They said the deluded persons, most of whom were emigrants from a great distance, believed their Deity countenanced their reception here of a baptism of regeneration, as proxies for whomsoever they held in warm affection in the countries from which they had come: That here parents "went into the water" for their lost children, children for their parents, widows for their spouses, and young persons for their lovers: That thus the Great Vase came to be for them associated with all dear and distant memories, and was therefore the object, of all others in the building, to which they attached the greatest degree of idolatrous affection. On this account, the victors had so diligently desecrated it, as to render the apartment in which it was contained too noisome to abide in.

They permitted me also to ascend into the steeple to see where it had been lightning-struck on the Sabbath before; and to look out east and south on wasted farms like those I had seen near the City, extending till they were lost in the distance. Here, in the face of the pure day, close to the scar of Divine wrath left by the thunderbolt, were fragments of food, cruises of liquor and broken drinking vessels, with a bass drum and a steamboat bell, of which I afterwards learned the use with pain.

It was after nightfall when I was ready to cross the river on my return. The wind had freshened after sunset, and the water beating roughly into my little boat, I headed higher up the stream than the point I had left in the morning, and landed where a faint glimmering light invited me to steer. Here among the dock and rushes, sheltered only by the darkness, without roof between them and the sky, I came upon a crowd of several hundred creatures, whom my movements roused from uneasy slumber upon the ground.

Passing these on my way to the light, I found it came from a tallow candle in a paper funnel-shade, such as is used by street venders of apples and peanuts, and which flaring and guttering away in the bleak air off the water, shone flickeringly on the emaciated faces of a man in the last stage of a bilious remittant fever. They had done their best for him. Over his head was something like a tent, made of a sheet or two, and he rested on a but partially ripped open old straw mattress, with a hair sofa cushion under his head for a pillow. His gaping jaw and glazing eye told how short a time he would monopolize these luxuries, though a seemingly bewildered and excited person, who might have been his wife, seemed to find hope in occasionally forcing him to swallow awkwardly measured sips of the tepid river water from a burned and battered bitter smelling tin coffee-pot. Those who knew better had furnished [the] apothecary he needed—a toothless old bald-head, whose manner had the repulsive dulness of a man familiar with death scenes. He, so long as I remained, mumbled in his patient's ear a monotonous and melancholy prayer, between the pauses of which I heard the hiccup and sobbing of two little girls, who were sitting upon a piece of driftwood outside.

Dreadful, indeed, the suffering of these forsaken beings. Bowed and cramped by cold and sunburn, alternating as each weary day and night dragged on, they were, almost all of them, the crippled victims of disease. They were there because they had no homes, nor hospital nor poorhouse nor friends to offer them any. They could not satisfy the feeble cravings of their sick: they had not bread to quiet the fractious hunger cries of their children. Mothers and babes, daughters and grandparents, all of them alike, were bivouacked in tatters, wanting even covering to comfort those whom the sick shiver of fever was searching to the marrow.

These were the Mormons, famishing, in Lee County, Iowa, in the fourth week of the month of September, in the year of our Lord 1846. The city—it was Nauvoo, Illinois. The Mormons were the owners of that city, and the smiling country round. And those who stopped their ploughs, who had silenced their hammers, their axes, their shuttles and their workshop wheels; those who had put out their fires, who had eaten their food, spoiled their orchards, and trampled under foot their thousands of acres of unharvested bread; these were the keepers of their dwellings—the carousers in their Temple—whose drunken riot insulted the ears of their dying. . . .

They were, all told, not more than six hundred and forty persons who were thus lying on the river flats. But the Mormons in Nauvoo had numbered the year before over twenty thousand. Where were they? They had last been seen, carrying in mournful trains their sick and wounded, halt and blind, to disappear behind the western horizon, pursuing the phantom of another home. Hardly anything else was known of them: and people asked with curiosity, What had been their fate—what their fortunes?

Thomas L. Kane, Discourse delivered before The Historical Society of Pennsylvania (Philadelphia: King & Baird, Printers, Sansom Street, 1850), pp. 3–11.

"THE QUAILS DESCEND"

THOMAS BULLOCK

On the 9th of October several wagons with oxen having been sent by the Twelve to fetch the poor Saints away, were drawn out in a line on the river banks ready to start. But hark! what is that? See! the quails descend. They alight close by our little camp of twelve wagons, run past each wagon tongue, when they arise, fly around the camp three times, descend and again run the gauntlet past each wagon. See! the sick knock them down with sticks and the little children catch them alive with their hands! Some are cooked for breakfast.

While my family were seated on the wagon tongue and ground, having a washtub for a table, behold they come again! One descends upon our tea-board in the midst of our cups, while we were actually around the table eating our breakfast, which a little boy eight years old catches alive with his hands. They rise again, the flocks increase in number, seldom going seven rods from our camp, continually flying around the camp, sometimes under the wagons, sometimes over, and even into the wagons where the poor, sick Saints are lying in bed; thus having a direct manifestation from the Most High that although we are driven by men He has not forsaken us, but that His eyes are continually over us for good. At noon, having caught alive about fifty and killed about fifty more, the captain gave orders not to kill any more, as it was a direct manifestation and visitation from the Lord. In the afternoon hundreds were flying at a time. When our camp started at three P.M. there could not have been less then five hundred, some said there were fifteen hundred, flying around the camp.

Thus am I a witness to this visitation. Some Gentiles who were at the camp marveled greatly. Even passengers on a steamboat going down the river looked with astonishment.

James A. Little, *From Kirtland to Salt Lake City* (Salt Lake City: James A. Little, 1890), pp. 74–75.

A BRIGHT RED SHAWL

CAMILLA WOODBURY JUDD

In May, 1856, [Robert and Ann Hartley Parker] with their four children, Max, 12; Martha Alice, 10; Arthur, 5; and Ada, one year old, left England by sailing vessel to join the Saints in Utah. . . . They went by rail to Iowa City where they continued their journey by handcart. All had their share of the work. Robert and Ann pulled the heavily loaded cart, Maxie pushed and Martha Alice followed with the younger children, taking care of little brother Arthur.

. . . Robert Parker was stricken with fever that was sweeping the company [and had to be] placed in one of the wagons. [This meant that] Martha Alice [his daughter] had to leave her little brother to the care of other children while she lent her child-strength to the heavy cart.

One day, while going through the timberlands of Nebraska, Arthur became feverish and ill, and unnoticed by the other children, sat down to rest beside the trail. He was soon fast asleep. In the afternoon a sudden storm came up and the company hurried to make camp. Finding that Arthur was not with the children, they hurriedly organized a posse and went back to search for him. They returned with grim faces after two days' searching. The captain ordered the company to move on. Ann pleaded with him, but he set his jaw hard—the food was giving out and not another day could be lost.

Ann Parker pinned a bright shawl about the thin shoulders of her husband and sent him back alone on the trail to search again for their child. If he found him dead he was to wrap him in the shawl; if alive, the shawl would be a flag to signal her. Ann and her children took up their load and struggled on with the company, while Robert retraced the miles of forest trail, calling, searching, and praying for his helpless little son. At last he reached a mail and trading station where he learned that his child had been cared for by a woodsman and his wife. He had been ill from exposure and fright. [But] God had heard the prayers of his people.

Out on the trail each night Ann and her children kept watch, and when, on the third night, the rays of the setting sun caught the glimmer of a bright red shawl, the brave little mother sank in a pitiful heap in the sand. Completely exhausted, Ann slept for the first time in six long days and nights. God indeed was kind and merciful, and in the gladness of their hearts the Saints sang, "All is well. . . ."

Kate B. Carter, comp., *Treasures of Pioneer History* (Salt Lake City: Daughters of Utah Pioneers, 1956), 5:240–41.

"THE CATTLE ARE GONE!"

JOSEPH FIELDING SMITH

There had been an arrangement between the authorities of the Church and the leaders of the mob, that the Saints should remain in Nauvoo until the spring of 1846, excepting the poor who would be unable to leave at that time because of their poverty. This agreement was never kept; but it was impossible for all the Saints to evacuate the city as early as the mob desired.

Mary Smith with her family remained in Nauvoo until the

summer of 1846. It was only a day or two before the battle of Nauvoo, when, under threats, she hastily loaded her children in a flat boat with such household effects as could be carried, and crossed the Mississippi to a point near Montrose. There under the trees on the bank of the river the family pitched camp that night, and there they experienced the horror of listening to the bombardment of Nauvoo. The oldest son, John, had been privileged to cross the river with a company some time before, but Joseph, then but a boy in his eighth year, heard the roar of guns and was aware of the fact that the remaining Saints were being murdered or driven from their homes.

Here necessity required the mother to leave her little flock camped on the bank of the Mississippi river as she made her way down the river to Keokuk, Iowa, and there negotiated and effected the sale of real estate in Hancock County, Illinois. She received in exchange for this property some wagons, oxen for teams, some horses, cows, etc., and in this manner provided for the transportation of her family across Iowa to Winter Quarters. Although Joseph was not yet eight years of age, he was required to drive one of the ox teams most of the way from Montrose to Winter Quarters. At this place the family sojourned until the spring of 1848, endeavoring in the meantime, by help from friends who were not prepared to continue on the journey, and by constant toil, to gather sufficient teams and necessities to make the journey across the plains. During the winter of 1847–48 Mary Smith made two trips down the Missouri to purchase provisions, and trade for necessities for the family, which numbered in all, about eleven souls. Her son Joseph writing of these trips has said:

"Once I accompanied her, along with my Uncle Joseph Fielding, at which time we went down to St. Joseph, Missouri, and purchased corn and had it ground at Savannah. We also went for the purpose of obtaining provisions and clothing for the family for the coming winter, and for the journey across the plains the following spring. We

took two wagons with two yoke of oxen on each. I was almost nine
years of age at this time. The weather was unpropitious, the roads
were bad, and it rained a great deal during the journey, so that the
trip was a very hard, trying and unpleasant one. At St. Joseph we purchased our groceries and dry goods, and at Savannah we laid in our
store of flour, meal and corn, bacon and other provisions.

"Returning to Winter Quarters, we camped one evening in an
open prairie on the Missouri River bottoms, by the side of a small
spring creek, which emptied into the river about three quarters of
a mile from us. We were in plain sight of the river, and could
apparently see over every foot of the little open prairie where we
were camped, to the river on the southwest, to the bluffs on the
northwest, and to the timber which skirted the prairie on the right
and left. Camping nearby, on the other side of the creek, were
some men with a herd of beef cattle, which they were driving to
Savannah and St. Joseph for market. We usually unyoked our oxen
and turned them loose to feed during our encampments at night,
but this time, on account of the proximity of this herd of cattle,
fearing that they might get mixed up and driven off with them, we
turned our oxen out to feed in their yokes.

"Next morning when we came to look them up, to our great
disappointment our best yoke of oxen was not to be found. Uncle
Fielding and I spent all the morning, well nigh until noon, hunting for them, but to no avail. The grass was tall, and in the morning was wet with heavy dew. Tramping through this grass and
through the woods and over the bluff, we were soaked to the skin,
fatigued, disheartened and almost exhausted.

"In this pitiable plight I was the first to return to our wagons,
and as I approached I saw my mother kneeling down in prayer. I
halted for a moment and then drew gently near enough to hear
her pleading with the Lord not to suffer us to be left in this helpless condition, but to lead us to recover our lost team, that we
might continue our travels in safety. When she arose from her

91

knees I was standing nearby. The first expression I caught upon her precious face was a lovely smile, which discouraged as I was, gave me renewed hope and an assurance I had not felt before.

"A few moments later Uncle Joseph Fielding came to the camp, wet with the dews, faint, fatigued and thoroughly disheartened. His first words were: 'Well, Mary, the cattle are gone!' Mother replied in a voice which fairly rang with cheerfulness, 'Never mind; your breakfast has been waiting for hours, and now, while you and Joseph are eating, I will just take a walk out and see if I can find the cattle.' My uncle held up his hands in blank astonishment, and if the Missouri River had suddenly turned to run up stream, neither of us could have been much more surprised. 'Why, Mary,' he exclaimed, 'what do you mean? We have been all over this country, all through the timber and through the herd of cattle, and our oxen are gone—they are not to be found. I believe they have been driven off, and it is useless for you to attempt to do such a thing as to hunt for them.'

"'Never mind me,' said mother, 'get your breakfast and I will see,' and she started towards the river, following down spring creek. Before she was out of speaking distance the man in charge of the herd of beef cattle rode up from the opposite side of the creek and called out: 'Madam, I saw your oxen over in that direction this morning about daybreak,' pointing in the opposite direction from that in which mother was going. We heard plainly what he said, but mother went right on, and did not even turn her head to look at him. A moment later the man rode off rapidly toward his herd, which had been gathered in the opening near the edge of the woods, and they were soon under full drive for the road leading toward Savannah, and soon disappeared from view.

"My mother continued straight down the little stream of water, until she stood almost on the bank of the river, and then she beckoned to us. I was watching her every moment and was determined that she should not get out of my sight. Instantly we rose from the 'mess-chest,' on which our breakfast had been spread, and started toward her, and like John, who outran the other disciple to the sepulchre, I outran my uncle and came first to the spot where my mother stood.

"There I saw our oxen fastened to a clump of willows growing in the bottom of a deep gulch which had been washed out of the sandy bank of the river by the little spring creek, perfectly concealed from view. We were not long in releasing them from bondage and getting back to our camp, where the other cattle had been fastened to the wagon wheels all the morning, and we were soon on our way home rejoicing. The worthy herdsmen had suddenly departed when they saw mother would not heed them; I hope they went in search of estray honesty, which I trust they found."

Joseph Fielding Smith, *Life of Joseph F. Smith* (Salt Lake City: Deseret Book Co., 1938), pp. 130–33.

MARY FIELDING SMITH'S
OXEN ARE HEALED

JOSEPH FIELDING SMITH

After this," says President [Joseph F.] Smith, "we moved smoothly until we reached a point about mid-way between the Platte and Sweetwater, when one of our best oxen laid down in the yoke as if poisoned and all supposed he

93

would die." The ox stiffened out spasmodically evidently in the throes of death. The death of this faithful animal would have been fatal to the progress of Widow Smith on the journey to the valley. She knew this, so also did Father _____. Naturally when the ox dropped to the ground all the wagons that were following came to a sudden stop.

"At this Father _____ came up and seeing the cause of the disturbance he blustered about," President Smith has said, "as if the world were about at an end. 'There,' said he, 'I told you you would have to be helped and that you would be a burden on the company.' But in this he was mistaken."

Producing a bottle of consecrated oil, Widow Smith asked her brother and James Lawson if they would please administer to the ox just as they would do to a sick person, for it was vital to her interest that the ox be restored that she might pursue her journey. Her earnest plea was complied with. These brethren poured oil on the head of the ox and then laid their hands upon it and rebuked the power of the destroyer just as they would have done if the animal had been a human being. Immediately the ox got up and within a very few moments again pulled in the yoke as if nothing had ever happened. This was a great astonishment to the company.

Before the company had proceeded very far another of her oxen fell down as the first, but with the same treatment he also got up, and this was repeated the third time; by administration the oxen were fully healed. This brought great chagrin to the countenance of the captain of the company.

Widow Smith was not disturbed again until the company reached the Rattlesnake bend on the Sweetwater. At this place "Old Bully," one of the old oxen, laid down and died of sheer old age. He was hardly missed, however, as he had been unable to render but little service for some time.

On reaching the last crossing of the Sweetwater, three of the

Captain's oxen and his best mule laid down near the camp-ground and died. This was a sore trial to him, and, says President Joseph F. Smith, "a very great loss, as he was obliged to get help for himself before he could proceed."

Joseph Fielding Smith, *Life of Joseph F. Smith* (Salt Lake City: Deseret Book Co., 1938), pp. 150–51.

"We Beat Them into the Valley"

JOSEPH F. SMITH

Early next morning, the captain gave notice to the company to arise, hitch up and roll over the mountain into the valley.

To our consternation, when we gathered up our cattle, the essential part of our means of transportation, for some reason had strayed away, and were not to be found with the herd. A brother of mine (John) who was also a boy scout at that time, then obtained a horse and rode back over the road in search of the lost cattle. The captain ordered the march to begin, and, regardless of our predicament, the company started out, up the mountain. The morning sun was then shining brightly, without a cloud appearing anywhere in the sky! I had happened to hear the promise of my dear mother that we would beat the captain into the valley, and would not ask any help from him either. I sat in the front of the wagon with the teams we had in hand hitched to the wheels, while my brother was absent hunting the others. I saw the company wending its slow way up the hill, the animals struggling to pull their heavy loads. The forward teams now had almost reached the summit of the hill, and I said to myself, "True enough, we have come thus far, and we have been blessed, and not the slightest help from anyone has been asked by us." But the last promise seemed to be now impossible; the last hope of getting into the valley before the rest of our company was vanishing in my opinion.

You have doubtless heard descriptions of the terrific thunder storms that sometimes visit the mountains. The pure, crystal streams a few moments before flow gently down their channels; but after one of these rains, in a few minutes they become raging torrents, muddy and sometimes bringing down fallen trees and roots and rocks. All of a sudden, and in less time than I am taking to tell you, a big, dark, heavy cloud rose from the northwest, going directly southeast. In a few minutes it burst in such terrific fury that the cattle could not face the storm, and the captain seemed forced to direct the company to unhitch the teams, turn them loose, and block the wheels to keep the wagons from running back down the hill. The cattle fled before the storm down into the entrance into Parley's canyon, from the Park, into and through the brush. Luckily, the storm lasted only a short time. As it ceased to rain, and the wind ceased to blow, my brother, John, drove up with our lost cattle. We then hitched them to the wagon, and the question was asked by my uncle . . . : "Mary, what shall we do? Go on, or wait for the company to gather up their teams?" She said: "Joseph (that was her brother's name), they have not waited for us, and I see no necessity for us to wait for them."

So we hitched up and rolled up the mountain, leaving the company behind, and this was on the 23rd day of September, 1848. We reached the Old Fort about 10 o'clock that Saturday night. The next morning, in the Old Bowery, we had the privilege of listening to President Brigham Young and President Kimball, Erastus Snow, and some others, give some very excellent instructions. Then, on the afternoon of that Sunday, we went out and met our friends coming in, very dusty, and very footsore and very tired!

The prediction of the widow was actually fulfilled; we beat them into the valley, and we asked no help from them either!

Joseph Fielding Smith, *Life of Joseph F. Smith* (Salt Lake City: Deseret Book Co., 1938), pp. 154–55.

"WE MET MR. BRIDGER"

BRIGHAM YOUNG

We had to have faith to come here. When we met Mr. [Jim] Bridger on the Big Sandy River, said he, "Mr. Young, I would give a thousand dollars if I knew an ear of corn could be ripened in the Great Basin." Said I, "Wait eighteen months and I will show you many of them." Did I say this from knowledge? No, it was my faith; but we had not the least encouragement—from natural reasoning and all that we could learn of this country—of its sterility, its cold and frost, to believe that we could ever raise anything. But we travelled on, breaking the road through the mountains and building bridges until we arrived here, and then we did everything we could to sustain ourselves. We had faith that we could raise grain; was there any harm in this? Not at all. If we had not had faith, what would have become of us? We would have gone down in unbelief, have closed up every resource for our sustenance and should never have raised anything. I ask the whole world, is there any harm in having faith in God? Have you faith? . . . You know James says, "Show me your faith without works, and I will show you my faith by my works." . . . We show our faith by our works. Is there any harm in this? I ask the whole Christian world, is there any harm in believing in God, in a supreme power and influence?

Journal of Discourses, 26 vols. (London: Latter-day Saints' Book Depot, 1854–86), 13:173.

THE MISHAPS OF MARY BATHGATE AND ISABELLA PARKS

DANIEL D. MCARTHUR

On 16 August 1856 on the pioneer trail] Sister Mary Bathgate was badly bitten by a large rattlesnake, just above the ankle, on the back part of her leg. She [and Sister Isabella Park were] about half a mile ahead of the camp at the time it happened. . . . They were both old women, over sixty years of age, and neither of them had ridden one inch since they had left Iowa campground. Sister Bathgate sent a little girl hurrying back to have me and Brothers Leonard and Crandall come with all haste, and bring the oil with us, for she was bitten badly.

As soon as we heard the news, we left all things, and, with the oil, we went posthaste. When we got to her she was quite sick, but said that there was power in the priesthood, and she knew it. So we took a pocketknife, cut the wound larger, and squeezed out all the bad blood we could. . . . We then . . . anointed her . . . and laid our hands on her in the name of Jesus, and felt to rebuke the influence of the poison, and she felt full of faith. We then told her that she must get into the wagon, so she called witnesses to prove that she did not get into the wagon until she was compelled to because of the cursed snake. We started on and traveled two miles, when we stopped to take some refreshment. Sister Bathgate continued to be quite sick, but was full of faith, and after stopping one and a half hours we hitched up our teams. As the word was given for the teams to start, old Sister Isabella Park ran in before the wagon to see how her companion was. The driver, not seeing her, hallooed at his team, and they being quick to mind, Sister Park could not get out of the way, and the fore wheel struck her and threw her down and passed over both her hips. Brother Leonard grabbed hold of her to pull her out of the way, before the hind wheel could catch her. He only got her part way and the hind wheel passed over her ankles.

We all thought that she would be all mashed to pieces, but to the joy of us all, there was not a bone broken, although the wagon had something like two tons burden on it, a load for four yoke of oxen. We went right to work and applied the same medicine to her that we did to the sister who was bitten by the rattlesnake, and although quite sore for a few days, Sister Park got better, so that she was [back walking] before we got into the Valley, and Sister Bathgate was right by her side, to cheer her up.

LeRoy R. and Ann W. Hafen, *Handcarts to Zion: The Story of a Unique Western Migration 1856–1860* (Glendale, Calif.: Arthur H. Clark Co., 1960), pp. 216–17.

RESCUE OF THE WILLIE AND MARTIN HANDCART COMPANIES

SOLOMON F. KIMBALL

On the evening of the 20th [of October], they [the rescue party] turned down to a sheltered place on the Sweetwater, and camped for the night, for men and animals were completely exhausted. Just as they were located, here came Captain Willie and Joseph B. Elder, on two worn-out mules, with news that their company, east of Rocky Ridge, was in a freezing, starving condition, and would perish unless immediate relief was given.

The boys [sent on the rescue] soon hitched their teams again and continued on their way as long as their animals could stand it. At daylight the next morning another start was made, and they continued going until the Willie camp was reached. Before they had time to alight from their wagons they witnessed sights that were enough to move the hardest heart. These poor unfortunates, numbering a little less than five hundred, were caught in a place where there was neither wood nor shelter. They had not had anything to eat for forty-eight hours, and were literally freezing and starving to death.

The Salt Lake boys were soon mounted on harnessed mules, with axes in hand, and in a short time dragged from the distant hills several cords of wood to the Willie camp below. Bonfires were soon made, and the cooking began in earnest, every available person taking a hand. This was kept up until every member of the Willie company had enough to eat and to spare. Soon there was an improvement in camp, but the relief came too late for some, and nine deaths occurred that night.

This is what Brother John Chislett, a member of that ill-fated company, had to say about that portion of the journey:

"We traveled on in misery and sorrow, day after day, sometimes going quite a distance, and at other times we were only able to walk a few miles. We were finally overtaken by a snowstorm which the fierce winds blew furiously about our ears, but we dare not stop, as we had sixteen miles to make that day in order to reach wood and water. . . .

"Just as the sun was sinking behind the distant cliffs west of our camp, several covered wagons were seen coming towards us. The news spread through the camp like wildfire, and all who were able turned out en masse. Shouts of joy rent the air, strong men wept, and children danced with gladness. As the brethren entered our camp the sisters fell upon them and deluged them with their tears and kisses. Our rescuers were so overcome that they could hardly speak, but in choking silence attempted to repress the emotions that evidently mastered them. Soon, however the feeling was somewhat abated, and such a shaking of hands, such words of comfort, and such invocations of God's blessings were never before witnessed. . . ."

The next morning, agreeable to plans adopted by the relief party, at a meeting held the evening before, Captain George D. Grant, with seventeen men and nine teams, pushed on to the relief of the Martin, Hodgett and Hunt companies, taking most of the provisions with him, while William H. Kimball, with the remainder of the outfit, started back to Salt Lake in charge of the Willie company. It was late in the day before Elder Kimball got the handcart people started, as they were in such a weakened condition. About forty of their number had already perished, and others were dying. . . .

On the morning of October 22, 1856, fifteen members of the

relief party, under the leadership of Captain George D. Grant, bade farewell to the handcart folks, at Rocky Ridge, and proceeded to their journey to the east. . . .

Sunday, 26th, was a day of rest in very deed, a good, necessary thing for both men and beasts. After traveling more than three hundred miles, in a little less than nineteen days, over almost impassable roads, the boys were so completely exhausted that Captain Grant was compelled to call a halt. The day was spent in fasting and prayer, and in preparing themselves to receive the mind and the will of the Lord in relation to their future movements. . . .

[Several days later], "We found the Martin company in a deplorable condition, they having lost fifty-six of their number since crossing the North Platte, nine days before. Their provisions were nearly gone, and their clothing almost worn out. Most of their bedding had been left behind, as they were unable to haul it, on account of their weakened condition. We advised them to move on, every day, just as far as they could, as that was the only possible show they had to escape death. . . .

"When we overtook the Martin company, we found them strung out for miles. Old men were tugging at loaded carts, women pulling sick husbands, children struggling through the deep snow, and so it went. They camped that night in a place where there was neither wood nor shelter, and the weather was bitter cold. Several deaths occurred that night, and others were dying." . . .

On the morning of November 3, Captain Grant sent by couriers the following dispatch to President Brigham Young:

"There is not much use for me to attempt to give a description of these people; for this you will learn from your son, Joseph, and from Brother Garr, who are the bearers of this message. You can imagine between five and six hundred men, women and children, worn down by drawing carts through mud and snow, fainting by the wayside, children crying with cold, their limbs stiffened, their feet bleeding, and some of them bare to the frost. The sight is too much for the stoutest of us, but we go on doing our duty, not doubting, nor despairing. Our party is too small to be much of a help. The assistance we give is only a drop in the bucket, as it were, in comparison to what is needed. I believe that not more than one-third of the Martin company will be able to walk any further. You may think this extravagant, but, nevertheless, it is true. Some of the emigrants have good courage, but a great many of them are like children, and do not realize what is before them.

"I have never felt so much interest in any mission that I have ever before been called to perform, and all the boys who came with me feel the same. We have prayed without ceasing, and the blessings of the Lord have been with us. Brother Charles F. Decker, who has traveled this road forty-nine times, declares that he never before saw so much snow on the Sweetwater as there is at the present time.

"Brother Hunt's company is two days back on the road, and Cyrus H. Wheelock and some of the other brethren are with him. We will try to move towards the Valley every day, even if we have to shovel snow to do it, the Lord being our helper. I have never before seen such energy and faith among the boys as is manifested on this trip." . . .

To describe conditions surrounding the old fort at Devil's Gate during the first few days of November, 1856, would be a difficult task. About twenty-five out of the nine hundred emigrants who had arrived there since the 2nd of the month, had already perished, and others were lying at the point of death. Their food supply was nearly exhausted, and there were no signs of help. The snow was eighteen inches deep on the level, and the weather intensely cold. Feed was scarce, and cattle were dying by the score. Wood was almost out of the question, and the more feeble among the Saints were literally freezing to death. Unless immediate steps were taken to relieve the situation, all would perish together.

Captain Grant, thoroughly conversant with these facts, ordered his men to make a start for the west in charge of the Martin company even if they accomplished no more than to find a better camping ground where wood and feed could be secured in greater abundance. Those of the handcart people who were unable to walk were crowded into the overloaded wagons, and a start was made; the balance of the company hobbling along behind with their carts as best as they could.

When the boys came to the first crossing of the Sweetwater west of Devil's Gate, they found the stream full of floating ice, making it dangerous to cross, on account of the strong current. However, the teams went over in safety and continued on their way until they came to a sheltered place, afterwards called "Martin's Hollow." Here they camped for the night and, after burying a number of Saints who had died during the day, busied themselves in getting ready to receive the remainder of the company who were expected at any moment.

When the people who were drawing carts came to the brink of this treacherous stream, they refused to go any further, realizing what it meant to do so, as the water in places was almost waist deep, and the river more than a hundred feet wide by actual measurement. To cross that mountain torrent under such conditions to them meant nothing short of suicide, as it will be remembered that nearly one-sixth of their number had already perished from the effects of crossing North Platte, eighteen days before. They believed that no earthly power could bring them through that place alive, and reasoned that if they had to die it was useless to add to their suffering by the perpetration of such a rash act as crossing the river here. They had walked hundreds of miles over an almost trackless plain, pulling carts as they went, and after making such tremendous sacrifices for the cause of truth, to lay down their lives in such a dreadful manner was awful to contemplate. They became alarmed, and cried mightily unto the Lord for help, but received no answer. All the warring elements of nature appeared to be against them, and the spirit of death itself seemed to be in the very air.

After they had given up in despair, after all hopes had vanished, after every apparent avenue of escape seemed closed, three eighteen-year-old boys belonging to the relief party came to the rescue, and to the astonishment of all who saw, carried nearly every member of that ill-fated handcart company across the snowbound stream. The strain was so terrible, and the exposure so great, that in later years all the boys died from the effects of it. When President Brigham Young heard of this heroic act, he wept like a child, and later declared publicly, "that act alone will ensure C. Allen Huntington, George W. Grant and David P. Kimball an everlasting salvation in the Celestial Kingdom of God, worlds without end." . . .

On the evening of the 11th, the food supply was found to be exhausted, and no signs of relief in sight. A half dozen or more deaths were occurring daily, and the strongest emigrants in camp were fast becoming discouraged. The snow was badly drifted, and the weather bitter cold. Not a word from the Valley had reached the ears of Captain Grant since the company of rescuers left there thirty-six days before, and unless substantial aid reached them within the next few days, that region of country would become a veritable graveyard.

Just before sundown, a dark something in the distance, was seen working its way through the deep snow. It was thought to be a wild beast of some kind. At first but little attention was paid to it, but as it drew nearer, all eyes were turned in that direction. It finally took the form of a man, and two animals, which caused a general sensation throughout the camp. Everybody by this time was on the tiptoe of expectancy and in a few moments their surprise was complete when the chief scout of all scouts, Ephraim K. Hanks, came limping into camp with horses loaded with buffalo meat.

In substance the following is the story told by Elder Hanks and verified in many instances by those who were well acquainted with most of the circumstances:

"I was down to Provo on a fishing expedition, and felt impressed to go to Salt Lake, but for what reason I knew not. On my way there, I stopped overnight with Gurney Brown at Draper. Being somewhat fatigued after the hard day's journey, I retired to rest early, and as I lay awake in my bed, I heard a voice calling me by name and then saying: 'The handcart people are in trouble, and you are wanted; will you go help them?' I turned instantly in the direction from whence the voice came, and beheld an ordinary-sized man in the room. Without any hesitation I answered, 'Yes, I will go.' I then turned over to go to sleep, but had slept only a few minutes when the voice called a second time, repeating almost the same words as on the first occasion. My answer was the same as before. This was repeated the third time.

"When I got up the next morning, I said to Brother Brown, 'The handcart people are in trouble, and I have promised to go out and help them.'

"After breakfast I hastened on to Salt Lake and arrived there on the Saturday preceding the Sunday on which the call was made for volunteers to go and help the last handcart company in. When some of the brethren responded by saying that they would be ready to start in a few days, I spoke out at once, saying, 'I am ready now.'

"The next day I was wending my way eastward over the mountains with a light wagon, all by myself. About ten miles east of Green River, I met quite a number of teams that had been sent to the relief of the belated companies but had turned back on account of the deep snow. Those in charge had come to the conclusion that the emigrants as well as the twenty-seven heroes who had gone to their relief, had all perished, and they did not propose to risk their lives by going any further.

"I helped myself to such things as I was in need of, and continued on my way. Just before I reached South Pass, I was overtaken by one of the worst storms that I ever witnessed. Near the summit, I came to a wagon partly loaded with provisions in charge of Redick N. Allred. After enjoying a needed rest, I secured from him a saddled horse and pack animal, and continued on my way in snow almost to my waist.

"After traveling for a day or two, I met Joseph A. Young and one of the Garr boys on their way to Salt Lake with important messages for Brigham Young. The next evening as I was making my bed, I thought to myself how nice it would be to have a buffalo robe to lie on, and some fresh meat for supper. I kneeled down and asked the Lord to send me a buffalo. Looking around, imagine my surprise when I beheld a big, fat, buffalo bull within fifty yards of my camp. As soon as I could get my gun I brought him down with the first shot. After eating tongue and tenderloin to my heart's content, I went to sleep while my horses were loading up on sagebrush.

"The next day I reached Ice Spring Bench, about sixty miles west of Devil's Gate, and killed another big, fat, buffalo. I cut the meat into long, thin, strips, and lashed it onto my horses. I traveled on until towards evening when I spied in the distance a black streak in the snow. As I drew nearer, it seemed to move, and then I knew what it was.

"About sundown, I reached the ill-fated handcart camp, and the sight that met my eyes was enough to rouse the emotions of the hardest heart. The starving forms and haggard looks of those poor, dejected creatures can never be blotted from my mind. Flocking around me, one would say, 'Please give me some meat for my hungry children.' Shivering urchins with tears streaming down their cheeks would cry out, 'Please, mister, give me some,' and so it went. In less than ten minutes the meat was all gone, and in a short time everybody was eating bison with a relish that did one's eyes good to behold.

"During the evening, a woman passed by the fire where I was sitting and seemed to be in great trouble. Out of curiosity I followed her to Daniel Tyler's tent, some distance away. She asked him if he would please come and administer to her sick husband. Brother Tyler accompanied her, and when he looked at the man he said, 'I cannot administer to a dead man,' and returned to his tent, as he was almost sick himself. I went over to the campfire where Captain Grant and Heber P. Kimball were sitting, and asked them if they would assist me for a few moments, which they consented to do. We washed the man from head to foot with warm water, and then administered to him. During the administration I commanded him in the name of Jesus Christ to breathe and live. The effect was almost instantaneous, and he immediately sat up in bed and sang a song. His wife was so overjoyed that she ran through the camp crying, 'My husband was dead, but the man who has brought the meat has healed him.'

"This event caused general sensation throughout the camp, and many drooping spirits took fresh courage from that very moment. After that the most of my time was spent in looking after the sick and afflicted. Some days I anointed and administered to as many as one or two hundred and in scores of instances they were healed almost instantly.

"Notwithstanding these wonderful manifestations of God's power, many of the Saints lost their limbs either whole or in part. Many I washed with warm water and castile soap until the frozen parts would fall off, after which I would sever the shreds of flesh from the remaining portions of their limbs with my scissors. Some lost toes, some fingers, and others whole hands and feet. One woman lost both of her lower limbs to her knees.

"As the company moved on from day to day, I would leave the road with my pack animals and hunt game. On these trips I killed many buffaloes, and distributed the meat among the hungry Saints. The most remarkable thing about it was that I had traveled that road more than fifty times, and never before saw so many buffaloes in that part of the country. There was not a member of the party but what believed that the Lord had sent them to us in answer to prayer."

On the 17th, the emigrants were filled with delight when they met William H. Kimball at the head of another relief party. It will be remembered that Elder Kimball took charge of the Willie company, at Rocky Ridge, on the morning of October 22, and remained with it until it reached the Valley on the 9th of November. After remaining in Salt Lake one day, he started back with several light wagons loaded with provisions, clothing, and medicines. . . .

The company reached South Pass on the 18th, after facing a terrible snow storm all day. There was considerable wailing among those of the emigrants who were compelled to walk, as their feet, by this time, were in dreadful condition. From there on, they met teams almost every day and soon had wagons enough to carry them all.

On November 30, the four hundred and thirteen survivors of the Martin company reached Salt Lake, and the emigrants that belonged to the Hunt and Hodgett wagon trains came straggling along until the middle of the next month. Nearly all the cattle that were taken from Devil's Gate perished before they reached Fort Bridger.

Probably no greater act of heroism was ever recorded in the annals of history than that performed by the twenty-seven young men who, on the morning of October 7, 1856, went from the city of the Great Salt Lake to the relief of the 1,550 belated emigrants, who were caught in the early snows of a severe winter, hundreds of miles from human habitation, without food and without shelter. By their indefatigable labors these brave mountain boys were instruments in the hands of the Lord in saving 1,300 of that number. Had it not been for their heroic efforts, not enough emigrants would have been left to tell the dreadful tale.

Improvement Era 17:112–17, 201–10, 287–99.

BRIGHAM YOUNG
AND THE RESCUE PARTIES

B. H. ROBERTS

The men with one group of relief wagons, not yet met by the emigrants, concluded from their long delay in appearing that the rear companies of the emigration had perished in the snow, and were for turning back to Salt Lake; but Ephraim K. Hanks, commonly known as "Eph Hanks," who was connected with the mail carrying service, was determined to ascertain the fate of the emigrants, and accordingly mounted one team horse, and leading another, rode on alone. He met the emigrants while yet on the Sweetwater. He had killed a buffalo—two of them, in fact—and cutting the meat into strips, packed it on the horse he was leading; and this with other buffalo he had killed after joining the company, materially added to the meat supply.

By the time South Pass was reached enough relief teams had arrived to allow of some passing on to help the wagon trains still further back, and at the same time admit of all the emigrants riding in the wagons. The journey now was more rapid. By the 21st of November Green river was reached. On the 28th the company camped on the Weber. Meantime other parties had been at work keeping the road open over the mountain passes east of Salt Lake City. By this time the relief wagons numbered one hundred and four, and the emigrants were welcomed by throngs of people into Salt Lake City, where they arrived on Sunday, the 30th of November.

Every relief that shelter, and food, and clothing, and kindness, and devoted attention could bring to these belated emigrants was accorded them. The usual Sunday morning services were in progress at the "Old Tabernacle" when President Young learned of the approach of Martin's company to the city. In dismissing the congregation that the people might meet the emigrants and care for them, he said:

"When those persons arrive I do not want to see them put into houses by themselves. I want to have them distributed in this city among the families that have good, comfortable houses; and I wish the sisters now before me, and all who know how and can, to nurse and wait upon the newcomers, and prudently administer medicine and food to them. . . . The afternoon meeting will be omitted, for I wish the sisters to go home and prepare to give those who have just arrived a mouthful of something to eat, and to wash them, and nurse them up. . . . Prayer is good, but when (as on this occasion) baked potatoes, and pudding, and milk are needed, prayer will not supply their place. Give every duty its proper time and place. . . . I want you to understand that I desire this people to nurse them up; we want you to receive them as your own children, and to have the same feelings for them. . . . Now that the most of them are here, we will continue our labors of love until they are able to take care of themselves, and we will receive the blessing. You need not be distrustful about that, for the Lord will bless this people."

B. H. Roberts, *A Comprehensive History of The Church of Jesus Christ of Latter-day Saints,* 6 vols. (Salt Lake City: The Church of Jesus Christ of Latter-day Saints, 1930), 4:99–101.

"MY FEET WERE FROZEN"

MARY GOBLE PAY

We traveled from fifteen to twenty-five miles a day . . . till we got to the Platte River. . . . We caught up with the handcart companies that day. We watched them cross the river. There were great lumps of ice floating down the river. It was bitter cold. The next morning there were fourteen dead. . . . We went back to camp and had our prayers and . . . sang "Come, Come, Ye Saints, No Toil nor Labor Fear." I wondered what made my mother cry that night. . . . The next morning my little sister was born. It was the twenty-third of September. We named her Edith. She lived six weeks and died. . . . She was buried at the last crossing of the Sweetwater.

When we arrived at Devils Gate, it was bitter cold. We left many of our things there. . . . My brother, James . . . was as well as he ever was when we went to bed that night. In the morning he was dead.

My feet were frozen; also my brother's and my sister's. It was nothing but snow. We could not drive the pegs in our tents. . . . We did not know what would become of us. Then one night a man came to our camp and told us . . . Brigham Young had sent men and teams to help us. . . . We sang songs; some danced, and some cried.

My mother had never got well. . . . She died between the Little and Big Mountains. . . . She was 43 years of age. . . .

We arrived in Salt Lake City nine o'clock at night the eleventh of December, 1856. Three out of the four that were living were frozen. My mother was dead in the wagon.

Early next morning Brigham Young came. . . . When he saw

our condition, our feet frozen and our mother dead, tears rolled down his cheeks.

The doctor amputated my toes, using a saw and a butcher knife. The sisters were dressing mother for her grave. . . . When my feet were fixed they carried us in to see our mother for the last time. . . . That afternoon she was buried.

I have thought often of my mother's words before we left England. "Polly, I want to go to Zion while my children are small so they can be raised in the Gospel of Jesus Christ, for I know this is the true church."

Autobiography of Mary Goble Pay, Church Archives, The Church of Jesus Christ of Latter-day Saints.

"THE ANGELS OF GOD WERE THERE"

DAVID O. MCKAY

A teacher, conducting a class, said it was unwise ever to attempt, even to permit [the Martin handcart company] to come across the plains under such conditions.

[According to a class member] some sharp criticism of the Church and its leaders was being indulged in for permitting any company of converts to venture across the plains with no more supplies or protection than a handcart caravan afforded.

An old man in the corner sat silent and listened as long as he could stand it, then he arose and said things that no person who heard him will ever forget. His face was white with emotion, yet he spoke calmly, deliberately, but with great earnestness and sincerity.

In substance [he] said, "I ask you to stop this criticism. You are discussing a matter you know nothing about. Cold historic facts mean nothing here, for they give no proper interpretation of the questions involved. Mistake to send the Handcart Company out so late in the season? Yes. But I was in that company and my wife was in it and Sister Nellie Unthank whom you have cited was there, too. We suffered beyond anything you can imagine and many died of exposure and starvation, but did you ever hear a survivor of that company utter a word of criticism? Not one of that company ever apostatized or left the Church, because everyone of us came through with the absolute knowledge that God lives for we became acquainted with him in our extremities.

"I have pulled my handcart when I was so weak and weary from illness and lack of food that I could hardly put one foot ahead of the other. I have looked ahead and seen a patch of sand or a hill slope and I have said, I can go only that far and there I must give up, for I cannot pull the load through it. . . . I have gone on to that sand and when I reached it, the cart began pushing me. I have looked back many times to see who was pushing my cart, but my eyes saw no one. I knew then that the angels of God were there.

"Was I sorry that I chose to come by handcart? No. Neither then nor any minute of my life since. The price we paid to become acquainted with God was a privilege to pay, and I am thankful that I was privileged to come in the Martin Handcart Company."

Relief Society Magazine, January 1948, p. 8.

"THIS IS THE PLACE"

~

JAMES A. LITTLE

The 24th of July has been celebrated as the anniversary of the arrival of the pioneers in the valley of the Great Salt Lake from the circumstance that on that day, 1847, Brigham Young, who had been detained by sickness, and those who had remained with him, first emerged from the defile in the Wasatch mountains and followed the track of the main body who preceded them. It was the culmination of a long series of efforts to find a place of rest, where the Saints could enjoy immunity from the pursuit of enemies.

There is a slight elevation of table land a short distance in front of Emigration canyon. This hides the valley from the traveler until the top of it is reached. From this point Brigham Young and those who were with him, among whom were his brother L. D. Young, Apostles Wilford Woodruff and Heber C. Kimball, had their first view of the object of their toils, the valley of the Great Salt Lake. It requires no stretch of the imagination to comprehend that a feeling of joy, of exhilaration and thanksgiving filled to overflowing the hearts of these weary pilgrims. The faith that had sustained them through years of suffering and hope enabled them to discern in the near future the attainment of the object of their sacrifices. They experienced the same impulse to shout for joy as those who had preceded them.

President Young, still feeble from the effects of his late illness, was riding under the cover of Elder Woodruff's carriage. As the teams halted he came to the front, took a general view of the country before him, then uncovered his head, swung his hat and shouted with all the energy his feeble condition permitted, "Hurrah! Hurrah!! Hurrah!!!" Then turning to Heber C. Kimball who was near, he exclaimed, "Brother Heber, *this is the place.*" The circumstances emphasized the expression with a world of meaning. "This is the place" that has been prophesied of from the days of Kirtland, where the Saints are to be gathered from the nations of the earth and acquire strength to further contend for the right. Here is the place where we will build temples to the Lord our God and make greater preparations than we have been able to do, surrounded by enemies, for the redemption of our race.

James A. Little, *From Kirtland to Salt Lake City* (Salt Lake City: James A. Little, 1890), pp. 117–19.

"WE WILL MAKE THE DESERT BLOSSOM LIKE THE ROSE"

JOSEPH F. SMITH

When President Young set his foot down here, upon this desert spot, it was in the midst of persuasion, prayers and petitions on the part of some Latter-day Saints who had gone forward and landed upon the coast of California, that beautiful, rich country, semi-tropical, abounding in resources that no inland country could possess, inviting and appealing for settlers at that time, and just such settlers as President Brigham

116

Young could have taken there—honest people, people who were firm in their faith, who were established in the knowledge of truth and righteousness and in the testimony of Jesus Christ—which is the spirit of prophecy—and in the testimony of Joseph Smith which was a confirmation of the spirit of Christ and His mission—these people pleaded with President Young. "Come with us," they said, "and let us go to the coast. Go where the roses bloom all the year round, where the fragrance of flowers scents the air, from May until May; where beauty reigns; where the elements of wealth are to be found, and only need to be developed. Come with us."

"No," said President Young; "we will remain here, and we will make the desert blossom like the rose. We will fulfill the Scriptures by remaining here."

Utah Genealogical and Historical Magazine, 8 [1917]:156.

CRICKETS AND SEAGULLS

B. H. ROBERTS

The pioneers when entering the valley, it will be remembered, noted that in the foothills there were great numbers of large, black crickets, which then excited but a passing remark. Now, however, in this month of May, [1848], they came swarming from the foothills literally by millions, and descended upon the new-made fields of grain. They devoured all before them as they came to it. Their appetite never abated. They were cutting and grinding day and night, leaving the fields bare and brown behind them. There seemed to be no end to their numbers. They could not fly; their only means of locomotion was by clumsily hopping a scant foot at a time—hence, once in the fields, the difficulty of getting them out; and they came in myriads, increasing daily. Holes were dug; and for the radius of a rod the pests were surrounded by women and children, and driven into them and buried—bushels of them at a time; and this was repeated again and again; but what was the use? This method seemed not to affect the numbers of the pests. Then the men plowed ditches around the wheat fields, turned in the water, and drove the black vermin into the running streams and thus carried them from the fields and destroyed them by hundreds of thousands—all to no purpose; as many as ever seemed to remain, and more were daily swarming from the hills. Fire was tried, but to no better purpose. Man's ingenuity was baffled. He might as well try to sweep back the rising tide of the ocean with a broom as prevail against these swarming pests by the methods tried. Insignificant, these inch or inch and a half long insects separately, but in millions, terrible. The incident illustrates the formidableness of mere numbers. Since the days of Egypt's curse of locusts there was probably nothing like it. The failure to destroy these pests spelled famine to these first settlers of Salt Lake Valley. It meant starvation to the companies of thousands of women and children then en route across the plains. Small wonder if the hearts of the colonists failed them. They looked at one another in helpless astonishment. They were beaten. That is something awful for strong men to admit, especially when beaten by units so insignificant. Meantime the ceaseless gnawing of the ruthless and insatiable invader went on. The brown patches of the wheat fields grew larger. Soon all would be bare and brown, and hope of food and life would disappear with the recently green wheat fields.

Then the miraculous happened. I say it deliberately, the miraculous happened, as men commonly view the miraculous. There was heard the shrill, half-scream, half-plaintive cry of some seagulls hovering over the wheat fields. Presently they alight and begin devouring the crickets. Others come—thousands of them—from over the lake. The upper feathers of the gull's wings are tinted with a delicate grey, and some of the flight feathers, primaries, to be exact, are marked with black, but the prevailing color is white; and as they came upon the new wheat fields, stretched upward and then gracefully folded their wings and began devouring the devourers, to the cricket-vexed colonists they seemed like white-winged angels of deliverance—these gulls. They were tireless in their destructive—nay, their saving work. It was noted that when they were glutted with crickets they would go to the streams, drink, vomit, and return again to the slaughter. And so it continued, day after day, until the plague was stayed, and the crops of the pioneers saved.

B. H. Roberts, *A Comprehensive History of The Church of Jesus Christ of Latter-day Saints,* 6 vols. (Salt Lake City: The Church of Jesus Christ of Latter-day Saints, 1930), 331–33.

"CHEAPER THAN IN NEW YORK"

ORSON F. WHITNEY

I t was during this time of famine, when the half-starved, half-clad settlers scarcely knew where to look for the next crust of bread or for rags to hide their nakedness—for clothing had become almost as scarce with them as bread-stuffs—that Heber C. Kimball, filled with the spirit of prophecy, in a public meeting declared to the astonished congregation that, within a short time, "States goods" would be sold in the streets of Great Salt Lake City cheaper than in New York and that the people should be abundantly supplied with food and clothing.

"I don't believe a word of it," said Charles C. Rich; and he but voiced the sentiment of nine-tenths of those who had heard the astounding declaration.

Heber himself was startled at his own words, as soon as the Spirit's force had abated and the "natural man" had reasserted itself. On resuming his seat, he remarked to the brethren that he was afraid he "had missed it this time." But they were not his own words, and He who had inspired them knew how to fulfill.

The occasion for the fulfillment of this remarkable prediction was the unexpected advent of the gold-hunters, on their way to California. The discovery of gold in that land had set on fire, as it were, the civilized world, and hundreds of richly laden trains now began pouring across the continent on their way to the new El Dorado. Salt Lake Valley became the resting place, or "half-way house" of the nation, and before the Saints had had time to recover from their surprise at Heber's temerity in making such a prophecy, the still more wonderful fulfillment was brought to their very doors.

The gold-hunters were actuated by but one desire; to reach the Pacific Coast. . . . Impatient at their slow progress, in order to lighten their loads, they threw away or "sold for a song" the valuable merchandise with which they had stored their wagons to cross the Plains. Their choice, blooded, though now jaded stock, they eagerly exchanged for the fresh mules and horses of the pioneers, and bartered off, at almost any sacrifice, dry goods, groceries, provisions, tools, clothing, etc., for the most primitive outfits, with barely enough provisions to enable them to reach their journey's end.

Thus, as . . . Heber had predicted, "States goods" were actually sold in the streets of Great Salt Lake City cheaper than they could have been purchased in the City of New York.

Orson F. Whitney, *Life of Heber C. Kimball,* 2d ed. (Salt Lake City: Stevens & Wallis, 1945), pp. 389–91.

SCANTY PIONEER FARE

LORENZO D. YOUNG

Oliver G. Workman, a Battalion man, without family, came to Salt Lake with others from California in the autumn of 1847, and there he met his brother Jacob and family and assisted in providing food. The following spring, flour became so scarce that it was very difficult for the needy to obtain even a moiety. Mr. Workman came to me twice and stated that he had tried to get a little and could not. I told him I had none to sell at any price, but I let him have a few pounds each time.

In a few days he came to me the third time and stated that he had tried to get a little flour until he was discouraged. He expressed his regret at being under the necessity of coming again but, said he, "What can I do? My brother's wife is famishing!" I remarked that I had only a little flour left and I stepped into another room where Mrs. Young lay on the bed sick. I stated the case to her and asked, "What shall we do?" The question was quite as important to us as to Mr. Workman; but she replied, "We cannot see anyone starve. Divide to the last pound." I weighed what I thought we might spare. It was seven pounds. As I handed the sack containing it to Mr. Workman he put his hand into his pocket, and, without counting handed out a handful of gold. I again told him I had no flour to sell; that I would not exchange him a pound of flour for a pound of gold. He returned to the gold to his pocket, and, as he turned to go away he was overpowered by his feelings and shed tears.

Soon after this occurrence myself and family were entirely out of food. It had been necessary to work my oxen very hard through the winter, and all my cattle were too poor for food. I heard of a man on Mill Creek who had a three-year-old steer which he was keeping for beef, with the design of going to California in the spring. I succeeded in trading him a pair of large oxen by agreeing to give him one quarter of the animal after it was dressed. I drove the steer home, butchered it and hung the hide on the fence with the flesh side out. This furnished a feast for the magpies as they picked off what little meat remained on it. My share of the beef, with what little food could be gathered from other sources, kept us along for several weeks. During that time I made every possible exertion to obtain more food, but without success.

Circumstances again seemed desperate. I took the hide off the fence and put it to soak in City creek. When it became soft and pliable I cut it into strips for convenience in handling. I labored on it about two days, scraping the flesh side clean and getting the hair off the other. After I became satisfied with its condition, I turned it over to Mrs. Young. To prepare a meal, a piece of raw-hide was boiled until it became a glue soup, when salt was added to season. This being a native product was abundant while other condiments were as scarce as the food they were intended to season.

From the wreck of affairs in Nauvoo Mrs. Young saved a favorite set of china. I never knew more need of an inviting looking table than in those days of glue soup. Mrs. Young decked it out in the most inviting manner possible; the center piece, a pan of glue soup, with a ladle for dipping and conveying it to our plates. The Lord was always asked to bless the scanty fare. We satisfied our appetites as best we could, with a thankful feeling that we had that much to sustain life. Mrs. Young's health was generally poor, and on that diet she daily grew weaker. I felt that something must be done or she would die for want of nourishment. I went to a man that I understood had considerable flour and offered him a horse for a few pounds. He was one of a few Saints who had but little faith that we could remain in the country, and he designed going to California when spring was sufficiently advanced. His fears that he might be short prevented him from letting me have any flour. I met Bishop E. Hunter and made known my situation. Said he, "I have but little flour, but Sister Young must not die for want of some." He let me have seven pounds. Mrs. Young ever after believed that the kindness of Brother Hunter saved her life. On her dying bed, and about an hour and a half before she expired, she spoke of the circumstance and blessed him.

On the bottom lands along the river Jordan, thistles grew in abundance. The roots of these afforded considerable nourishment. As the large, dry top usually remained attached to the root until a new growth in the spring, they could be found and dug in the winter. They were a great help to the Saints in times of scarcity. In the spring of 1848 many acres of bottom land had been dug over. I, at times, as well as others, was compelled to avail myself of this means of sustaining life. As vegetation grew in the spring, other roots and herbs were used for food. Segoes for a time were in considerable demand, but several persons were poisoned by eating the wrong variety. Three persons died in as many weeks from this cause. After the sad occurrence they were not much used as edibles.

One morning I met Brother Welcome Chapman with a basket of cowslips. As I had been accustomed to these for early spring greens in my youth, to me at that time they seemed a great luxury. That they grew in this mountain region surprised me. Only those who have longed for something palatable and refreshing can appreciate the feelings that caused me to exclaim with considerable enthusiasm, "Brother Chapman, where on earth did you get them?" He replied, "I have found a little spot up the canyon where they grow, and I go and get a basket of them in the morning to last us during the day." I asked him if the supply was sufficient to let me have some. He thought so, and gave me what he then had. When cooked we enjoyed them very much. They were a change, a variety. Brother Chapman continued to furnish a few greens, from which we realized much benefit. In those times faith was an important factor in our lives. The prayer that the Lord would bless our food that it might strengthen us was made up of no idle words. It came from the heart, and in return the blessing was often realized. With the meager fare I was able to accomplish considerable labor.

James A. Little, *From Kirtland to Salt Lake City* (Salt Lake City: James A. Little, 1890), pp. 170–74.

FAITH

PRAYER AND JOHNNYCAKE

JOHN LYMAN SMITH

In my early years I used to often eat at the table with Joseph the Prophet. At one time he was called to dinner. I being at play in the room with his son Joseph, he called us to him, and we stood one each side of him. After he had looked over the table he said, "Lord, we thank Thee for this Johnnycake, and ask Thee to send us something better. Amen." The corn bread was cut and I received a piece from his hand.

Before the bread was all eaten, a man came to the door and asked if the Prophet Joseph was at home. Joseph replied he was, whereupon the visitor said, "I have brought you some flour and a ham."

Joseph arose and took the gift, and blessed the man in the name of the Lord. Turning to his wife, Emma, he said, "I knew the Lord would answer my prayer."

Juvenile Instructor 27:172.

"WHAT DO YOU KNOW
ABOUT OLD JOE SMITH?"

FROM
EDWIN RUSHTON JOURNAL

After sailing from England, our immigrant company reached Nauvoo, April 13, 1843. Father was very anxious to find the members of his family already established there, and hurried towards the town in search of them. He had gone only a short distance when he met a man riding a beautiful black horse. The man accosted him, saying, "Hey, Bub, is that a company of Mormons just landed?"

In much surprise, Father answered, "Yes, sir."

"Are you a Mormon?" the stranger continued.

"Yes sir," Father again answered.

"What do you know about old Joe Smith?" the stranger asked.

"I know that Joseph Smith is a prophet of God," said Father.

"I suppose you are looking for an old man with a long, gray beard. What would you think if I told you I was Joseph Smith?" the man continued.

"If you are Joseph Smith," said Father, "I know you are a prophet of God."

In a gentle voice, the man explained, "I am Joseph Smith. I came to meet those people, dressed as I am in rough clothes and speaking in this manner, to see if their faith is strong enough to stand the things they must meet. If not, they should turn back right now."

Edwin Rushton, Pioneer Journals, unpublished.

JOSEPH SMITH TESTS
EDWIN D. WOOLLEY'S FAITH

TRUMAN MADSEN

Bishop Edwin D. Woolley was a forebear of President Spencer W. Kimball. He was a stubborn man (he himself said it)—*contrary* was the word they used in those days. It was said of him, "If he dies by drowning, look for the body upstream." Edwin D. Woolley had a store in Nauvoo, and one day the Prophet said to him, "Brother Woolley, we want all your goods for the building up of the kingdom of God," or words to that effect. Brother Woolley did as he was asked, packing his whole stock ready to be moved. Then he went to ask Joseph what he wished him to do about the goods he had received for sale on commission. Was he ready to hand all the other goods over to the Church? the Prophet asked. Brother Woolley said he was. His eyes moist, the Prophet put his hand on the other man's shoulder and said, "The Lord bless you. Put them back on the shelves."

Truman Madsen, *Joseph Smith the Prophet* (Salt Lake City: Bookcraft, 1989), p. 92.

"YOU PRAYED ME HERE"

ORSON F. WHITNEY

Six months after the Church was organized, Oliver Cowdery, Parley P. Pratt, and other Elders started upon a mission to the Lamanites; and, coming to Kirtland, in northern Ohio, they preached the Gospel there, and gathered into the fold quite a number, among them Edward Partridge, who became the first Bishop of the Church; Algernon Sidney Gilbert, Frederick G. Williams, Sidney Rigdon, and my grandfather, Newel K. Whitney, with his wife, Elizabeth Ann Whitney. These disciples, hearing that the Church would probably move westward, began to pray for the coming of the Prophet.

I have heard my grandmother and my father relate that when the Prophet came to Kirtland he drove in a sleigh and halted in front of the mercantile store of Gilbert and Whitney. He sprang out, went into the store, walked up to the junior partner, and said: "Newel K. Whitney, thou art the man." Grandfather was astonished; he had never seen Joseph Smith till then—Joseph had never seen him with his natural eyes—and he answered: "Stranger, you have the advantage of me; I could not call you by name, as you have me." And the stranger then said: "I am Joseph, the Prophet. You have prayed me here. Now, what do you want of me?"

Conference Report, April 1912, p. 50.

FAITH AND PRAYERS OF A MOTHER

LUCY MACK SMITH

On the first of August [1834], Joseph and Hyrum returned [from Zion's Camp]. They were overjoyed to meet us again in health, more especially on account of the perils which they had passed through during their absence. Joseph and Hyrum sat down beside me, each holding one of my hands in his, while they related the following story:

"When we started on our journey, we made arrangements to have everyone made as comfortable as possible; but the sufferings which are incident to such an excursion made some of the brethren discontented, and they began to murmur against us, saying, The Lord never required them to take such a tiresome journey, and that it was folly for them to suffer such fatigue and inconvenience just to gratify us. We warned them, in the name of the Lord, to stop their murmuring; for, if they did not, the displeasure of the Almighty would be manifested in judgments in their midst. But many of them paid no attention to what we said, until one morning when they went out to harness up their horses, and found them all so lame as to be unable to travel. We then told them that this was a curse which had come upon them because of transgression; but, if they would repent, it might be removed—if not, a greater curse would come upon them. They believed what we said and repented of their folly. . . . It was not long, however, till the spirit of dissension arose again. . . .

"Soon after arriving at the point of destination, the cholera broke out in our midst; the brethren were so violently attacked that it seemed impossible to render them any assistance. They immediately sent for us to lay hands on them, but we soon discovered that this, also, was a judgment from the Almighty; for, when we laid our hands upon them, in the name of the Lord, the disease immediately fastened itself upon us and in a few minutes we were in awful agony. We made signals to each other . . . in order to join in prayer to God that he would deliver us from this dreadful influence. . . . We were hardly able to stand upon our feet, and we feared that we should die in that western wilderness without the privilege of blessing our children, or giving them one word of parting counsel. We . . . fell upon our knees and cried unto the Lord that he would deliver us from this awful calamity, but we arose worse than before. We kneeled down the second time, and when we commenced praying the cramp seized us, gathering the cords in our arms and legs in bunches and operating equally severe throughout our system. We still besought the Lord, with all our strength, to have mercy upon us, but all in vain. It seemed as though the heavens were sealed against us. . . . We then kneeled down the third time, concluding never to rise to our feet again until one or the other should get a testimony that we should be healed; and that the one who should get the first intimation of the same from the Spirit, should make it known to the other."

They stated further, that after praying some time the cramp began to release its hold; and, in a short time, Hyrum sprang to his feet and exclaimed, "Joseph, we shall return to our families. I have had an open vision, in which I saw mother kneeling under an apple tree; and she is even now asking God, in tears, to spare our lives, that she may again behold us in the flesh. The Spirit testifies, that her prayers, united with ours, will be answered."

"Oh, my mother!" said Joseph, "how often have your prayers been the means of assisting us when the shadows of death encompassed us."

Lucy Mack Smith, *History of Joseph Smith,* edited by Preston Nibley (Salt Lake City: Bookcraft, 1958), pp. 227–29.

FAITH OF A CHILD

HEBER C. KIMBALL

My wife, one day, when going out on a visit, gave my daughter Helen Mar charge not to touch the dishes, for if she broke any during her absence she would give her a whipping when she returned. While my wife was absent my daughter broke a number of the dishes by letting the table leaf fall, and then she went out under an apple tree and prayed that her mother's heart might be softened, that when she returned she might not whip her. Her mother was very punctual when she made a promise to her children, to fulfill it, and when she returned she undertook, as a duty, to carry this promise into effect. She retired with her into her room, but found herself powerless to chastise her; her heart was so softened that it was impossible for her to raise her hand against the child. Afterwards, Helen told her mother she had prayed to the Lord that she might not whip her.

Orson F. Whitney, *Life of Heber C. Kimball*, 2d ed. (Salt Lake City: Stevens & Wallis, 1945), p. 69.

"A PRESENT
FOR HIS FAITHFULNESS"

CAROLINE CROSBY

Times became very hard in Kirt[land]. It seemed that our enemies were determined to drive us away if they could possibly, by starving us. None of the business men would employ a Mormon scarcely, on any conditions. And our prophet was continually harassed with vexatious lawsuits. Besides, the great apostacy in the church added a double portion of distress and suffering to those who wished to abide in the faith, and keep the commandments.

We became very short of provisions, several times ate the last we had and knew not where the next meal was coming from. We then had an opportunity to try the charity of the brethren, who were many of them in the same predicament as ourselves. I recollect that Wm Cahoon called in to see us one night, as he was going home with a few quarts of corn meal, and inquired if we had any breadstuff on hand, we told him we had not. He said he would divide what he had with us, and if my husband would go home with him, he would also divide his potatoes and meat which bore the same proportion to his meal. Joseph Young also divided with us several times in the same way, and we with him. We had numerous opportunities of dividing almost our last loaf with the brethren.

Mr C worked on br Joseph's house, as he was building tolerably large, but frequently got so straitened that he had nothing to give the workmen when Saturday night came, and they were obliged to borrow or do without. They all left at one time, except

Mr C, he worked on for several days alone. Sister Emma observing that he was laboring there alone, came in one day, and inquired of him whether or where he got his provision. He told her he was entirely without, and knew not where to look, as he had no money and the boss who employed him had no means in his hands. She then went into her chamber, and brought him a nice ham [weighing] 20 lbs., telling him that it was a present for his faithfulness, and that he should bring a sack, and get as much flour as he could to take home. Accordingly he came home rejoicing, considering it a perfect Godsend. It was a beautiful white flour, and the ham was very sweet. I thought nothing ever tasted half as good.

Kenneth W. Godfrey, Audrey M. Godfrey, Jill Mulvay Derr, *Women's Voices: An Untold History of the Latter-day Saints, 1830–1900* (Salt Lake City: Deseret Book Co., 1982), pp. 55–56.

"The Lord Will Provide"

DRUSILLA DORRIS HENDRICKS

We started March 17th 1839 for Quincy, Illinois. On the first of April as soon as the brethren found we were there, [they] secured a bottle of oil, consecrated it, and came with Father Joseph Smith at their head, (seven in number) while we were camped out and got him [her husband, James] on a chair and anointed and administered to him again, then assisted him to his feet and he walked, between two of them, some thirty yards and back.

We soon got into a room, partly underground and partly on top of the ground. The room was very close and he took sick and I had to lift him at least fifty times a day and in doing so I had to strain every nerve.

We had the cattle which had hauled us here but could not sell them, but could hire them out for a small sum to break prairie, so we hired them. We had one small heifer that the mob did not take that gave us a little milk for twice a day, but in less than two weeks there came a drove of cattle from Missouri and they drove her off with them, so we were like Job of old and my husband was as sore for his blood cankered and he broke in sores all over his body so that you could not put a pin point on him without putting it on a sore, from the crown of his head to the soles of his feet.

In two weeks we neither had bread or meat so we sent our oldest son, William, three miles out on the prairie to the man who had hired our cattle. We had one spoonful of sugar and one saucer full of corn meal so I made mush of the meal and put the sugar on it and gave it to my children. That was the last of eatables of any kind we had in the house or on the earth. We were in a strange land and among strangers. The conflict began in my mind. "Your folks told you your husband would be killed and are you not sorry you did not listen to them." I said, No I am not. I did what was right if I die I am glad I was baptized, for the remission of my sins for I have an answer of a good conscience. But after that a third person spoke, it was a still small voice this time saying hold on for the Lord will provide. I said I would for I would trust him and not grumble.

I went to work and washed everything and cleaned the house thoroughly as I said to myself, If I die I will die clean. Along in the afternoon Brother Rubin Alred came. He lived fifteen miles away. He went to the bed where my husband lay and asked him if we had any prospects for bread at all and received the answer that we had none. He asked me for a sack and then went to his wagon and brought in a sack of meal and he also made me a present of a washboard saying you had to leave everything and I felt you were out of bread so I came by the mill to get my grinding done before I came here and it made me late. I thanked him and he started home. In a few moments my son, William, came in with only fifty cents. We thought he would get three dollars as that is what was due us for the hire of our cattle. The man had lost the cattle and wanted the boy to go and find them. I made the best of what we had for I took the money and went down to the river and purchased flour 6 lbs., pork 2 1/2 lbs. and 1/2 bushel of potatoes, so I had quite a supply and we were thankful but could [not] take the honor to ourselves, so we lived sparingly for at least two weeks but when that was gone we were in the same condition again for we had nothing. I felt awful but the same voice that gave me comfort before was there to comfort me again and it said, hold on, the Lord will provide for his Saints. I said if He provided for us this time I should think He owned us for his children. I washed and cleaned as before and was just finishing the doorstep when Brother Alexander Williams came up to my back door with two bushels of meal on his shoulder. I looked up and said Brother Williams, I have just found out how the widows crust and barrel held out through the famine. He asked how. I said just as it was out someone was sent to fill it. He said he was so busy with his crop that he could hardly leave it, but the Spirit strove with him saying Brother Hendricks' family is suffering, so I dropped everything and came by and had it ground lest you would not get it soon enough. I soon baked a cake of the meal and he blessed it and we all partook of it and water. Hunger makes sweet, cakes without sugar.

He told us that he had baptized the man and his wife that he was living with. He was tending the farm and that he should come again. But when he wanted more corn, the man he was working for, whose name was Edwards, said to him, "You shall not work for me for corn and take it to the Saints who have been driven and robbed." "Tell me where you go and I will go myself." So he came just as we were out. I remarked that the Scriptures said, "In the mouth of two or three witnesses shall every word be established and the D. & C. says it is the Lord's duty to look after and provide for his Saints, which has been proven true to me to a demonstration.

Carol Cornwall Madsen, *In Their Own Words: Women and the Story of Nauvoo* (Salt Lake City: Deseret Book Co., 1994), pp. 162–64.

"WHAT A DINNER WE HAD THAT DAY"

HANNAH CORNABY

One morning having, as usual, attended to family prayer, in which, with greater significance than is often used, we asked, "give us this day our daily bread;" and having eaten a rather scanty breakfast—every morsel we had in the house—Edith was wondering what we should have for dinner, and why Pa had not sent us some fish. I, too, was anxious, not having heard from Provo for some days; so, telling my darlings I would go and see if Sister Ellen Jackson, (whose husband was also one of the fishing party), had heard any news, I started off. Sister Jackson had not heard from the fishery, but was quite cheerful; and telling me how well her garden was growing, added that the radishes were fit for use, and insisted that I must have some. It was good to see something to eat; and, quite pleased, I bade her good morning. I passed on my way the house of Brother Charles Gray, and Sister Gray asked me where I had got such fine radishes. I told her, and offered to divide them with her, to which she agreed, providing I would take in exchange some lettuce and cress, of which she had plenty. She filled a pan with these; and I hurried away thinking how pleased my children would be, if only we had bread to eat with them.

As I was passing Brother Simon Baker's house, Sister Baker saw me, and invited me in. I told her I had left my children and could not stop long. She then asked me where I had got such nice green stuff, and when I told her, and offered her some, she replied, "If I could exchange some for butter, I would be glad." She then gave me a piece of nice fresh butter, which had just come from their dairy on the Jordan; and also a large slice of cheese. If I only had bread, I thought, how good these would be! Just then my eyes rested upon a large vessel full of broken bread. Sister Baker, seeing I had noticed it, told me its history. It had been sent the day before, in a sack, to the canyon where her husband had a number of men working. On the way it had fallen from the wagon and been crushed under the wheel. She did not know what to do with it, remarking that she would offer me some of it but feared I would feel insulted, although she assured me it was perfectly clean. I accepted her offer, and, after filling a large pan, she sent her daughter home with me to carry it.

The children were watching for my return; and when they saw the bread, they clapped their hands with delight. Bread, butter, cheese, radishes, lettuce, and cress! What a dinner we had that day! Elijah never enjoyed the dinner the ravens brought him more than I did that meal; nor did he more fully understand that a kind Providence had furnished it.

Hannah Cornaby, *Autobiography and Poems* (Salt Lake City: J. C. Graham Co., 1881), pp. 41–42.

DEATH OF ORSON SPENCER'S WIFE

JOHN R. YOUNG

Orson Spencer was a graduate from an eastern college, who having studied for the ministry, became a popular preacher in the Baptist Church. Meeting with a "Mormon" elder, he became acquainted with the teachings of Joseph Smith and accepted them. Before doing so, however, he and his highly educated young wife counted the cost, laid their hearts on the altar and made the sacrifice! How few realize what it involved to become a "Mormon" in those early days! Home, friends, occupation, popularity, all that makes life pleasant, were gone. Almost over night they were strangers to their own kindred.

After leaving Nauvoo, his wife, ever delicate and frail, sank rapidly under the ever accumulating hardships. The sorrowing husband wrote imploringly to the wife's parents, asking them to receive her into their home until the Saints should find an abiding place. The answer came, "Let her renounce her degrading faith and she can come back, but never until she does."

When the letter was read to her, she asked her husband to get his Bible and to turn to the book of Ruth and read the first chapter, sixteenth and seventeenth verses: "Entreat me not to leave thee or to return from following after thee: for whither thou goest I will go, and where thou lodgest I will lodge. Thy people shall be my people and thy God my God."

Not a murmur escaped her lips. The storm was severe and the wagon covers leaked. Friends held milk pans over her bed to keep her dry. In those conditions, in peace and without apparent suf-

140

fering, the spirit took its flight and her body was consigned to a grave by the wayside.

Memoirs of John R. Young (Salt Lake City: Deseret News Press, 1920), pp. 17–18.

"THE LORD TOLD HIM TO GO TO JOSEPH MILLETT"

JOSEPH MILLETT

One of my children came in, said that Brother Newton Hall's folks were out of bread. Had none that day. I put . . . our flour in [a] sack to send up to Brother Hall's. Just then Brother Hall came in. Says I, "Brother Hall, how are you out for flour." "Brother Millett, we have none." "Well, Brother Hall, there is some in that sack. I have divided and was going to send it to you. Your children told mine that you were out." Brother Hall began to cry. Said he had tried others. Could not get any. Went to the cedars and prayed to the Lord and the Lord told him to go to Joseph Millett. "Well, Brother Hall, you needn't bring this back if the Lord sent you for it. You don't owe me for it." You can't tell how good it made me feel to know that the Lord knew that there was such a person as Joseph Millett.

Journal of Joseph Millett (Library-Archives, Historical Department, The Church of Jesus Christ of Latter-day Saints), pp. 88–89.

"THEY COUNSELED ME
TO BURN THE BOOK"

DON VINCENT DI FRANCESCA

As I think back over the events of my life leading up to a cold morning in February 1910, I cannot escape the feeling that God had been mindful of my existence. That morning the caretaker of the Italian chapel delivered a note to me from the pastor, advising me he was ill in bed and asking me to come to his house, as he had important matters to discuss with me regarding the affairs of the parish.

As I walked down Broadway [in New York City], the strong wind from the open sea blew cold against me, so I held my head down and turned my face away from the wind. It was then I saw what appeared to be a book lying on top of an open barrel of ashes, set there to be picked up by the garbage collection wagon. The form of the pages and the manner in which they were bound gave me the impression that it was a religious book. Curious, I picked up the book and knocked it against the side of the barrel to shake the ashes from its pages. The book was written in the English language. I looked for the frontispiece, but it had been torn away.

As I stood there with the book in my hands, the fury of the wind turned the pages, and one by one, the names Nephi, Mosiah, Alma, Moroni, and Isaiah appeared before my eyes. Since the cold wind was bitter, I hurriedly wrapped the soiled book in a newspaper and continued my journey.

At the parish house I gave a few words of comfort to my colleague Scarillo and agreed to the services he requested of me during his illness. As I walked back to my own lodgings, my mind dwelt on the book in my hand and the strange names I had read. Who were these men? Who was this prophet Isaiah? Was he the one I had read about in the Bible, or was he some other Isaiah?

Back in my room I carefully turned the torn pages and came to the words of Isaiah, which I read most carefully. What could be the name of the church that taught such doctrine in words so easily understood? The cover of the book and the title page were missing. I read the declaration of witnesses in the opening pages and was strongly impressed by the strength of their testimonies, but there was no other clue to the book's identity.

I purchased some alcohol and cotton from the drugstore beneath my lodgings and began cleaning the soiled pages. Then for several hours I read what was written in the book. When I had read chapter ten of the book of Moroni, I locked the door of my room; and with the book held in my hands, I knelt down and asked God, the Eternal Father, in the name of his Son Jesus Christ, to tell me if the book was of God. As I prayed, I felt my body becoming cold. Then my heart began to pound, and a feeling of warmth and gladness came over me and filled me with such joy that I cannot find words to express. I knew that the words of the book came from God.

I continued my services in the parish, but my preaching was tinged with the new words I had found in the book. The members of my congregation were so interested in my words that they became dissatisfied with the sermons of my colleagues, and they asked them why they did not preach the sweet arguments of Don Vincent. This was the beginning of troubles for me. When members began leaving the chapel during the sermons of my colleagues and remained when I occupied the pulpit, my colleagues became angry with me.

The beginning of real discord began Christmas eve, 1910. In

my sermon that evening, I told the story of the birth and mission of Jesus Christ as given in my new book. When I had finished, some of my colleagues, without any shadow of shame, publicly contradicted all I had said. The absurdities of their assertions so upset me that I openly rebelled against them. They denounced me and turned me over to the committee of censure for disciplinary action.

When I appeared before this committee, the members gave me what was supposed to be fatherly advice. They counseled me to burn the book, which they said was of the devil, since it was the cause of so much trouble and had destroyed the harmony of the pastoral brothers. I replied by giving my witness that the book they asked me to burn was the word of God, but because of the missing pages I did not know the name of the church that had brought forth the book. I declared that if I were to burn the book, I would displease God. I would rather go out of the congregation of the church than offend him. When I had so stated, the president of the council ended the discussion, stating the council would decide on the matter later.

It was not until 1914 that I was once again brought before the council. The vice venerable spoke in a friendly tone, suggesting that the sharp words of the committee members at the previous hearing may have provoked me, which was regrettable, since they all loved me and were mindful of the valuable assistance I had always so freely given. However, he said, I must remember that obedience—complete and absolute—is the rule. The long suffering of the members, to whom I had continued to preach falsehoods, had come to an end, and I must burn the book.

In reply, I stated I could not deny the words of the book nor would I burn it, since in doing so I would offend God. I said I looked forward with joy to the time when the church to which the book belonged would be made known to me and I would become a part of it. At this, the vice venerable cried, "Enough! Enough!"

He then read the decision that had been made by the council: I was to be stripped of my position as a pastor of the church and of every right and privilege I had previously enjoyed.

Three weeks later I was called before the supreme synod. After giving me an opportunity to retract my previous statements, which I refused to do, the synod confirmed the judgment of the council. I was thus completely cut off from the body of the church.

In November 1914, I was called into the Italian army and sent to the Port of Naples. I saw action in France, where I experienced all of the sadness and suffering associated with the battles of World War I. Remembering the lessons of the book I had read, I related to some of the men in my company the story of the people of Ammon—how they refused to shed the blood of their brothers and buried their arms rather than be guilty of so great crimes. The chaplain reported me to the colonel, and the next day I was escorted to the colonel's office. He asked me to tell him the story I had related to the soldiers, as it is recorded in the twenty-fourth chapter of Alma. Then he asked me how I had come into possession of the book, and why I retained a book written in the English language and published by an unnamed church. I received as punishment a ten-day sentence on bread and water, with the order that I was to speak no more of the book and its stories.

After the end of the war I returned to New York, where I met an old friend who was a pastor of my former church and who knew the history of my troubles. He felt I had been unfairly dealt with, and he began interceding for me with members of the synod. I was finally admitted to the congregation as a lay member. As an experiment, it was agreed that I should accompany one of the pastors on a mission to New Zealand and to Australia.

In Sydney, Australia, we met some Italian immigrants who asked questions about the errors in the translations of the Bible as published by the Catholic Church. They were not satisfied with the answers given by my companion, and he became angry with them. Then they asked me about it, and, knowing I had the truth in the Book of Mormon, I once again told the story of Christ's appearance to the people of the land described there, and that Christ had said, "That other sheep I have which are not of this fold; them also I must bring, and they shall hear my voice; and there shall be one fold, and one shepherd" (3 Ne. 15:17). When they asked me where I had learned such teachings, I told them of the book I had found. The story was sweet to them but very bitter for my colleague. He reported me to the synod, and once again their previous judgment was confirmed, and I was cut off from the church forever. Soon after, I returned to Italy.

In May 1930, while I was seeking in a French dictionary for some information, I suddenly saw the entry "Mormon." I read the words carefully and found that a Mormon Church had been established in 1830 and that this church operated a university at Provo, Utah. I wrote to the president of the university at Provo, asking for information about the book and its missing pages. I received an answer two weeks later, and was told that my letter had been passed on to the President of The Church of Jesus Christ of Latter-day Saints and that he would inform me about the book with the missing pages, which book did indeed belong to the Mormon Church.

On June 16, 1930, President Heber J. Grant answered my letter and sent a copy of the Book of Mormon, which had been translated into the Italian language in 1852 by President Lorenzo Snow while he was a missionary. President Grant informed me that Elder John A. Widtsoe was president of the Church's European Mission, with headquarters in Liverpool, England, and he would give my request to him. A few days later, Elder Widtsoe wrote to me from Liverpool and sent me a pamphlet that contained the story of the Prophet Joseph Smith, telling of the gold plates and the coming forth of the Book of Mormon. At long last I had learned the rest of the story begun so long ago when, guided by the hand of God, I found the torn book lying on top of a barrel of ashes on a street in New York City.

On June 5, 1932, Elder Widtsoe came to Naples to baptize me, but a revolution between the Fascists and anti-Fascists on the island of Sicily had broken out, and the police at Palermo refused permission for me to leave the island. I was thus denied a chance for baptism at that time.

The following year Elder Widtsoe asked me to translate the Joseph Smith pamphlet into Italian and to have 1,000 copies published. I took my translation to the printer, Joseph Gussio, who took the material to the Catholic bishop of the diocese of Cefalu. The bishop ordered the printer to destroy the material. I brought suit against the printer, but all I received from the court was an order to him to return the original booklet, which he had thrown into some waste paper in a cellar.

When Elder Widtsoe was released as president of the mission in 1934, I started correspondence with Elder Joseph F. Merrill, who had succeeded him. He put my name on the mailing list for the *Millennial Star,* which I received until 1940 when the subscription was stopped because of World War II. In January 1937, Elder Richard R. Lyman, successor to President Merrill, wrote to me, advising me that he and Elder Hugh B. Brown would be in Rome on a certain day and I could meet them there and be baptized. The letter was delayed because of war conditions, and I did not receive it in time.

From then until 1949, I was cut off from all news of the Church, but I remained a faithful follower and preached the gospel of the dispensation of the fulness of times. I had copies of the standard works, and I translated chapters into Italian and sent them to acquaintances with the greeting: "Good day. The morning breaks—Jehovah speaks!"

On February 13, 1949, I resumed correspondence with Elder Widtsoe at Church headquarters in Salt Lake City. Elder Widtsoe answered by letter October 3, 1950, explaining that he had been in Norway. I sent him a long letter in reply in which I asked him to help me to be quickly baptized, because I felt that I had proven myself to be a faithful son and pure servant of God, observing the laws and commandments of his kingdom. Elder Widtsoe asked President Samuel E. Bringhurst of the Swiss Mission if he would go to Sicily to baptize me. On January 18, 1951, President Bringhurst arrived on the island, and I was baptized at Imerese, Province of Palermo. According to the records of the Church, this was apparently the first baptism performed on the Island of Sicily. Then on April 28, 1956, I entered the temple at Bern, Switzerland, and received my endowments.

At last, to be in the presence of my Heavenly Father! I felt I had now proved faithful in my second estate, after having searched for and found the true Church by means of an unknown book that I found so many years ago, lying on an open barrel of ashes in the city of New York.

Improvement Era, May 1968, pp. 4–7.

"WOULD YOU DENY ME A BLESSING?"

JOSEPH F. SMITH

I recollect most vividly a circumstance that occurred in the days of my childhood. My mother was a widow, with a large family to provide for. One spring when we opened our potato pits she had her boys get a load of the best potatoes, and she took them to the tithing office; potatoes were scarce that season. I was a little boy at the time, and drove the team. When we drove up to the steps of the tithing office, ready to unload the potatoes, one of the clerks came out and said to my mother, "Widow Smith, it's a shame that you should have to pay tithing." He said a number of other things that I remember well, but they are not necessary for me to repeat here. The . . . name of that tithing clerk was William Thompson, and he chided my mother for paying her tithing, called her anything but wise or prudent; and said there were others who were strong and able to work that were supported from the tithing office. My mother turned upon him and said:

"William, you ought to be ashamed of yourself. Would you deny me a blessing? If I did not pay my tithing, I should expect the Lord to withhold His blessings from me. I pay my tithing, not only because it is a law of God, but because I expect a blessing by doing it. By keeping this and other laws, I expect to prosper and to be able to provide for my family." Though she was a widow, you may turn to the records of the Church from the beginning unto the day of her death, and you will find that she never received a farthing from the Church to help her support herself and her family; but she paid in thousands of dollars in wheat, potatoes, corn, vegetables, meat, etc. The tithes of her sheep and cattle, the tenth pound of her butter, her tenth chicken, the tenth of her eggs, the tenth pig, the tenth calf, the tenth colt—a tenth of everything she raised was paid. Here sits my brother, who can bear testimony to the truth of what I say, as can others who knew her. She prospered because she obeyed the laws of God. She had abundance to sustain her family. We never lacked so much as many others did; for while we found nettle greens most acceptable when we first came to the valley; and while we enjoyed thistle roots, segoes and all that kind of thing, we were no worse off than thousands of others, and not so bad off as many, for we were never without corn-meal and milk or butter, to my knowledge. Then that widow had her name recorded in the book of the law of the Lord. That widow was entitled to the privileges of the house of God. No ordinance of the Gospel could be denied her, for she was obedient to the laws of God, and she would not fail in her duty when though discouraged from observing a commandment of God by one who was in an official position.

Conference Report, April 6, 1900, pp. 48–49.

THE STORY OF A GENEROUS MAN

GEORGE ALBERT SMITH

One day on the street I met a friend whom I had known since boyhood. I had not visited with him for some time, and I was interested in being brought up to date concerning his life, his problems, and his faith, therefore I invited him to go to a conference in Utah County with me. He drove his fine car (the make of car I was driving had not been received into society at that time). He took his wife, and I took mine.

At the conference, I called on him to speak. I did not know what it might do to him, but I thought I would take a chance. He made a fine talk. He told of his trips to the East, how he explained the gospel to the people he met, and how grateful he was for his heritage. He stated that his opportunities in the world had been magnified and multiplied because his father and mother had joined the Church in the Old World.

As we drove home, he turned to me and said: "My, this has been a wonderful conference. I have enjoyed it."

I thought to myself, he was like one of our sisters who came home from fast meeting and said to her family: "That is the best meeting I ever attended."

One of the daughters asked: "Well, Mother, who spoke?" And then her mother replied, "I did."

I thought he had enjoyed it because he himself had participated. I was glad he had. Then he said: "You know I have heard many things in this conference, but there is only one thing that I do not understand the way you do."

I said: "What is it?"

151

"Well," he said, "it is about paying tithing."

He thought I would ask him how he paid his tithing, but I did not. I thought if he wanted to tell me, he would. He said: "Would you like me to tell you how I pay my tithing?"

I said, "If you want to, you may."

"Well," he said, "if I make ten thousand dollars in a year, I put a thousand dollars in the bank for tithing. I know why it's there. Then when the bishop comes and wants me to make a contribution for the chapel or give him a check for a missionary who is going away, if I think he needs the money, I give him a check. If a family in the ward is in distress and needs coal or food or clothing or anything else, I write out a check. If I find a boy or a girl who is having difficulty getting through school in the East, I send a check. Little by little I exhaust the thousand dollars, and every dollar of it has gone where I know it has done good. Now, what do you think of that?"

"Well," I said, "do you want me to tell you what I think of it?"

He said, "Yes."

I said: "I think you are a very generous man with someone else's property." And he nearly tipped the car over.

He said, "What do you mean?"

I said, "You have an idea that you have paid your tithing?"

"Yes," he said.

I said: "You have not paid any tithing. You have told me what you have done with the Lord's money but you have not told me that you have given anyone a penny of your own. He is the best partner you have in the world, He gives you everything you have, even the air you breathe. He has said you should take one-tenth of what comes to you and give it to the Church as directed by the Lord. You haven't done that; you have taken your best partner's money, and have given it away."

Well, I will tell you there was quiet in the car for some time. We rode on to Salt Lake City and talked about other things.

About a month after that I met him on the street. He came up, put his arm in mine, and said: "Brother Smith, I am paying my tithing the same way you do." I was very happy to hear that.

Not long before he died, he came into my office to tell me what he was doing with his own money.

George Albert Smith, *Sharing the Gospel with Others,* selected and compiled by Preston Nibley (Salt Lake City: Deseret Book Co., 1948), pp. 44–47.

"NEVER WRITE A SERMON"

MATTHEW COWLEY

I had a particular assignment or instruction from President George Albert Smith when I was called [as an apostle]. He called me into his office one day and took hold of my hand, and while he was holding my hand and looking at me he said, "I want to say something to you, Brother Cowley."

I said, "Well, I'm willing to listen."

"This is just a particular suggestion to you, not to all the brethren, but to you." He said, "Never write a sermon. Never write down what you are going to say."

I said, "What on earth will I do?"

He said, "You tell the people what the Lord wants you to tell them while you are standing on your feet."

I said, "That certainly is putting some responsibility on the Lord."

But I've tried to live up to that instruction. And I've had some great experiences. There have been times when the Lord has forsaken me. But when he hasn't, I've had some miraculous—well, I shouldn't say miraculous—it is the normal experience of the priesthood, of having the inspiration of the Holy Spirit. I can bear witness to you . . . that God can work through his priesthood and that he does work through it. I know that without any question of doubt. I've had too many experiences. I'm an expert witness about these things.

Matthew Cowley, *Matthew Cowley Speaks* (Salt Lake City: Deseret Book Co., 1954), pp. 237–38.

"THAT IS GOD'S PEARL SHELL"

MATTHEW COWLEY

Down in Tahiti . . . our people . . . have a seasonal occupation of pearl shell diving, and our men are the best shell divers in the islands of French Oceania. Why are they the best divers? Because they keep the Word of Wisdom, and they can stay under the water longer than the others who do not. They stay under the water at a depth of ninety feet for upwards of two minutes and forty seconds. They dive to that depth and bring up the pearl shell which gives them part of their means of support for the remainder of the year until the next season approaches.

. . . One young Latter-day Saint placed his pearl shells on the shore in two piles, one was a large one and one a rather small one, and when the trader came around with whom he had the contract to sell his pearl shells, the trader asked him about the small pile. He said: "Is that yours?"

He said: "No, that is not mine."

The trader said: "Where did it come from?"

He said: "Oh, I dove for it."

"Well, why is it not yours?"

He said: "That is God's pearl shell."

"Who has the right to sell it?"

He said: "I can sell it."

"Well, then, I will buy it."

"Yes, you may buy it, but not at the contract price. You will have to pay the market price for God's pearl shell"; because the market price had gone up since he had signed the contract.

And so he sold God's pearl shell at the market price and his own at the price for which he had contracted. And when I inquired what he would have done had the price gone down instead of up, he said: "I would not have segregated God's pearl shell. I would have left it with mine. I would always see to it that God gets the top price for his pearl shell."

Matthew Cowley, *Matthew Cowley Speaks* (Salt Lake City: Deseret Book Co., 1954), pp. 5–6.

"Now I Can Shake Hands with the Priesthood of God"

MATTHEW COWLEY

I had a little mother, and I still have her down in New Zealand. I knew her on my first mission when I was just a young boy. In those days she called me her son. When I went back to preside, she called me her father. I am fearfully and wonderfully made.

Now, on one occasion I called in, as I always did when I visited that vicinity, to see this grand little woman, then in her eighties, and blind. She did not live in an organized branch, had no contact with the priesthood except as the missionaries visited there. We had no missionaries in those days. They were away at war.

I went in and greeted her in the Maori fashion. She was out in her back yard by her little fire. I reached forth my hand to shake hands with her, and I was going to rub noses with her, and she said: "Do not shake hands with me, Father."

I said: "Oh, that is clean dirt on your hands. I am willing to shake hands with you. I am glad to. I want to."

She said: "Not yet." Then she got on her hands and knees and crawled over to her little house. At the corner of the house there was a spade. She lifted up that spade and crawled off in another direction, measuring the distance she went. She finally arrived at a spot and started digging down into the soil with that spade. It finally struck something hard. She took out the soil with her hands and lifted out a fruit jar. She opened that fruit jar and reached down in it, took something out and handed it to me, and it turned out to be New Zealand money. In American money it would have been equivalent to one hundred dollars.

She said: "There is my tithing. Now I can shake hands with the priesthood of God."

I said: "You do not owe that much tithing."

She said: "I know it. I do not owe it now, but I am paying some in advance, for I do not know when the priesthood of God will get around this way again."

And then I leaned over and pressed my nose and forehead against hers, and the tears from my eyes ran down her cheeks, and as I left her, I asked God in my heart to bring down upon me a curse if from that day henceforth and forever I did not return to God . . . one-tenth of all that should ever come into my hands.

Matthew Cowley, *Matthew Cowley Speaks* (Salt Lake City: Deseret Book Co., 1954), pp. 7–8.

"Throw It Here, Sissy!"

HEBER J. GRANT

Becuase I was] an only child, my mother reared me very carefully. Indeed, I grew more or less on the principle of a hothouse house plant, the growth of which is "long and lanky" but not substantial. I learned to sweep, and to wash and wipe dishes, but did little stone throwing and little indulging in those sports which are interesting and attractive to boys, and which develop their physical frames. Therefore, when I joined a baseball club, the boys of my own age and a little older played in the first nine; those younger than I played in the second, and those still younger in the third, and I played with them.

One of the reasons for this was that I could not throw the ball from one base to the other. Another reason was that I lacked physical strength to run or bat well. When I picked up a ball, the boys would generally shout:

"Throw it here, sissy!"

So much fun was engendered on my account by my youthful companions that I solemnly vowed that I would play baseball in the nine that would win the championship of the Territory of Utah.

My mother was keeping boarders at the time for a living, and I shined their boots until I saved a dollar which I invested in a baseball. I spent hours and hours throwing the ball at Bishop Edwin D. Woolley's barn, which caused him to refer to me as the laziest boy in the Thirteenth Ward. Often my arm would ache so that I could scarcely go to sleep at night. But I kept on practicing and finally succeeded in getting into the second nine of our club. Subsequently I joined a better club, and eventually played in the nine that won the championship of the territory and beat the nine that had won the championship for California, Colorado, and Wyoming. Having thus made good my promise to myself, I retired from the baseball arena.

Heber J. Grant, *Gospel Standards,* compiled by G. Homer Durham (Salt Lake City: Improvement Era, 1969), pp. 342–43.

"BY WHAT RIGHT DO YOU ROB ME?"

HEBER   J.   GRANT

I remember as a young man I had fifty dollars in my pocket on one occasion which I intended to deposit in the bank. When I went on Thursday morning to Fast meeting—the Fast meetings used to be held on Thursdays instead of Sundays—and the bishop made an appeal for a donation, I walked up and handed him the fifty dollars. He took five of it and put it in the drawer and gave the forty-five back to me and said that was my full share.

I said, "Bishop Woolley, by what right do you rob me of putting the Lord in my debt? Didn't you preach here today that the Lord rewards fourfold? My mother is a widow, and she needs two hundred dollars."

He said: "My boy, do you believe that if I take this other forty-five dollars you will get your two hundred dollars quicker?"

I said: "Certainly."

Well, he took it.

While walking from that Fast meeting to the place where I worked, an idea popped into my head. I sent a telegram to a man asking him how many bonds of a certain kind he would buy at a specified price within forty-eight hours and allow me to draw a draft on him through Wells-Fargo's bank. He was a man whom I did not know. I had never spoken to him in my life, but I had seen him a time or two on the streets of Salt Lake. He wired back that he wanted as many as I could get. My profit on that transaction was $218.50.

The next day I walked down to the bishop and said: "Bishop, I made $218.50 after paying that $50.00 donation the other day and so I owe $21.85 in tithing. I will have to dig up the difference between $21.85 and $18.50. The Lord did not quite give me the tithing in addition to a four to one increase."

Someone will say that it would have happened anyway.

I do not think it would have happened. I do not think I would have got the idea. I do not think I would have sent the telegram.

Heber J. Grant, *Gospel Standards,* compiled by G. Homer Durham (Salt Lake City: Improvement Era, 1969), pp. 296–97.

LEARNING TO SING

HEBER J. GRANT

My voice at ten years of age, must have made a very deep impression upon Brother Thomas, seeing that he had remembered it for thirty-three years. Noticing that he seemed quite skeptical, I asked him to walk over with me into the corner of the building, so as not to disturb the people who had not yet left the meetinghouse and I sang to him in a low voice, "God Moves in a Mysterious Way." At the close he said: "That's all right."

At the end of two or three months, I was able to sing not only, "O My Father," but "God Moves in a Mysterious Way," "Come, Come, Ye Saints," and two or three other hymns. Shortly after this, while taking a trip south, I sang one or more hymns in each of the Arizona stakes, and in Juarez, Mexico. Upon my return to Salt Lake City, I attempted to sing "O My Father," in the big Tabernacle, hoping to give an object lesson to the young people, and to encourage them to learn to sing. I made a failure, getting off the key nearly every verse, and instead of my effort encouraging the young people, I fear it tended to discourage them.

When first starting to practice, if some person would join in and sing bass, tenor, or alto, I could not carry the tune. Neither could I sing, if anyone accompanied me on the piano or organ, as the variety of sounds confused me.

I am pleased to be able to say that I can now sing with piano or organ accompaniment, and can also sing the lead in "God Moves in a Mysterious Way," in a duet, a trio, or quartet. I have learned quite a number of songs, and have been assured by Brother Ensign, and several others well versed in music, to whom I have sung within the past few weeks, that I succeeded without making a mistake in a single note, which I fear would not be the case were the attempt to be made in public. However, I intend to continue trying to sing the hymn "O My Father," in the assembly hall or big tabernacle until such time as I can sing it without an error.

How did I succeed so far? Brother Ensign adopted the plan of having me sing a line over and over again, trying to imitate his voice. He kept this up until the line was learned and could be "pronounced musically," on the same principle as learning the sound of a word. The child may be taught to pronounce correctly the word "incomprehensibility," not withstanding the length, even if the child does not understand the phonetic sounds. I learned to sing upon the same principle, starting, figuratively speaking, in the eighth grade, with not even a knowledge of the contents of the primary. It required a vast amount of practice to learn, and my first hymn was sung many hundreds of times before I succeeded in getting it right.

Upon my recent trip to Arizona, I asked Elders Rudger Clawson and J. Golden Kimball if they had any objections to my singing one hundred hymns that day. They took it as a joke and assured me that they would be delighted. We were on the way from Holbrook to St. Johns, a distance of about sixty miles. After I had sung about forty tunes, they assured me that if I sang the remaining sixty they would be sure to have nervous prostration. I paid no attention whatever to their appeal, but held them to their bargain and sang the full one hundred. One hundred and fifteen songs in one day, and four hundred in four days, is the largest amount of practicing I ever did.

. . . My musical deafness is disappearing, and by sitting down to a piano and playing the lead notes, I can learn a song in less than one-tenth the time required when I first commenced to practice.

Heber J. Grant, *Gospel Standards,* compiled by G. Homer Durham (Salt Lake City: Improvement Era, 1969), pp. 351–54.

"THE BEST IS
NONE TOO GOOD FOR GOD"

⌒

DAVID O. MCKAY

I thank my earthly father for the lesson he gave to two boys in a hayfield at a time when tithes were paid in kind. We had driven out to the field to get the tenth load of hay, and then over to a part of the meadow where we had taken the ninth load, where there was "wire grass" and "slough grass." As we started to load the hay, Father called out, "No, boys, drive over to the higher ground." There was timothy and redtop there. But one of the boys called back (and it was I), "No, let us take the hay as it comes!"

"No, David, that is the *tenth* load, and the best is none too good for God."

That is the most effective sermon on tithing I have ever heard in my life, and it touches, I found later in life, this very principle of the law of sacrifice. You cannot develop character without obeying that law. Temptation is going to come to you in this life. You sacrifice your appetites; you sacrifice your passions for the glory of God; and you gain the blessing of an upright character and spirituality. That is a fundamental truth.

David O. McKay, *Cherished Experiences from the Writings of President David O. McKay*, compiled by Clare Middlemiss (Salt Lake City: Deseret Book Co., 1955), pp. 19–20.

"ARE YOU IN TROUBLE?"

HUGH B. BROWN

I should like to introduce a story coming out of the first world war. I had a companion, a fellow officer, who was a very rich man, highly educated. He was a lawyer, had great power, was self-sufficient, and he said to me as we often talked of religion (because he knew who I was), "There is nothing in life that I would like to have that I cannot buy with my money."

Shortly thereafter he and I with two other officers were assigned to go to the city of Arras, France, which was under siege. It had been evacuated, and upon arrival there we thought there was no one in the city. We noted that the fire of the enemy was concentrated on the cathedral. We made our way to that cathedral and went in. There we found a little woman kneeling at an altar. We paused, respecting her devotion. Then shortly she arose, wrapped her little shawl around her frail shoulders, and came tottering down the aisle. The man among us who could speak better French said, "Are you in trouble?"

She straightened her shoulders, pulled in her chin, and said, "No, I'm not in trouble. I was in trouble when I came here, but I've left it there at the altar."

"And what was your trouble?"

She said, "I received word this morning that my fifth son has given his life for France. Their father went first, and then one by one all of them have gone. But," straightening again, "I have no trouble; I've left it there because I believe in the immortality of the soul. I believe that men will live after death. I know that I shall meet my loved ones again."

When the little soul went out, there were tears in the eyes of the men who were there, and the one who had said to me that he could purchase anything with money turned to me and said, "You and I have seen men in battle display courage and valor that is admirable, but in all my life I have never seen anything to compare with the faith, the fortitude and the courage of that little woman."

Then he said, "I would give all the money I have if I could have something of what she has."

Conference Report, October 1969, pp. 106–7.

"IF WE ONLY LIVE RIGHT"

LEGRAND RICHARDS

A few weeks ago, a young lady phoned me for an appointment; and when she came to the office, she sat there and cried for a little while, and then she said: "I guess I'm jittery."

"Well," I said, "that's all right." Then when she had composed herself, she said, "Bishop, what is there for the young people today? We have war. They are taking all the boys; it looks like another great war is ahead of us. What do we young people have to live for?"

I looked at her for a few minutes and said, "Have you ever thought of the other side of the story?"

She said, "What side?"

"Well," I said, "you remember the story of the two buckets that went down in the well; as the one came up, it said, 'This is surely a cold and dreary world. No matter how many times I come up full, I always have to go down empty.' Then the other bucket laughed and said, 'With me it is different. No matter how many times I go down empty, I always come up full.'"

I said, "Have you ever stopped to realize that of all the millions of our Father's children, you are one of the most favored? You are privileged to live in the Dispensation of the Fullness of Times that the prophets of old have looked forward to, when there is more revealed truth upon the earth than there has ever been in any other dispensation of the world's history, and where we enjoy blessings and comforts of life that kings did not enjoy a few years ago. Have you ever stopped to think of that side of the story?"

And before she left, she decided that probably it wasn't as cold and dreary a world, after all, as it might be.

I said, "You just go on, and live right, and don't you lose your courage, and don't think that life isn't worthwhile and isn't worth living. Whether you live or whether you die or whether you are permitted to live a long life or a short life isn't going to be the thing that is going to determine the success or failure of your life; it's how you live. And if we only live right, it will not matter whether the time is short or long; we won't have to worry much about it."

Conference Report, April 1951, pp. 39–40.

"Were Your Prayers Answered?"

~

BRYANT S. HINCKLEY

In 1903 at one of the meetings of a stake conference of the Utah Stake of Zion, held at Provo, sat a mother and her eight-year-old son [Creed Haymond]. Reed Smoot, as an apostle, promised the boys who were there that if they would do certain things, referring to the Word of Wisdom, they would be blessed accordingly. After the meeting, on their way home to Springville (this was in the horse and buggy days), this fond mother stopped the horses and said to her boy, "Will you promise me that you will never use tobacco or liquor?" He promised her, and she kissed him on his forehead. . . .

[Years later, Dr. Creed Haymond related a wonderful experience associated with that promise:] "It was in 1903, when I was only eight years of age, that I gave the promise. Then a period of sixteen years passed, and I found myself in Boston, representing the University of Pennsylvania, running in the I.C.A.A.A. track meet. The night before the finals, Lawson Robertson, coach of the University of Pennsylvania track team and coach of five Olympic teams, came to me and said: 'Creed, you are captain of this track team, and on your shoulders rests the responsibility of winning this championship tomorrow. You have been training faithfully since Christmas. (It was then June.) I want you to take this glass of sherry wine, because I fear that by tomorrow you may go stale.' I had a great shock. A deep emotion went through my soul. I said, 'Robbie, ask me anything but that, and I will do it. But that I cannot do.' He replied, 'I ought to know what is best for you. I have been in this business for a long time, and I know that men overtrain and go stale. I am not trying to corrupt your morals or your

167

ideals. I am doing this for your benefit.' I said, 'I can't do it, Robbie, and I won't do it.' He said, 'All right, but if we lose, you must shoulder the responsibility.'

"I felt very badly. This was one of the crucial events of my life. I had won the championship the previous year in the sprints and wished to repeat, as it never had been repeated two years in succession. I went to my room, undressed and kneeled beside the bed to pray, having decided to take the problem to the Lord. I prayed: 'Heavenly Father, I have been taught all my life that the Word of Wisdom was divinely given to the Prophet Joseph Smith, and was meant for the benefit of Thy children of the Covenant. Will Thou manifest to me if this principle is true in its portents, that I might know for myself of its divine authenticity, and whether or not I have acted wisely in this matter. If Thou will bless me with a witness—a testimony of this principle—I will pledge my life in Thy service wherever I may be called. This I will do if Thou will bless me with a witness.'

"I jumped into bed and for the only time in my life, on the night preceding a track meet, I slept soundly for nine hours without waking. The next morning at seven o'clock, hearing a knock on my door, I jumped up and opened the door, and there stood my coach. He was pale and concerned. He inquired, 'How are you?' I told him that I felt fine. He informed me that all the men were ill and were vomiting. I asked the cause of their illness, and if it could have been the wine. He answered that he did not know the cause.

"This was event number two of a series of startling events. We went out to the field, and these things happened: Carl Johnson, sprinter of the University of Michigan, was six feet one inch tall. When you start in a race, you dig holes in the ground so that you can get a fast start. In the semi-finals, he had picked lane number two, and the spread between his feet was long. In the finals of the one hundred, I had picked the same lane. Being short-legged, the spread between my feet was shorter than his. I dug my holes in front of the place where his holes had been dug, which place was filled with soft dirt. There were six men in the final event, having won through the elimination of fifty-four starters the day before. Every man was keyed for the one-hundred-yard sprint championship of America. We got on our mark; the starter pulled the gun, and we went. I made a terrific surge and my hold broke, and I slipped and fell on my knee. I didn't stay there, but in desperation I got up and was after the other men, the leading man being four yards ahead of me. It seemed an impossible task; I gave everything that I had. When I got to eighty-five yards, I still was in third place; at ninety-five yards I was in second place. It seemed that I was literally picked off my feet as I hit the tape, winner of the one-hundred-yard dash championship. I know I shouldn't have won the race, and couldn't have done so under any conditions dependent upon myself alone.

"Then another startling thing happened. It was the only time of my life of eleven years of running that I have ever seen a condition exist where the field events were completed before the finals of the track events. The semi-final of the two hundred twenty was held after all other events were finished. I was in the last semifinal. Just before I got on my marks, it was announced to the crowd that Haymond of Pennsylvania was going to try for a world's record in the two hundred twenty straight-away, as I already had broken the record on a curved track in the two hundred twenty in 1915. In desperation to break a record, I gave everything I had. Instead of running out easy and free, I was bound up and ran straight up and down and ran the two hundred twenty in twenty-one and three-fifths of a second, which missed the world's record by two-fifths of a second. As I finished the race, the clerk of the course came over and said, 'Go right back to the start; the day is late and they are going to run the two hundred twenty finals.'

"I was out of breath and said, 'I cannot run in this condition!'

"He stated, 'But you have to!'

"So, as I went to the start of the two hundred twenty, Billy

Moore, captain of the Harvard team, who had run just previous to me, came up and said: 'Haymond, they are going to make us run now. You are in no condition to run and you have a right to demand a rest.' So I went over to the starter and said, 'Mr. Reynolds, you can see that I am in no condition to run. I demand a rest before the finals.' He said, 'All right, Haymond, I will give you ten minutes.' Just as he said that, the telephone rang and the referee said: 'Run the race immediately.' The clerk of the course said, 'Gentlemen, I am sorry, but come to your marks.'

"I was exhausted. As trained, the runner should take a deep breath. As I took a deep breath, it seemed that a draft went through me and cleared my whole system of exhaustion. I was as rested and as free of exhaustion as I was in the early morning. When the gun went off, we were gone. In place of running tied up, I ran free and easy and won the race. I was thrilled, having won under these conditions, and started off the field without inquiring as to the time. Halfway to the gymnasium, I felt someone pick me up in his arms. It was my coach. He weighed two hundred twenty pounds and I weighed one hundred thirty-five. As he took me in his arms and squeezed me, he said: 'I wanted to be the first to tell you that you just ran the fastest two hundred twenty of any human who ever ran. You just ran twenty-one seconds flat.'

"Of course I was thrilled. I dressed, went back to the hotel, and being very tired, I went to bed early. I suppose this was the first time in my life that I had ever gone to bed without saying my prayers, but I am human. I had broken a record; I had received congratulations from men of all stations; I was somewhat of a hero. When I went to bed, I wasn't thinking of prayer. I was thinking of the thrills of the day. I was just about to drop off to sleep when I heard within my mind these words, 'Were your prayers answered?'

"I woke up with a start. Then, as I thought of the conditions that existed, having slept all the previous night without waking; the other men having taken the wine were sick; and although we had five intercollegiate champions, not one of the other four placed better than third place in times that were slower than their try-out times the previous week; having won the one hundred when I shouldn't have won it—I know I wouldn't have won it and God knows I would not have won it alone; having won the two hundred and twenty and broken the record under conditions which normally would have made it impossible for me to win; as I meditated and reflected upon this series of events, I decided that my prayers had been answered. Now I hoped that I would be able to fulfill my part of the pledge, and that in the great future following 1919 I would be able to live and give service according to the promises I made with my Father in Heaven."

Bryant S. Hinckley, *The Faith of Our Pioneer Fathers* (Salt Lake City, Deseret Book Co., 1965), pp. 195–201.

"I Would Henceforth
Be a Full Tithe Payer"

ELEANOR KNOWLES

Early spring in 1931, Claire and Howard [W. Hunter] were talking seriously about marriage. In his history he wrote: "I had not given up the hope of going on a mission and I had saved some money with that in mind. Claire offered to help support me and wait for me until I returned. Even though I

171

appreciated the offer, I could not accept the proposal of having her work and support me. We finally decided that it would be better for us to get married and at a later time, as soon as conditions might permit, we would go on a mission together.

"One beautiful spring evening, we drove to Palos Verdes and parked on the cliffs where we could watch the waves roll in from the Pacific and break over the rocks in the light of a full moon. We talked about our plans and I put a diamond ring on her finger. We made many decisions that night and some strong resolutions regarding our lives. The moon was setting in the west and dawn was just commencing to break when we got home."

The couple decided to be married in the Salt Lake Temple in June. Howard went to his bishop, told him of his plans, and asked for a temple recommend. He was stunned when Bishop Brigham J. Peacock said he couldn't understand how Howard could support a wife on his small income.

"When I told him how much I was making," Howard wrote, "he said the reason for his doubt as to my ability to support a wife was based on the amount of tithing I had paid. Suddenly I became conscious of the seriousness of not being a full tithe payer.

"Because my father had not been a member of the Church during my years at home, tithing had never been discussed in our family and I had never considered its importance. As we talked, I realized that the bishop did not intend to give me a temple recommendation. In his kindly way he taught me the importance of the law and when I told him I would henceforth be a full tithe payer, he continued the interview and relieved my anxiety by filling out and signing a recommendation form."

Howard related his experience to Claire, who had always been a full tithe payer. As a result, he said, "we resolved that we would live this law throughout our marriage and tithing would come first."

Eleanor Knowles, *Howard W. Hunter* (Salt Lake City: Deseret Book Co., 1994), pp. 80–81.

A TESTIMONY OF TITHING

PRESTON NIBLEY

While visiting in Providence, Rhode Island, on April 25, 1926, I remarked to the president of the branch that he must have an outstanding testimony of the law of tithing, since I had noted that he paid a large tithing and paid it so regularly. He replied that he had, and I asked him if he would mind relating the same to me, which he did in about the following manner.

He said that his wife and children joined the Church in England some years before, and when he indicated the name of the Elder who preached the gospel to them, I found that he was one of my early M.I.A. teachers. He said that the reason he didn't join the Church was because he did not have faith to pay his tithing and he did not want to be a hypocrite. Some time later when one of the young missionaries was being released to return home he came to this brother and told him he wanted to baptize him before returning home, to which the brother replied: "You cannot because I haven't the faith to pay my tithing, and I do not want to be a hypocrite."

The spirit of the Lord seemed to rest upon the young missionary, and he replied in words something like this, "Brother _____, if you will let me baptize you before I return home, I promise you that within a year from now you will be in America with your family, and will be earning three times as much as you are at the present."

The brother said he could not resist availing himself of such a promise, and so he was baptized. He said he could not feel that

173

the promise could come true, as he at the time was under contract to work for the company he was with for an additional two years. It was during the time of the world war when we had such a difficult time to get cloth in this country that would hold its color, and the dye workers of America sent representatives to England to induce some of the dye workers there to come to America and teach them how to make dyes. Representatives of the American firms called on this man's father, and he indicated that he was not interested, but his son might be. So they approached the son. He said that he could not accept their offer because he was bound to work for his company for an additional two years. They asked if he would be willing to go if they would buy [his contract] so the company would release him from his contract, and he indicated that he would.

"Now," he said, "the Lord just threw in a little for good measure. Within a year's time according to the promise of the Elder, I was in America with my wife and children, and was earning four times as much as I was when he made me that promise." The genuineness of this experience is attested by the faithfulness of this brother in the payment of his tithing, following his baptism into the Church.

Preston Nibley, *Missionary Experiences* (Salt Lake City: Deseret News Press, 1942), pp. 310–11.

COURAGE

JOSEPH SMITH'S LEG OPERATION

LUCY MACK SMITH

Joseph, our third son, having recovered from the typhus fever, after something like two weeks' sickness, one day screamed out while sitting in a chair, with a pain in his shoulder, and, in a very short time he appeared to be in such agony that we feared the consequence would prove to be something very serious. We immediately sent for a doctor. When he arrived and had examined the patient, he said that it was his opinion that this pain was occasioned by a sprain. But the child declared this could not be the case as he had received no injury in any way whatever, but that a severe pain had seized him all at once, of the cause of which he was entirely ignorant.

Notwithstanding the child's protestations, still the physician insisted that it must be a sprain, and consequently he anointed his shoulder with some bone linament, but this was of no advantage to him, for the pain continued the same after the anointing as before.

When two weeks of extreme suffering had elapsed, the attendant physician concluded to make closer examination, whereupon he found that a large fever sore had gathered between his breast and shoulder. He immediately lanced it, upon which it discharged fully a quart of matter.

As soon as the sore had discharged itself the pain left it, and shot like lightning (using his own terms) down his side into the marrow of the bone of his leg and soon became very severe. My poor boy, at this, was almost in despair, and he cried out "Oh, father! the pain is so severe, how can I bear it!"

His leg soon began to swell, and he continued to suffer the greatest agony for the space of two weeks longer. During this period I carried him much of the time in my arms in order to mitigate his suffering as much as possible; in consequence of which I was taken very ill myself. The anxiety of mind that I experienced, together with physical over-exertion, was too much for my constitution and my nature sank under it.

Hyrum, who was rather remarkable for his tenderness and sympathy, now desired that he might take my place. As he was a good, trusty boy, we let him do so, and, in order to make the task as easy for him as possible, we laid Joseph upon a low bed and Hyrum sat beside him, almost day and night for some considerable length of time, holding the affected part of his leg in his hands and pressing it between them, so that his afflicted brother might be enabled to endure the pain which was so excruciating that he was scarcely able to bear it.

At the end of three weeks, we thought it advisable to send again for the surgeon. When he came he made an incision of eight inches, on the front side of the leg, between the knee and ankle. This relieved the pain in a great measure, and the patient was quite comfortable until the wound began to heal, when the pain became as violent as ever.

The surgeon was called again, and he this time enlarged the wound, cutting the leg even to the bone. It commenced healing the second time, and as soon as it began to heal it also began to swell again, which swelling continued to rise till we deemed it wisdom to call a council of surgeons; and when they met in consultation they decided that amputation was the only remedy.

Soon after coming to this conclusion, they rode up to the door and were invited into a room apart from the one in which Joseph lay. They being seated, I addressed them thus: "Gentlemen, what can you do to save my boy's leg?" They answered, "We can do nothing; we have cut it open to the bone and find it so affected that we consider his leg incurable and that amputation is absolutely necessary in order to save his life."

This was like a thunderbolt to me. I appealed to the principal surgeon, saying, "Dr. Stone, can you not make another trial? Can you not, by cutting around the bone, take out the diseased part, and perhaps that which is sound will heal over, and by this means you will save his leg? You will not, you must not, take off his leg, until you try once more. I will not consent to let you enter his room until you make me this promise."

After consulting a short time with each other, they agreed to do as I had requested, then went to see my suffering son. One of the doctors, on approaching his bed, said, "My poor boy, we have come again." "Yes," said Joseph, "I see you have; but you have not come to take off my leg, have you, sir?" "No," replied the surgeon, "it is your mother's request that we make one more effort, and that is what we have now come for."

The principal surgeon, after a moment's conversation, ordered cords to be brought to bind Joseph fast to a bedstead; but to this Joseph objected. The doctor, however, insisted that he must be confined, upon which Joseph said very decidedly, "No, doctor, I will not be bound, for I can bear the operation much better if I have my liberty."

"Then," said Dr. Stone, "will you drink some brandy?"

"No," said Joseph, "not one drop."

"Will you take some wine?" rejoined the doctor. "You must take something, or you can never endure the severe operation to which you must be subjected."

"No," exclaimed Joseph, "I will not touch one particle of liquor, neither will I be tied down; but I will tell you what I will do—I will have my father sit on the bed and hold me in his arms, and then I will do whatever is necessary in order to have the bone taken out." Looking at me, he said, "Mother, I want you to leave the room, for I know you cannot bear to see me suffer so; father can stand it, but you have carried me so much, and watched over me so long, you are almost worn out." Then looking up into my face, his eyes swimming in tears, he continued. "Now, mother, promise me that you will not stay, will you? The Lord will help me, and I shall get through with it."

To this request I consented, and getting a number of folded sheets, and laying them under his leg, I retired, going several hundred yards from the house in order to be out of hearing.

The surgeons commenced operating by boring into the bone of his leg, first on one side of the bone where it was affected, then on the other side, after which they broke it off with a pair of forceps or pincers. They thus took away large pieces of the bone. When they broke off the first piece, Joseph screamed out so loudly, that I could not forbear running to him. On my entering the room, he cried out, "Oh, mother, go back, go back; I do not want you to come in—I will try to tough it out, if you will go away."

When the third piece was taken away, I burst into the room again—and oh, my God! what a spectacle for a mother's eye! The wound torn open, the blood still gushing from it, and the bed literally covered with blood. Joseph was pale as a corpse, and large drops of sweat were rolling down his face, whilst upon every feature was depicted the utmost agony!

I was immediately forced from the room, and detained until the operation was completed; but when the act was accomplished, Joseph put upon a clean bed, the room cleared of every appearance of blood, and the instruments which were used in the operation removed, I was permitted again to enter.

Joseph immediately commenced getting better, and from this onward, continued to mend until he became strong and healthy. When he had so far recovered as to be able to travel, he went with his uncle, Jesse Smith, to Salem, for the benefit of his health, hoping the sea-breezes would be of service to him, and in this he was not disappointed.

Having passed through about a year of sickness and distress, health again returned to our family, and we most assuredly realized the blessing; and indeed, we felt to acknowledge the hand of God, more in preserving our lives through such a tremendous scene of affliction, than if we had, during this time, seen nothing but health and prosperity.

Lucy Mack Smith, *History of Joseph Smith,* edited by Preston Nibley (Salt Lake City: Bookcraft, 1958), pp. 54–58.

"I Should Not Like to Be Murdered by Inches"

LUCY MACK SMITH

A few days subsequent to [a mob attack], Joseph was at our house writing a letter. While he was thus engaged, I stepped to the door, and looking towards the prairie, I beheld a large company of armed men advancing towards the city, but, as I supposed it to be training day, said nothing about it.

Presently the main body came to a halt. The officers dismounting, eight of them came into the house. Thinking they had come for some refreshment, I offered them chairs, but they refused to be seated, and, placing themselves in a line across the floor, continued standing. I again requested them to sit, but they replied, "We do not choose to sit down; we have come here to kill Joe Smith and all the 'Mormons.'"

"Ah," said I, "what has Joseph Smith done, that you should want to kill him?"

"He has killed seven men in Daviess county," replied the foremost, "and we have come to kill him, and all his Church."

"He has not been in Daviess county," I answered, "consequently the report must be false. Furthermore, if you should see him, you would not want to kill him."

"There is no doubt that the report is perfectly correct," rejoined the officer; "it came straight to us, and I believe it; and we were sent to kill the Prophet and all who believe in him, and I'll be d—— if I don't execute my orders."

"I suppose," said I, "you intend to kill me, with the rest?"

"Yes, we do," returned the officer.

"Very well," I continued, "I want you to act the gentleman about it, and do the job quick. Just shoot me down at once, then I shall be at rest; but I should not like to be murdered by inches."

"There it is again," said he. "You tell a 'Mormon' that you will kill him, and they will always tell you, 'that is nothing—if you kill us, we shall be happy.'"

Joseph, just at this moment finished his letter, and, seeing that he was at liberty, I said, "Gentlemen, suffer me to make you acquainted with Joseph Smith, the Prophet." They stared at him as if he were a spectre. He smiled, and stepping towards them, gave each of them his hand, in a manner which convinced them that he was neither a guilty criminal nor yet a hypocrite.

Joseph then sat down and explained to them the views, feelings, etc., of the Church, and what their course had been; besides the treatment which they had received from their enemies since the first. He also argued, that if any of the brethren had broken the law, they ought to be tried by the law, before anyone else was molested. After talking with them some time in this way, he said, "Mother, I believe I will go home now—Emma will be expecting me." At this two of the men sprang to their feet, and declared that he should not go alone, as it would be unsafe that they would go with him, in order to protect him. Accordingly the three left together. . . .

The men who went home with my son promised to disband the militia under them and go home, which they accordingly did, and we supposed that peace was again restored.

Lucy Mack Smith, *History of Joseph Smith,* edited by Preston Nibley (Salt Lake City: Bookcraft, 1958), pp. 254–56.

"I Was Willing to Suffer for the Sake of Christ"

EDWARD PARTRIDGE

I was taken from my house by the mob, George Simpson being their leader, who escorted me about half a mile, to the court house, on the public square in Independence; and then and there, a few rods from said court house, surrounded by hundreds of the mob, I was stripped of my hat, coat and vest and daubed with tar from head to foot, and then had a quantity of feathers put upon me; and all this because I would not agree to leave the county, and my home where I had lived two years.

Before tarring and feathering me I was permitted to speak. I told them that the Saints had suffered persecution in all ages of the world; that I had done nothing which ought to offend anyone; that if they abused me, they would abuse an innocent person; that I was willing to suffer for the sake of Christ; but, to leave the country, I was not then willing to consent to it. By this time the multitude made so much noise that I could not be heard: some were cursing and swearing, saying, "call upon your Jesus," etc.; others were equally noisy in trying to still the rest, that they might be enabled to hear what I was saying.

Until after I had spoken, I knew not what they intended to do with me, whether to kill me, to whip me, or what else I knew not. I bore my abuse with so much resignation and meekness, that it appeared to astound the multitude, who permitted me to retire in silence, many looking very solemn, their sympathies having been touched as I thought; and as to myself, I was so filled with the Spirit and love of God, that I had no hatred towards my persecutors or anyone else.

Joseph Smith, *History of The Church of Jesus Christ of Latter-day Saints,* 7 vols., 2d ed. rev., edited by B. H. Roberts (Salt Lake City: The Church of Jesus Christ of Latter-day Saints, 1932–51), 1:390–91.

"MAJESTY HAVE I SEEN BUT ONCE"

PARLEY P. PRATT

Our brethren, some fifty in number, were penned up in the cold, dreary court house. It was a very severe time of snow and winter weather, and we suffered much. During this time Elder Rigdon was taken very sick, from hardship and exposure, and finally lost his reason; but still he was kept in a miserable, noisy and cold room, and compelled to sleep on the floor with a chain and padlock round his ankle, and fastened to six others. Here he endured the constant noise and confusion of an unruly guard, the officer of which was Colonel Sterling Price, since Governor of the State.

These guards were composed generally of the most noisy, foul mouthed, vulgar, disgraceful rabble that ever defiled the earth. . . .

In one of those tedious nights we had lain as if in sleep till the hour of midnight had passed, and our ears and hearts had been pained, while we had listened for hours to the obscene jests, the horrid oaths, the dreadful blasphemies and filthy language of our guards, Colonel Price at their head, as they recounted to each other their deeds of rapine, murder, robbery, etc., which they had committed among the *"Mormons"* while at Far West and vicinity. They even boasted of defiling by force wives, daughters and virgins, and of shooting or dashing out the brains of men, women and children.

I had listened till I became so disgusted, shocked, horrified, and so filled with the spirit of indignant justice that I could scarcely refrain from rising upon my feet and rebuking the guards; but had said nothing to Joseph, or any one else, although I lay next to him and knew he was awake. On a sudden he arose to his feet, and spoke in a voice of thunder, as the roaring lion, uttering, as near as I can recollect, the following words:

"SILENCE, ye fiends of the infernal pit. In the name of Jesus Christ I rebuke you, and command you to be still; I will not live another minute and bear such language. Cease such talk, or you or I die THIS INSTANT!"

He ceased to speak. He stood erect in terrible majesty. Chained, and without a weapon; calm, unruffled and dignified as an angel, he looked upon the quailing guards, whose weapons were lowered or dropped to the ground; whose knees smote together, and who, shrinking into a corner, or crouching at his feet, begged his pardon, and remained quiet till a change of guards.

I have seen the ministers of justice, clothed in magisterial robes, and criminals arraigned before them, while life was suspended on a breath, in the courts of England; I have witnessed a Congress in solemn session to give laws to nations; I have tried to conceive of kings, of royal courts, of thrones and crowns; and of emperors assembled to decide the fate of kingdoms; but dignity and majesty have I seen but *once,* as it stood in chains, at midnight, in a dungeon in an obscure village of Missouri.

Parley P. Pratt, *Autobiography of Parley P. Pratt,* edited by Parley P. Pratt Jr., Classics in Mormon Literature ed. (Salt Lake City: Deseret Book Co., 1985), pp. 179–80.

"SENTENCED TO BE SHOT"

FROM *MILLENNIAL STAR*

In October, 1838, after learning that Far West was surrounded by a mob, [Lyman Wight] raised fifty-three volunteers in Adam-ondi-Ahman (25 miles distant) and repaired immediately to Far West to aid in its defence, where with Joseph and Hyrum Smith and others, he was betrayed into the hands of his enemies, by Colonel George M. Hinkle, on the 31st; and was sentenced by a court-martial to be shot the next morning (November 1st) [1838] at

8 o'clock. During the evening, General Moses Wilson took him out by himself, and tried to induce him to betray Joseph Smith, and swear falsely against him; at which time the following conversation took place.

General Wilson said, "Colonel Wight, we have nothing against you, only that you are associated with J[oseph] Smith. He is our enemy and a d—— rascal, and would take any plan he could to kill us. You are a d—— fine fellow; and if you will come out and swear against him, we will spare your life, and give you any office you want; and if you don't do it, you will be shot tomorrow at 8 o'clock."

Colonel Wight replied, "General Wilson, you are entirely mistaken in your man, both in regard to myself and Joseph Smith. Joseph Smith is not an enemy to mankind, he is not your enemy; but is as good a friend as you have got. Had it not been for him, you would have been in hell long ago, for I should have sent you there [myself], and no other man but Joseph Smith could have prevented me and you may thank him for your life. And, now, if you will give me the boys I brought from [Adam-ondi-Ahman] yesterday, I will whip your whole army."

Wilson said, "Wight, you are a strange man; but if you will not accept my proposal, you will be shot tomorrow morning at 8."

Colonel Wight replied, "Shoot and be damned."

Millennial Star 27:457.

"IT IS COLD-BLOODED MURDER"

$\sim$

FROM *HISTORY OF THE CHURCH*

Elder Parley P. Pratt in his Autobiography [pp. 203–5] referring to [the] betrayal of the brethren on the part of Hinkle
and their reception and treatment by the mob, says:

"Colonel George M. Hinkle, who was at that time the highest
officer of the militia assembled for the defense of Far West, waited
on Messrs. Joseph Smith, Sidney Rigdon, Hyrum Smith, Lyman
Wight, George W. Robinson and myself, with a request from
General Lucas that we would repair to his camp, with the assurance that as soon as peaceable arrangements could be entered
into we should be released. We had no confidence in the word of
a murderer and robber, but there was no alternative but to put
ourselves into the hands of such monsters, or to have the city
attacked, and men, women and children massacred. We, therefore, commended ourselves to the Lord, and voluntarily surren-
dered as sheep into the hands of wolves.

"As we approached the camp of the enemy, General Lucas
rode out to meet us with a guard of several hundred men. The
haughty general rode up, and, without speaking to us, instantly
ordered his guards to surround us. They did so very abruptly, and
we were marched into camp surrounded by thousands of savage
looking beings, many of whom were dressed and painted like
Indian warriors. These all set up a constant yell, like so many
bloodhounds let loose upon their prey, as if they had achieved one
of the most miraculous victories that ever graced the annals of the
world. If the vision of the infernal regions could suddenly open to
the mind, with thousands of malicious fiends, all clamoring, exult-

ing, deriding, blaspheming, mocking, railing, raging and foaming
like a troubled sea, then could some idea be formed of the hell
which we had entered.

"In camp we were placed under a strong guard, and were without shelter during the night, lying on the ground in the open air,
in the midst of a great rain. The guards during the whole night
kept up a constant tirade of mockery, and the most obscene blackguardism and abuse. They blasphemed God; mocked Jesus Christ;
swore the most dreadful oaths; taunted Brother Joseph and others; demanded miracles; wanted signs, such as 'Come, Mr. Smith,
show us an angel.' 'Give us one of your revelations.' 'Show us a
miracle.' 'Come, there is one of your brethren here in camp
whom we took prisoner yesterday in his own house, and knocked
his brains out with his own rifle, which we found hanging over his
fireplace; he lays speechless and dying; speak the word and heal
him, and then we will all believe.' 'Or, if you are Apostles or men
of God, deliver yourselves, and then we will be Mormons.' Next
would be a volley of oaths and blasphemies; then a tumultuous
tirade of lewd boastings of having defiled virgins and wives by
force, etc., much of which I dare not write; and, indeed, language
would fail me to attempt more than a faint description. Thus
passed this dreadful night, and before morning several other cap-
tives were added to our number, among whom was Brother Amasa
Lyman." . . .

This incident of sentencing the Prophet and his companion
prisoners to be shot on the public square at Far West is also
referred to in the History of Caldwell county [p. 137], compiled
by the St. Louis National Historical Company, and the formal
orders of General Lucas to Brigadier-General Doniphan and also
Doniphan's reply are given. I quote the following:

"Yielding to the pressure upon him, it is alleged that General
Lucas, at about midnight, issued the following order to General
Doniphan, in whose keeping the hostages were:

Brigadier-General Doniphan:

SIR:—You will take Joseph Smith and the other prisoners into the public square of Far West, and shoot them at 9 o'clock tomorrow morning.

SAMUEL D. LUCAS,
Major-General Commanding.

But General Doniphan, in great and righteous indignation, promptly returned the following reply to his superior:

It is cold-blooded murder. I will not obey your order. My brigade shall march for Liberty tomorrow morning, at 8 o'clock; and if you execute these men, I will hold you responsible before an earthly tribunal, so help me God.

A. W. DONIPHAN,
Brigadier-General.

"The prisoners somehow heard of the order, and kneeled in prayer, and prayed fervently that it might not be executed. And it was not. Flagrantly insubordinate as was General Doniphan's refusal, he was never called to account for it. The 'Mormons' have always remembered General Doniphan's humanity on this occasion, as well as on others, and when, in 1873, he went to Salt Lake City, he was received with much feeling, and shown every regard and attention by Brigham Young and the other authorities of the Church and city, and by even the masses of the people." . . .

Parley P. Pratt, referring to this incident, says: "We are informed that the general officers held a secret council during most of the night, which was dignified by the name of court martial; in which, without a hearing, or, without even being brought before it, we were all sentenced to be shot. The day and hour was also appointed for the execution of this sentence, viz., next morning at 8 o'clock, in the public square at Far West. Of this we were informed by Brigadier-General Doniphan, who was one of the council, but who was so violently opposed to this cold-blooded murder that he assured the council that he would revolt and withdraw his whole brigade, and march them back to Clay county as soon as it was light, if they persisted in so dreadful an undertaking. Said he, 'It is cold-blooded murder, and I wash my hands of it.' His firm remonstrance, and that of a few others, so alarmed the haughty murderer and his accomplices that they dared not put the decree in execution."

Joseph Smith, *History of The Church of Jesus Christ of Latter-day Saints,* 7 vols., 2d ed. rev., edited by B. H. Roberts (Salt Lake City: The Church of Jesus Christ of Latter-day Saints, 1932–51), 3:189–91.

SAVING THE BOOK OF
COMMANDMENTS

M A R Y   E L I Z A B E T H
R O L L I N S   L I G H T N E R

When the mob [at Independence, Missouri, in 1833] was tearing down the printing office, a two story building [in which the Book of Commandments was being printed], driving Brother [William W.] Phelps' family out of the lower part of the house, they (the mob) brought out some large sheets of paper, saying, "Here are the Mormon commandments." My sister [Caroline], 12 years old (I was then 14) and myself were in a corner of a fence watching them. When they spoke about them being the commandments, I was determined to have some of them. So while their backs were turned, prying out the gable

191

end of the house, we ran and gathered up all we could carry in our arms. As we turned away, two of the mob got down off the house and called for us to stop, but we ran as fast as we could, through a gap in the fence into a large corn field, and the two men after us. We ran a long way in the field, laid the papers on the ground, then laid down on top of them. The corn was very high and thick. They hunted all around us, but did not see us. After we were satisfied they had given up the search, we tried to find our way out of the field. The corn was so tall we thought we were lost. On looking up we saw some trees that had been girdled to kill them. We followed them and came to an old log stable, which looked like it had not been used for years. Sister Phelps and family were there, carrying in brush and piling it up on one side of the stable to make their beds on. She asked us what we had. We told her and also how we came by them. She took them and placed them between her beds. Subsequently Oliver Cowdery bound them in small books and gave me one.

Deseret Evening News, February 20, 1904, p. 24.

"IT WOULD MOST LIKELY COST ME MY LIFE"

JOHN TAYLOR *

In 1833 at the time of the destruction of the printing press in Independence, Jackson Co. the printed sheets of the Book of Commandments and the pied type and press were thrown in an old log stable by the mob. I asked Bp. Partridge if I might go and get out some copies of the Book of Commandments. He said it would most likely cost me my life if I attempted it. I told him I did not mind hazarding my life to secure some copies of the commandments. He then said I might go. I ran my hand into a crack between the logs and pulled out a few at a time until I got as many as I could carry, when I was discovered. A dozen men surrounded me and commenced throwing stones at me and I shouted out "Oh my God must I be stoned to death like Stephen for the sake of the word of the Lord." The Lord gave me strength and skill to elude them and make my escape without being hit by a stone. I delivered the copies to Bp. Partridge who said I had done a good work and my escape was a miracle.

---

*Note: This John Taylor was a twenty-year-old Latter-day Saint convert from Kentucky. He is not to be confused with John Taylor, third President of the Church.

Statement of John Taylor dictated to Leo Hawkins and George A. Smith, Salt Lake City, 15 April 1858, Church Archives, The Church of Jesus Christ of Latter-day Saints.

"THIS WILL CURE YOU
OF YOUR FAITH"

ELIZA R. SNOW

In Kirtland the persecution increased until many had to flee for their lives, and in the spring of 1838, in company with my father, mother, three brothers, one sister and her two daughters, I left Kirtland, and arrived in Far West, Caldwell county, Mo., on the 16th of July, where I stopped at the house of Sidney Rigdon, with my brother Lorenzo, who was very sick, while the rest of the family went farther, and settled in Adam-Ondi-Ahman, in Davies county. In two weeks, my brother being sufficiently recovered, my father sent for us and we joined the family group. My father purchased the premises of two of the "old settlers," and paid their demands in full. I mention this, because subsequent events proved that, at the time of the purchase, although those men ostensibly were our warm friends, they had, in connection with others of the same stripe, concocted plans to mob and drive us from our newly acquired homes, and repossess them. . . . While we were busy in making preparations for the approaching winter, to our great surprise, those neighbors fled from the place, as if driven by a mob, leaving their clocks ticking, dishes spread for their meal, coffee-pots boiling, etc., etc., and, as they went, spread the report in every direction that the "Mormons" had driven them from their homes, arousing the inhabitants of the surrounding country, which resulted in the disgraceful, notorious "exterminating order" from the Governor of the State; in accordance therewith, we left Davies county for that of Caldwell, preparatory to fulfilling the injunction of leaving the State "before grass grows" in the spring.

The clemency of our law-abiding, citizen-expelling Governor allowed us ten days to leave our county, and, till the expiration of that term, a posse of militia was to guard us against mobs; but it would be very difficult to tell which was better, the militia or the mob—nothing was too mean for the militia to perform—no property was safe within the reach of those men.

One morning, while we were hared at work, preparing for our exit, the former occupant of our house entered, and in an impudent and arrogant manner inquired how soon we should be out of it. My American blood warmed to the temperature of an insulted, free-born citizen, as I looked at him, and thought, poor man, you little think with whom you have to deal—God lives! He certainly overruled in that instance, for those wicked men never got possession of that property, although my father sacrificed it to American mobocracy.

In assisting widows and others who required help, my father's time was so occupied that we did not start until the morning of the 10th, and last day of the allotted grace. The weather was very cold and the ground covered with snow. After assisting in the arrangements for the journey, and shivering with cold, in order to warm my aching feet, I walked until the teams overtook me. In the mean time, met one of the so-called militia, who accosted me with, "Well, I think this will cure you of your faith!" Looking him steadily in the eye, I replied, "No, sir; it will take more than *this* to cure me of my faith." His countenance suddenly fell, and he responded, "I must confess, you are a better soldier than I am." I passed on, thinking that, unless he was above the average of his fellows in that section, I was not highly complimented by his confession.

Edward W. Tullidge, *The Women of Mormondom* (New York: Tullidge & Crandall, 1877), pp. 142–45.

JOSEPH SMITH AND
THE RUNAWAY COACH

JOSEPH SMITH

While on the mountains some distance from Washington, our coachman stepped into a public house to take his grog, when the horses took fright and ran down the hill at full speed. I persuaded my fellow travelers to be quiet and retain their seats, but had to hold one woman to prevent her throwing her infant out of the coach. The passengers were exceedingly agitated, but I used every persuasion to calm their feelings; and opening the door, I secured my hold on the side of the coach the best way I could, and succeeded in placing myself in the coachman's seat, and reining up the horses, after they had run some two or three miles, and neither coach, horses, or passengers received any injury. My course was spoken of in the highest terms of commendation, as being one of the most daring and heroic deeds, and no language could express the gratitude of the passengers, when they found themselves safe, and the horses quiet. There were some members of Congress with us, who proposed naming the incident to that body, believing they would reward such conduct by some public act; but on inquiring my name, to mention as the author of their safety, and finding it to be Joseph Smith the "Mormon Prophet," as they called me, I heard no more of their praise, gratitude, or reward.

Joseph Smith, *History of The Church of Jesus Christ of Latter-day Saints,* 7 vols., 2d ed. rev., edited by B. H. Roberts (Salt Lake City: The Church of Jesus Christ of Latter-day Saints, 1932–51), 4:23–24.

THEY REFUSED TO TAKE AN OATH

JOSEPH FIELDING SMITH

Some time in the spring of 1844 . . . , two young men, Robert Scott and Dennison L. Harris, were invited to attend a secret meeting of . . . conspirators [against the Prophet Joseph Smith]. Dennison L. Harris was the son of Emer Harris, brother of Martin Harris. . . . Robert Scott at the time of this incident was living at the home of William Law. It was on this account that he and his companion were invited to attend the secret meeting. . . . Young Harris was also asked to invite his father, Emer Harris. These boys considered well this invitation and then consulted with Emer Harris, who concluded to take the matter to the Prophet Joseph Smith.

After hearing the story Joseph Smith instructed the father to stay away, but said he thought it would be well for the two boys to attend, but before going they were to receive some advice from him and follow his instructions carefully. Following the Prophet's instructions they attended the first two meetings, and each time made their report to the Prophet. The conspirators gave the time to abuse and falsehood concerning President Joseph Smith, and the discussion of their future plans. When the young men reported the second time their attendance the Prophet seemed to be in doubt as to the wisdom of the young men attending further meetings. He asked them to visit him again before the third meeting to which they were invited, which, like the others, was held on a Sunday. When the time came for the meeting these youths called for the Prophet's instruction. He had made it a matter of prayer and he said to them, "This will be the last time that they will admit you into their councils. They will come to some determination, but be sure that you make no covenant, nor enter into any obligations whatever with them." When they arrived at the place of meeting the young men were astonished to see it guarded by men with muskets, and after due scrutiny they were admitted. In the meeting the Prophet and his brother Hyrum and others were accused of the most wicked acts. They said that President Joseph Smith was a fallen prophet and his death was necessary to save the Church. An oath had been prepared which each of those present was asked to take. The candidates in turn would step up to the table where Francis M. Higbee, a justice of the peace, was stationed, and he would ask: "Are you ready?" Receiving from each a favorable reply he administered the following oath:

"You solemnly swear, before God and all holy angels, and these your brethren by whom you are surrounded that you will give your life, your liberty, your influence, your all, for the destruction of Joseph Smith and his party, so help you God!"

The person taking this oath would then say, "I do," after which he would lay down the Bible on which the oath was taken, and sign his name to a written copy of the oath in a book, which would then be acknowledged by the justice of the peace.

No doubt the amazed boys were frightened, and wondered how these men, formerly faithful members in the councils of the Church who had pledged their faith and their loyalty to the Prophet only a few months before, could stoop so low as they found them at these secret meetings. Like members of the Gadianton secret band these conspirators had lost all sense of honor. This oath was administered to each of those present, among them three women who were heavily veiled.

At the last the turn came for the two boys to take the pledge, but this they resolutely and manfully refused to do, stating that Joseph Smith had done them no harm and they were too young to understand these things. The anger of the leaders of this secret band was aroused. They first coaxed and then argued and when this failed, they threatened them with death. "Come, boys," they said, "do as we have done. You are young, and will not have anything to do in the affair, but we want you should keep it a secret, and act with us; that is all." "No," they replied, "we cannot take an oath like that against any man who has never done us any injury." They tried to pass out of the place, but were stopped by one of the guards who said, "No! not by a _____ _____! You know all our plans and arrangements, and we don't propose that you should leave in that style. You've got to take the oath, or you'll never leave here alive. They were then surrounded by these fiends of the bottomless pit, who with drawn swords and knives were determined to take their lives. The leaders finally concluded that the deed of blood could not be committed there, as the house was too near the street. So the young men were taken to the cellar and preparations were made for the execution. At this point someone called attention to the fact that the parents of the boys evidently knew where they were, and if they did not return a search would be put on foot that might prove to be very dangerous for the plotters. After some more arguing and consultation the conspirators reluctantly released the boys with a threat if they ever divulged the actions of these secret meetings, they would be killed. Under a guard they were escorted from the place. Wisely they took their departure leaving the impression that they would hold their tongues. They immediately took their course towards the river in the opposite direction from their homes, conveying the impression to their enemies by word and act, that they would keep their secret. On the river bank they met the Prophet and an elder brother of Robert Scott, who were waiting for them. To the Prophet these two boys told their harrowing story.

Joseph Fielding Smith, *Church History and Modern Revelation*, Fourth Series (Salt Lake City: The Church of Jesus Christ of Latter-day Saints, 1949), pp. 181–83.

"WHAT I THERE
HAVE SAID IS TRUE"

ANDREW JENSON

After his excommunication, Oliver Cowdery engaged in law business and practiced for some years as a lawyer in Michigan, but he never denied the truth of the Book of Mormon. On the contrary he seems to have used every opportunity to bear testimony of its divine origin.

While practicing law in Michigan, a gentleman, on a certain occasion, addressed him as follows: "Mr. Cowdery, I see your name attached to this book (Book of Mormon). If you believe it to be true, why are you in Michigan?" The gentleman then read the names of the Three Witnesses and asked, "Mr. Cowdery, do you believe this book?"

"No, sir," was the reply.

"Very well," continued the gentleman, "but your name is attached to it, and you declare here (pointing to the book) that you saw an angel, and also the plates, from which the book purports to be translated; and now you say you don't believe it. Which time did you tell the truth?"

Oliver Cowdery replied with emphasis, "My name is attached to that book, and what I there have said is true. I did see this; I know I saw it, and faith has nothing to do with it, as a perfect knowledge has swallowed up the faith which I had in the work knowing, as I do, that it is true."

Andrew Jenson, *Latter-day Saint Biographical Encyclopedia,* 4 vols. (Salt Lake City: Andrew Jenson History Co., 1901), 1:249.

"TRUE BLUE, THROUGH AND THROUGH!"

JOSEPH FIELDING SMITH

An] incident which I have heard [Joseph F. Smith] relate which shows his courage and integrity, occurred when he was returning from his mission to the Sandwich Islands [Hawaii], in the fall of 1857. He came home by way of Los Angeles, by what was called the Southern Route. In that year Johnston's Army was on the move for Utah, and naturally enough there was much excitement and bitterness of feeling concerning the "Mormons." In southern California, just after the little train of wagons had traveled only a short distance and made their camp, several anti-"Mormon" toughs rode into the camp on horseback, cursing and swearing and threatening what they would do to the "Mormons." Joseph F. was a little distance from the camp gathering wood for the fire, but he saw that the few members of his own party had cautiously gone into the brush down the creek, out of sight. When he saw that, he told me, the thought came into his mind, "Shall I run from these fellows? Why should I fear them?" With that he marched up with his arm full of wood to the campfire where one of the ruffians, still with his pistol in his hand, shouting and cursing about the "Mormons," in a loud voice said to Joseph F.:

"Are you a 'Mormon'?"

And the answer came straight, "Yes, siree; dyed in the wool; true blue, through and through."

At that the ruffian grasped him by the hand and said:

"Well, you are the _____ pleasantest man I ever met! Shake hands, young fellow, I am glad to see a man that stands up for his convictions."

Joseph F. Smith, *Gospel Doctrine*, 5th ed. (Salt Lake City: Deseret Book Co., 1939), p. 518.

REVELATION

"Brigham Young Will Preside Over This Church"

BRIGHAM YOUNG

In September, 1832, Brother Heber C. Kimball took his horse and wagon, Brother Joseph Young and myself accompanying him, and started for Kirtland to see the Prophet. . . . We visited many friends on the way, and some branches of the church. We exhorted them and prayed with them, and I spoke in tongues. Some pronounced it genuine and from the Lord, and others pronounced it of the Devil.

We proceeded to Kirtland and stopped at John P. Greene's, who had just arrived there with his family. We rested a few minutes, took some refreshment, and started to see the Prophet. We went to his father's house and learned that he was in the woods, chopping. We immediately repaired to the woods, where we found the Prophet, and two or three of his brothers, chopping and hauling wood. Here my joy was full at the privilege of shaking the hand of the Prophet of God, and receiv[ing] the sure testimony, by the Spirit of prophecy, that he was all that any man could believe him to be, as a true Prophet. He was happy to see us, and bid us welcome. We soon returned to his house, he accompanying us.

"In the evening a few of the brethren came in, and we conversed upon the things of the kingdom. He called upon me to pray; in my prayer I spoke in tongues. As soon as we arose from our knees, the brethren flocked around him, and asked his opinion concerning the gift of tongues that was upon me. He told them it was the pure Adamic language. Some said to him they

expected he would condemn the gift Brother Brigham had, but
he said, "No, it is of God, and the time will come when Brother
Brigham Young will preside over this Church." The latter part of
this conversation was in my absence.

Millennial Star 25:439.

"SIDNEY IS NOT
USED TO IT AS I AM"

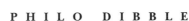

PHILO DIBBLE

The vision which is recorded in the Book of Doctrine and
Covenants [D&C 76] was given at the house of "Father
Johnson," in Hiram, Ohio, and during the time that
Joseph and Sidney were in the spirit and saw the heavens open,
there were other men in the room, perhaps twelve, among whom
I was one during a part of the time—probably two-thirds of the
time—I saw the glory and felt the power, but did not see the
vision.

The events and conversation, while they were seeing what is
written (and many things were seen and related that are not written), I will relate as minutely as is necessary.

Joseph would, at intervals, say: "What do I see?" as one might
say while looking out the window and beholding what all in the
room could not see. Then he would relate what he had seen or

what he was looking at. Then Sidney replied, "I see the same." Presently Sidney would say "what do I see?" and would repeat what he had seen or was seeing, and Joseph would reply, "I see the same."

This manner of conversation was repeated at short intervals to the end of the vision, and during the whole time not a word was spoken by any other person. Not a sound nor motion made by anyone but Joseph and Sidney, and it seemed to me that they never moved a joint or limb during the time I was there, which I think was over an hour, and to the end of the vision.

Joseph sat firmly and calmly all the time in the midst of a magnificent glory, but Sidney sat limp and pale, apparently as limber as a rag, observing which, Joseph remarked, smilingly, "Sidney is not used to it as I am."

Juvenile Instructor 27:303–4.

"I SAW MY SONS IN VISION"

LUCY MACK SMITH

Previous to our sickness in Quincy, my husband sent Brother Lamoreaux to Missouri, under strict instructions to see Joseph and Hyrum, or find out where they were before he should return. About the time that Lucy began to walk about a little, Brother Partridge and Brother Morley came to our house from Lima to see if Brother Lamoreaux had either written or returned. When they came we had heard nothing of him, but while they were with us he arrived in Quincy and sent us word that he had seen neither Joseph nor Hyrum. At this information Brother Partridge was in despair and said that when another messenger was to be sent, he would go himself, as he was instructed.

I listened to him some time in silence; at last the Spirit, which had so often comforted my heart, again spoke peace to my soul, and gave me an assurance that I should see my sons before the night should again close over my head. "Brother Partridge," I exclaimed, in tears of joy, "I shall see Joseph and Hyrum before tomorrow night." "No, mother Smith," said he, "I am perfectly discouraged; I don't believe we shall ever see them again in the world. At any rate, do not flatter yourself that they will be here as soon as that, for I tell you that you will be disappointed. I have always believed you before, but I cannot see any prospect of this prophecy being fulfilled, but if it is so, I will never dispute your word again." I asked him if he would stay in town long enough to prove my sayings whether they were true or false. He promised to do so. Brothers Partridge and Morley soon afterwards left the house in order to get further information upon the subject.

After falling asleep that night I saw my sons in vision. They were upon the prairie traveling, and seemed very tired and hungry. They had but one horse. I saw them stop and tie him to the stump of a burnt sapling, then lie down upon the ground to rest themselves; and they looked so pale and faint that it distressed me. I sprang up and said to my husband, "Oh, Mr. Smith, I can see Joseph and Hyrum, and they are so weak they can hardly stand. Now they are lying asleep on the cold ground! Oh, how I wish that I could give them something to eat!"

Mr. Smith begged me to be quiet, saying that I was nervous; but it was impossible for me to rest—they were still before my eyes—I saw them lie there full two hours; then one of them went away to get something to eat, but not succeeding, they traveled on. This time Hyrum rode and Joseph walked by his side, holding himself up by the stirrup leather. I saw him reel with weakness, but could render him no assistance. My soul was grieved; I rose from my bed and spent the remainder of the night in walking the floor.

The next day I made preparations to receive my sons, confident that the poor, afflicted wanderers would arrive at home before sunset. Sometime in the afternoon, Lucy and I were coming downstairs—she was before me. When she came to the bottom of the steps she sprang forward and exclaimed, "There is Brother Baldwin. My brothers—where are they?" This was Caleb Baldwin, who was imprisoned with them. He told us that Joseph and Hyrum were then crossing the river and would soon be in Quincy. Lucy, hearing this, ran to carry the tidings to Hyrum's family, but the excitement was not sufficient to keep up her strength. When she came to the door she fell prostrate. After recovering a little, she communicated the welcome news.

When Hyrum and Joseph landed, they went immediately to see their families, and the next day, they, together with their wives and the rest of our connections, visited us. The Quincy Grays also came to our house and saluted my sons in the most polite manner. During the afternoon, I asked Joseph and Hyrum, in the presence of the company, if they were not on the prairie the night previous in the situation which I have already related. They replied in the affirmative. I then asked Brother Partridge if he believed what I told him two days before. He answered that he would forever after that time acknowledge me to be a true prophetess. The day passed pleasantly and my sons returned to their homes, happy in their freedom and the society of their friends.

Lucy Mack Smith, *History of Joseph Smith,* edited by Preston Nibley (Salt Lake City: Bookcraft, 1958), pp. 300–302.

"ANGELS CLOTHED IN WHITE"

PRESCINDIA HUNTINGTON

In Kirtland we enjoyed many very great blessings, and often saw the power of God manifested. On one occasion I saw angels clothed in white walking upon the temple. It was during one of our monthly fast meetings, when the saints were in the temple worshipping. A little girl came to my door and in wonder called me out, exclaiming, "The meeting is on the top of the meetinghouse!" I went to the door, and there I saw on the temple angels clothed in white covering the roof from end to end. They seemed to be walking to and fro; they appeared and disappeared. The third time they appeared and disappeared before I realized that they were not mortal men. Each time in a moment they vanished, and their reappearance was the same. This was in broad daylight, in the afternoon. A number of the children in Kirtland saw the same.

When the brethren and sisters came home in the evening, they told of the power of God manifested in the temple that day, and of the prophesying and speaking in tongues. It was also said, in the interpretation of tongues, "That the angels were resting down upon the house."

At another fast meeting I was in the temple with my sister Zina. The whole of the congregation were on their knees, praying vocally, for such was the custom at the close of these meetings when Father Smith presided; yet there was no confusion; the voices of the congregation mingled softly together. While the congregation was thus praying, we both heard, from one corner of the room above our heads, a choir of angels singing most beautifully.

They were invisible to us, but myriads of angelic voices seemed to be united in singing some song of Zion, and their sweet harmony filled the temple of God.

We were also in the temple at the pentecost. In the morning Father Smith prayed for a pentecost, in opening the meeting. That day the power of God rested mightily upon the saints. There was poured out upon us abundantly the spirit of revelation, prophesy and tongues. The Holy Ghost filled the house; and along in the afternoon a noise was heard. It was the sound of a mighty rushing wind. But at first the congregation was startled, not knowing what it was. To many it seemed as though the roof was all in flames. Father Smith exclaimed, "Is the house on fire!"

"Do you not remember your prayer this morning, Father Smith?" inquired a brother.

Then the patriarch, clasping his hands, exclaimed, "The spirit of God, like a mighty rushing wind!"

At another time a cousin of ours came to visit us at Kirtland. She wanted to go to one of the saints' fast meetings, to hear someone sing or speak in tongues, but she said she expected to have a hearty laugh. Accordingly we went with our cousin to the meeting, during which a Brother McCarter rose and sang a song of Zion in tongues; I arose and sang simultaneously with him the same tune and words, beginning and ending each verse in perfect unison, without varying a word. It was just as though we had sung it together a thousand times. After we came out of meeting, our cousin observed, "Instead of laughing, I never felt so solemn in my life."

Edward W. Tullidge, *The Women of Mormondom* (New York: Tullidge & Crandall, 1877), pp. 207–9.

"GOD'S WRATH HANGS OVER JACKSON COUNTY"

L. W. LAWSON

On one occasion General Doniphan caused the sheriff of the county to bring Joseph Smith from the prison to his law office, for the purpose of consultation about his defense. During Smith's presence in the office, a resident of Jackson county, Missouri, came in for the purpose of paying a fee which was due by him to the firm of Doniphan and Baldwin, and offered in payment a tract of land in Jackson county.

Doniphan told him that his partner, Mr. Baldwin, was absent at the moment, but as soon as he had an opportunity he would consult him and decide about the matter. When the Jackson county man retired, Joseph Smith, who had overheard the conversation, addressed General Doniphan about [it] as follows:

"Doniphan, I advise you not to take Jackson county land in payment of the debt. God's wrath hangs over Jackson county. God's people have been ruthlessly driven from it, and you will live to see the day when it will be visited by fire and sword. The Lord of Hosts will sweep it with the besom of destruction. The fields and farms and houses will be destroyed, and only the chimneys will be left to mark the desolation."

General Doniphan said to me that the devastation of Jackson county forcibly reminded him of this remarkable prediction of the Mormon Prophet.

Improvement Era, November 1902, p. 9.

"You Will Aspire to the Presidency of the United States"

ORSON F. WHITNEY

Closely connected with events immediately preceding the Civil War, was another prophecy of Joseph Smith's, uttered May 18, 1843, and recorded at the time in the journal of his private secretary. On the date given, the Prophet dined with Stephen A. Douglas, at the home of Sheriff Backenstos, in Carthage, Illinois, the same town where the brothers Joseph and Hyrum afterwards met their tragic death. Judge Douglas was holding court there. The principal topic of conversation after dinner was the persecution of the Latter-day Saints in Missouri, not only the Jackson County affair of 1833, but the more sanguinary tragedy of 1838–1839, culminating in the mid-winter expulsion of the entire Church—then numbering twelve to fifteen thousand members—and its establishment in the adjoining State of Illinois. An account of these events, at the Judge's request, the "Mormon" leader gave. His narrative included a recital of the ineffectual attempts made by him and his people to obtain from the Federal Government a redress of grievances.

Douglas was deeply interested, and strongly condemned the conduct of Missouri. He was very friendly with the Prophet, who, continuing the conversation, predicted trouble for the Nation unless those wrongs were righted. Then, addressing Douglas, he said: "Judge, you will aspire to the Presidency of the United States; and if you ever turn your hand against me or the Latter-day Saints, you will feel the weight of the hand of the Almighty upon you. And you will live to see and know that I have testified the truth to you, for the conversation of this day will stick to you through life."

Judge Douglas reaped the full fruition of those fateful words. The prophecy concerning him was first published in the *Deseret News*, at Salt Lake City, September 24, 1856, and on February 26, 1859, it appeared in the *Millennial Star*, at Liverpool. Between those dates, Stephen A. Douglas, then a United States Senator—made such by the aid of "Mormon" votes in Illinois—turned his hand against his old-time friends and supporters. Joseph Smith was dead, but his followers, driven from the confines of civilization, were out in the wilderness, laying the foundations of the State of Utah. In a political speech, at Springfield, Illinois, June 12, 1857, Senator Douglas, basing a reference to the "Mormons" upon certain wild rumors afloat concerning them, virtually accused them of all manner of crimes and abominations. The speech was looked upon as a bid for popular favor.

Then came the Senator's race for the Presidency. His prospects at the outset were favorable. His party held the preponderance of the national vote, and he was the idol of his party. In June, 1860, he was enthusiastically nominated by the Democratic Convention at Baltimore. Men shouted for him, worked for him, and on election day voted for him; but all in vain. God's hand was against him! His party torn by dissension, divided its strength among three candidates, and was overwhelmingly defeated. "The Little Giant" was "snowed under," and his great rival Abraham Lincoln, was elevated to the Presidential chair. A few months later Senator Douglas died at his home in Chicago. He was only in the prime of life—aged forty-eight—but he had lived long enough to realize that God's prophets do not speak in vain.

Orson F. Whitney, *Saturday Night Thoughts*, revised edition (Salt Lake City: Deseret Book Co., 1927), pp. 52–54.

"Why Don't You Pray?"

Orson F. Whitney

I found myself in an overworked, run-down condition, manifesting a decided lack of physical and mental vigor. . . . One morning I was endeavoring to write the usual editorial [for the *Millennial Star* in Liverpool], but could make no headway, and wore out the whole day in a vain attempt to produce something worth reading. At last I threw down my pen and burst into tears of vexation.

Just then the Good Spirit whispered: "Why don't you pray?"

As if a voice had addressed me audibly, I answered, "I do pray." I was praying five times a day—secret prayers, morning, noon and night; and vocal prayers, with the rest of the household, at breakfast and dinner time. "I do pray—why can't I get some help," I asked, almost petulantly, for I was heartsick and half-discouraged.

"Pray now," said the Spirit, "and ask for what you want."

I saw the point. It was a special not a general prayer that was needed. I knelt and sobbed out a few simple words. I did not pray for the return of the Ten Tribes nor for the building of the New Jerusalem. I asked the Lord in the name of Jesus Christ to help me write that article. I then arose, seated myself, and began to write. My mind was now perfectly clear, and my pen fairly flew over the paper. All I needed came as fast as I could set it down—every thought, every word in place. In a short time the article was completed to my entire satisfaction.

Orson F. Whitney, *Through Memory's Halls: The Life Story of Orson F. Whitney* (Independence, Mo.: Zion's Printing and Publishing Co., 1930), pp. 151–52.

"I BEHELD JESUS"

ORSON F. WHITNEY

Then came a marvelous manifestation, an admonition from a higher source, one impossible to ignore. It was a dream, or a vision in a dream, as I lay upon my bed in the little town of Columbia, Lancaster County, Pennsylvania. I seemed to be in the Garden of Gethsemane, a witness of the Savior's agony. I saw Him as plainly as ever I have seen anyone. Standing behind a tree in the foreground, I beheld Jesus, with Peter, James and John, as they came through a little wicket gate at my right. Leaving the three Apostles there, after telling them to kneel and pray, the Son of God passed over to the other side, where He also knelt and prayed. It was the same prayer with which all Bible readers are familiar: "Oh my Father, if it be possible, let this cup pass from me; nevertheless not as I will, but as thou wilt."

As He prayed the tears streamed down his face, which was toward me. I was so moved at the sight that I also wept, out of pure sympathy. My whole heart went out to him; I loved him with all my soul, and longed to be with him as I longed for nothing else.

Presently He arose and walked to where those Apostles were kneeling—fast asleep! He shook them gently, awoke them, and in a tone of tender reproach, untinctured by the least show of anger or impatience, asked them plaintively if they could not watch with him one hour. There He was, with the awful weight of the world's sin upon his shoulders, with the pangs of every man, woman and child shooting through his sensitive soul—and they could not watch with him one poor hour!

. . . All at once the circumstances seemed to change, the scene

216

remaining just the same. Instead of before, it was after the crucifixion, and the Savior, with the three Apostles, now stood together
in a group at my left. They were about to depart and ascend into
Heaven. I could endure it no longer. I ran from behind the tree,
fell at his feet, clasped Him around the knees, and begged Him to
take me with Him.

I shall never forget the kind and gentle manner in which He
stopped, raised me up, and embraced me. It was so vivid, so real. I
felt the very warmth of his body, as He held me in His arms and
said in tenderest tones: "No, my son; these have finished their
work; they can go with me; but you must stay and finish yours."
Still I clung to Him. Gazing up into His face—for He was taller
than I—I besought him fervently: "Well, promise me that I will
come to you at the last." Smiling sweetly, He said: "That will
depend entirely upon yourself." I awoke with a sob in my throat,
and it was morning.

. . . I saw the moral clearly. I had never thought of being an
Apostle, nor of holding any other office in the Church, and it did
not occur to me even then. Yet I know that those sleeping Apostles
meant me. I was asleep at my post—as any man is who, having
been divinely appointed to do one thing, does another. [Though
serving on a mission, Elder Whitney had been spending much of
his time as a correspondent for the *Salt Lake Herald*.]

But from that hour all was changed. I was never the same man
again. I did not give up writing; for President Young, having
noticed some of my contributions to the home papers, advised me
to cultivate what he called my "gift for writing." "So that you can
use it," said he, "for the establishment of truth and righteousness."
I therefore continued to write, but not to the neglect of the Lord's
work. I held that first and foremost; all else was secondary.

Orson F. Whitney, *Through Memory's Halls: The Life Story of Orson F. Whitney*
(Independence, Mo.: Zion's Printing and Publishing Co., 1930), pp. 82–83.

HEAVENLY CITIES

LORENZO DOW YOUNG

While at Watertown, I married, and afterwards removed to Mendon, Monroe County [New York]. At this place I had a remarkable dream or vision. I fancied that I died. In a moment I was out of the body, fully conscious that I had made the change. At once, a heavenly messenger, or guide, was by me. I thought and acted as naturally as I had done in the body, and all my sensations seemed as complete without as with it. The personage with me was dressed in the purest white. For a short time, I remained in the room where my body lay. My sister Fanny (who was living with me when I had this dream) and my wife were weeping bitterly over my death. I sympathized with them deeply in their sorrow, and desired to comfort them. I realized that I was under the control of the man who was by me. I begged of him the privilege of speaking to them, but he said he could not grant it. My guide, for so I will call him, said, "Now let us go."

Space seemed annihilated. Apparently we went up, and almost instantly were in another world. It was of such magnitude that I formed no conception of its size. It was filled with innumerable hosts of beings, who seemed as naturally human as those among whom I had lived. With some I had been acquainted in the world I had just left. My guide informed me that those I saw had not yet arrived at their final abiding place. All kinds of people seemed mixed up promiscuously, as they are in this world. Their surroundings and manner indicated that they were in a state of expectation, and awaiting some event of considerable moment to them.

As we went on from this place, my guide said, "I will now show you the condition of the damned." Pointing with his hand, he said, "Look!"

I looked down a distance which appeared incomprehensible to me. I gazed on a vast region filled with multitudes of beings. I could see everything with the most minute distinctness. The multitude of people I saw were miserable in the extreme. "These," said my guide, "are they who have rejected the means of salvation, that were placed within their reach, and have brought up themselves the condemnation you behold."

The expression of the countenances of these sufferers was clear and distinct. They indicated extreme remorse, sorrow and dejection. They appeared conscious that none but themselves were to blame for their forlorn condition.

This scene affected me much, and I could not refrain from weeping.

Again my guide said, "Now let us go."

In a moment we were at the gate of a beautiful city. A porter opened it and we passed in. The city was grand and beautiful beyond anything that I can describe. It was clothed in the purest light, brilliant but not glaring or unpleasant.

The people, men and women, in their employments and surroundings, seemed contented and happy. I knew those I met without being told who they were. Jesus and the ancient apostles were there. I saw and spoke with the apostle Paul.

My guide would not permit me to pause much by the way, but rather hurried me on through this place to another still higher, but connected with it. It was still more beautiful and glorious than anything I had before seen. To me, its extent and magnificence were incomprehensible.

My guide pointed to a mansion which excelled everything else in perfection and beauty. It was clothed with fire and intense light. It appeared a fountain of light, throwing brilliant scintillations of glory all around it, and I could conceive of no limit to which these emanations extended. Said my guide, "That is where God resides." He permitted me to enter this glorious city but a short distance. Without speaking, he motioned that we would retrace our steps.

We were soon in the adjoining city. There I met my mother, and a sister who died when six or seven years old. These I knew at sight without an introduction.

After mingling with the pure and happy beings of this place a short time, my guide said again, "Let us go."

We were soon through the gate by which we had entered the city. My guide then said, "Now we will return."

I could distinctly see the world from which we had first come. It appeared to be a vast distance below us. To me, it looked cloudy, dreary and dark. I was filled with sad disappointment, I might say horror, at the idea of returning there. I supposed I had come to stay in that heavenly place, which I had so long desired to see; up to this time, the thought had not occurred to me that I would be required to return.

I plead with my guide to let me remain. He replied that I was permitted to only visit these heavenly cities, for I had not filled my mission in yonder world; therefore, I must return and take my body. If I was faithful to the grace of God which would be imparted to me, if I would bear a faithful testimony to the inhabitants of the earth of a sacrificed and risen Savior, and his atonement for man, in a little time I should be permitted to return and remain.

These words gave me comfort and inspired my bosom with the principle of faith. To me, these things were real. I felt that a great mission had been given me, and I accepted it in my heart. The responsibility of that mission has rested on me from that time until now.

We returned to my house. There I found my body, and it appeared to me dressed for burial. It was with great reluctance that I took possession of it to resume the ordinary avocations of life, and endeavor to fill the important mission I had received. I awoke and found myself in my bed. I lay and meditated the remainder of the night on what had been shown me.

Call it a dream, or vision, or what I may, what I saw was as real to every sense of my being as anything I have passed through. The memory of it is clear and distinct with me today, after the lapse of fifty years with its many changes.

From that time [1832], although belonging to no church, the Spirit was with me to testify to the sufferings and atonement of the Savior. As I had opportunity, I continually exhorted the people, in public and private, to exercise faith in the Lord Jesus Christ, to repent of their sins and live a life of righteousness and good works.

Wilford Woodruff, *Leaves from My Journal* (Salt Lake City: Juvenile Instructor's Office, 1882), pp. 27–30.

"I Have Been in the Spirit World"

HEBER C. KIMBALL

I went to see [Jedediah M. Grant] one day last week, and he reached out his hand and shook hands with me; he could not speak, but he shook hands warmly with me. . . . I laid my hands upon him and blessed him, and asked God to strengthen his lungs that he might be easier, and in two or three minutes he raised himself up and talked for about an hour as busily as he could, telling me what he had seen and what he understood, until I was afraid he would weary himself, when I arose and left him.

He said to me, "Brother Heber, I have been into the spirit world two nights in succession, and, of all the dreads that ever came across me, the worst was to have to again return to my body, though I had to do it. But O," says he, "the order and government that were there! When in the spirit world, I saw the order of righteous men and women; beheld them organized in their several grades, and there appeared to be no obstruction to my vision; I could see every man and woman in their grade and order. I looked to see whether there was any disorder there, but there was none; neither could I see any death nor any darkness, disorder or confusion." He said that the people he there saw were organized in family capacities; and when he looked at them he saw grade after grade and all were organized and in perfect harmony. He would mention one item after another and say, "Why, it is just as Brother Brigham says it is; it is just as he told us many a time."

That is a testimony as to the truth of what Brother Brigham teaches us, and I know it is true, from what little light I have.

He saw the righteous gathered together in the spirit world, and there were no wicked spirits among them. He saw his wife; she was the first person that came to him. He saw many that he knew, but did not have conversation with any except his wife, Caroline. She came to him, and he said that she looked beautiful and had their little child, that died on the Plains, in her arms, and said, "Mr. Grant, here is little Margaret; you know that the wolves ate her up, but it did not hurt her; here she is all right."

"To my astonishment," he said, "when I looked at families there was a deficiency in some, there was a lack, for I saw families that would not be permitted to come and dwell together, because they had not honored their calling here."

He asked his wife, Caroline, where Joseph and Hyrum and Father Smith and others were; she replied, "they have gone away ahead, to perform and transact business for us." The same as when Brother Brigham and his brethren left Winter Quarters and came here to search out a home; they came to find a location for their brethren.

He also spoke of the buildings he saw there, remarking that the Lord gave Solomon wisdom and poured gold and silver into his hands that he might display his skill and ability, and said that the temple erected by Solomon was much inferior to the most ordinary buildings he saw in the spirit world.

In regard to gardens, says Brother Grant, "I have seen good gardens on this earth, but I never saw any to compare with those that were there. I saw flowers of numerous kinds, and some with from fifty to a hundred different colored flowers growing upon one stalk." We have many kinds of flowers on the earth, and I suppose those very articles came from heaven, or they would not be here.

After mentioning the things that he had seen, he spoke of how much he disliked to return and resume his body, after having seen the beauty and glory of the spirit world, where the righteous spirits are gathered together.

Some may marvel at my speaking about these things, for many profess to believe that we have no spiritual existence. But do you not believe that my spirit was organized before it came to my body here? And do you not think there can be houses and gardens, fruit trees, and every other good thing there? The spirits of those things were made, as well as our spirits, and it follows that they can exist upon the same principle.

After speaking of the gardens and the beauty of everything there, Brother Grant said that he felt extremely sorrowful at having to leave so beautiful a place and come back to earth, for he looked upon his body with loathing, but was obliged to enter it again.

He said that after he came back he could look upon his family and see the spirit that was in them; and the darkness that was in them; and that he conversed with them about the Gospel, and what they should do, and they replied, "Well, Brother Grant, perhaps it is so, and perhaps it is not," and said that was the state of this people, to a great extent, for many are full of darkness and will not believe me.

I never had a view of the righteous assembling in the spirit world, but I have had a view of the hosts of hell, and have seen them as plainly as I see you today. The righteous spirits gather together to prepare and qualify themselves for a future day, and evil spirits have no power over them, though they are constantly striving for the mastery. I have seen evil spirits attempt to overcome those holding the Priesthood, and I know how they act.

Journal of Discourses, 26 vols. (London: Latter-day Saints' Book Depot, 1854–86), 4:135–37.

"THE HEAVENS
SEEMED LIKE BRASS"

LORENZO SNOW

I was baptized by Elder John Boynton, then one of the Twelve Apostles, June, 1836, in Kirtland, Ohio. Previous to accepting the ordinance of baptism, in my investigations of the principles taught by the Latter-day Saints, which I proved, by comparison, to be the same as those mentioned in the New Testament taught by Christ and His Apostles, I was thoroughly convinced that obedience to those principles would impart miraculous powers, manifestations and revelations. With sanguine expectation of this result, I received baptism and the ordinance of laying on of hands by one who professed to have divine authority; and, having thus yielded obedience to these ordinances, I was in constant expectation of the fulfillment of the promise of the reception of the Holy Ghost.

The manifestation did not immediately follow my baptism, as I had expected, but, although the time was deferred, when I did receive it, its realization was more perfect, tangible and miraculous than even my strongest hopes had led me to anticipate.

Some two or three weeks after I was baptized, one day while engaged in my studies, I began to reflect upon the fact that I had not obtained a *knowledge* of the truth of the work—that I had not realized the fulfillment of the promise "he that doeth my will shall know of the doctrine," and I began to feel very uneasy. I laid aside my books, left the house, and wandered around through the fields under the oppressive influence of a gloomy, disconsolate spirit, while an indescribable cloud of darkness seemed to envelop me. I had been accustomed, at the close of the day, to retire for secret prayer, to a grove a short distance from my lodgings, but at this time I felt no inclination to do so. The spirit of prayer had departed and the heavens seemed like brass over my head. At length, realizing that the usual time had come for secret prayer, I concluded I would not forego my evening service, and, as a matter of formality, knelt as I was in the habit of doing, and in my accustomed retired place, but not feeling as I was wont to feel.

I had no sooner opened my lips in an effort to pray, than I heard a sound, just above my head, like the rustling of silken robes, and immediately the Spirit of God descended upon me, completely enveloping my whole person, filling me, from the crown of my head to the soles of my feet, and O, the joy and happiness I felt! No language can describe the almost instantaneous transition from a dense cloud of mental and spiritual darkness into a refulgence of light and knowledge, as it was at that time imparted to my understanding. I then received a perfect knowledge that God lives, that Jesus Christ is the Son of God, and of the restoration of the holy Priesthood, and the fullness of the Gospel. It was a complete baptism—a tangible immersion in the heavenly principle or element, the Holy Ghost; and even more real and physical in its effects upon every part of my system than the immersion by water; dispelling forever, so long as reason and memory last, all possibility of doubt or fear in relation to the fact handed down to us historically, that the "Babe of Bethlehem" is truly the Son of God; also the fact that He is now being revealed to the children of men, and communicating knowledge, the same as in the Apostolic times. I was perfectly satisfied, as well I might be, for my expectations were more than realized, I think I may safely say in an infinite degree.

I cannot tell how long I remained in the full flow of the blissful enjoyment and divine enlightenment, but it was several minutes before the celestial element which filled and surrounded me began gradually to withdraw. On arising from my kneeling posture, with my heart swelling with gratitude to God, beyond the power of expression, I felt—I *knew* that He had conferred on me what only an omnipotent being can confer—that which is of greater value than all the wealth and honors worlds can bestow. That night, as I retired to rest, the same wonderful manifestations were repeated, and continued to be for several successive nights. The sweet remembrance of those glorious experiences, from that time to the present, bring them fresh before me, imparting an inspiring influence which pervades my whole being, and I trust will to the close of my earthly existence.

Eliza R. Snow, *Biography and Family Record of Lorenzo Snow* (Salt Lake City: Deseret News Co., 1884), pp. 7–9.

"As Man Now Is, God Once Was"

$\smile$

L E R O I   C .   S N O W

In the spring of 1840, just before leaving on his first mission to England, Lorenzo Snow spent an evening in the home of his friend Elder H. G. Sherwood, in Nauvoo. Elder Sherwood was endeavoring to explain the parable of the Savior about the husbandman who sent forth servants at different hours of the day to labor in the vineyard. While thus engaged in thought this most important event occurred, as told by President Snow himself:

"While attentively listening to his (Elder Sherwood's) explanation, the Spirit of the Lord rested mightily upon me—the eyes of my understanding were opened, and I saw as clear as the sun at noon-day, with wonder and astonishment, the pathway of God and man. I formed the following couplet which expresses the revelation, as it was shown to me, and explains Father Smith's [remarkable] saying to me at a blessing meeting in the Kirtland temple, prior to my baptism, as previously mentioned in my first interview with the Patriarch:

> *As man now is, God once was:*
> *As God now is, man may be.*

"I felt this to be a sacred communication which I related to no one except my sister Eliza, until I reached England, when in a confidential, private conversation with President Brigham Young in Manchester, I related to him this extraordinary manifestation."

Soon after his return from England, in January, 1843, Lorenzo Snow related to the Prophet Joseph Smith his experience in Elder

Sherwood's home. This was in a confidential interview in Nauvoo. The Prophet's reply was: "Brother Snow, that is true gospel doctrine, and it is a revelation from God to you."

Let us understand clearly that while Lorenzo Snow, through a revelation from God, was the author of the above couplet expression, the Lord had revealed this great truth to the Prophet and to Father Smith long before it was made known to Lorenzo Snow. In fact, it was the remarkable promise given to him in the Kirtland Temple, in 1836, by the Patriarch that first awakened the thought in his mind, and its expression in the frequently quoted couplet was not revealed to President Snow until the spring of 1840. We cannot emphasize the fact too strongly that this revealed truth impressed Lorenzo Snow more than perhaps all else; it sank so deeply into his soul that it became the inspiration of his life and gave him his broad vision of his own great future and the mighty mission and work of the Church.

Improvement Era, June 1919, p. 656.

THE GIFT OF
DISCERNING THE SPIRIT

~———~

TRUMAN MADSEN

A man acting as it were, as an undercover agent came to Nauvoo, tried to work his way into the good graces of the Prophet, then invited him out for a walk. On the crest of a hill the Prophet stopped, called him by name and said, "You have a boat and men in readiness to kidnap me, but you will not make out to do it." It was true. The man had planned to kidnap him, but instead he went away cursing. Joseph once wrote in a letter, "it is in vain to try to hide a bad spirit from the eyes of them who are spiritual, for it will show itself in speaking and in writing, as well as in all our other conduct. It is also needless to make great pretensions when the heart is not right: the Lord will expose it to the view of faithful Saints."

Truman Madsen, citing Diary of Oliver B. Huntington, 2:169–70; and *Journal of Discourses*, 26 vols. (London: Latter-day Saints' Book Depot, 1854–86), 26:359.

JOSEPH SMITH SEES THE ROCKY MOUNTAINS IN VISION

EDWARD TULLIDGE

O n the 6th of August, 1842, with quite a number of his brethren, [Joseph Smith] crossed the Mississippi river to the town of Montrose, to be present at the installation of the Masonic Lodge of the Risin Sun. A block schoolhouse had been prepared with shade in front, under which was a barrel of ice water. Judge James Adams was the highest Masonic authority in the state of Illinois, and had been sent there to organize this lodge. He and Hyrum Smith, being high Masons, went into the house to perform some ceremonies which the others were not entitled to witness. These, including Joseph Smith, remained under the bowery. Joseph, as he was tasting the cold water, warned the brethren not to be too free with it. With the tumbler still in his hand he prophesied that the saints would yet go to the Rocky Mountains; and, said he, this water tastes much like that of the crystal streams that are running from the snow-capped mountains. We will let Mr. Call describe this prophetic scene:

"I had before seen him in a vision, and now saw while he was talking his countenance change to white; not the deadly white of a bloodless face, but a living, brilliant white. He seemed absorbed in gazing at something at a great distance, and said: 'I am gazing upon the valleys of those mountains.' This was followed by a vivid description of the scenery of these mountains, as I have since become acquainted with it. Pointing to Shadrach Roundy and others, he said: 'There are some men here who shall do a great work in that land.' Pointing to me, he said: 'There is Anson, he shall go and shall assist in building up cities from one end of the country to the other; and you,' rather extending the idea to all those he had spoken of, 'shall perform as great a work as has been done by man, so that the nations of the earth shall be astonished, and many of them will be gathered in that land and assist in building cities and temples, and Israel shall be made to rejoice.'"

B. H. Roberts, *A Comprehensive History of The Church of Jesus Christ of Latter-day Saints,* 6 vols. (Salt Lake City: The Church of Jesus Christ of Latter-day Saints, 1930), 2:181–82.

"IT APPEARED TO BE JOSEPH SMITH"

GEORGE Q. CANNON

After the martyrdom of the Prophet, the Twelve soon returned to Nauvoo, and learned of the aspirations of Sidney Rigdon. He had claimed that the Church needed a guardian, and that he was that guardian. He had appointed the day for the guardian to be selected, and of course was present at the meeting, which was held in the open air. The wind was blowing toward the stand so strongly at the time that an improvised stand was made out of a wagon, which was drawn up at the back part of the congregation, and which he, William Marks, and some others occupied. He attempted to speak, but was much embarrassed. He had been the orator of the Church; but, on this occasion his oratory failed him, and his talk fell very flat.

In the meantime President Young and some of his brethren came and entered the stand. The wind by this time had ceased to blow. After Sidney Rigdon had spoken, President Young arose and addressed the congregation, which faced around to see and hear him, turning their backs towards the wagon occupied by Sidney. Now it is probable that there are some here today who were present on that occasion, and they, I doubt not, could, if necessary, bear witness that the power of God was manifested at that time, to the joy and satisfaction of the Saints.

It was necessary that there should be some manifestation of the power of God, because the people were divided. There was considerable of doubt as to who should lead the Church. People had supposed that Joseph would live to redeem Zion. They felt very much as the disciples did after the crucifixion: "We trusted," said they to the Savior, whom they knew not, while speaking of their Lord, "that it had been He which should have redeemed Israel." They were saddened in their hearts. So the Saints were when the Prophet Joseph was taken from them. Some even went so far as to think that perhaps God would resurrect him, they had such an idea about his continued earthly connection with this work.

But no sooner did President Young arise than the power of God rested down upon him in the face of the people. It did not appear to be Brigham Young; it appeared to be Joseph Smith that spoke to the people—Joseph in his looks, in his manner, and in his voice; even his figure was transformed so that it looked like that of Joseph, and everybody present, who had the Spirit of God, saw that he was the man whom God had chosen to hold the keys now that the Prophet Joseph had gone behind the veil, and that he had given him power to exercise them.

And from that time forward, notwithstanding the claims of Sidney Rigdon; notwithstanding the claims of Strang, notwithstanding the claims of William Smith, John E. Page and others who drew off from the Church in the days of Nauvoo; and notwithstanding the claims of other men who have since drawn off from the Church and made great pretensions, God has borne testimony to the acts and teachings of His servant Brigham, and those of his servants, the Apostles, who received the keys in connection with him. God sustained him and upheld him, and he blessed all those that listened to his counsel.

Journal of Discourses, 26 vols. (London: Latter-day Saints' Book Depot, 1854–86), 23:363–64.

"KEEP THE SPIRIT OF THE LORD"

MARION G. ROMNEY

In February, 1847, [Brigham Young] had a dream in which the Prophet Joseph Smith appeared to him. It was a glorious dream. You will find it in the history of the Church written by Brother Cannon. Brigham Young expressed his sorrow that he was separated from the companionship of President Smith, the Prophet, and asked him why he could not come with him. The Prophet told him he would have to wait awhile.

Then Brigham Young asked him if he had a message for them, and the Prophet stepped toward him, looking very earnestly, yet patiently, and said (I quote the words of the Prophet in that dream of Brigham Young's):

"Tell the brethren to be humble and faithful and be sure to keep the Spirit of the Lord, that it will lead them aright. Be careful and not turn away the still, small voice; it will teach them what to do and where to go; it will yield the fruits of the kingdom. Tell the brethren to keep their hearts open to conviction, so that when the Holy Ghost comes to them, their hearts will be ready to receive it. . . .

"They can tell the Spirit of the Lord from all other spirits—it will whisper peace and joy to their souls; it will take malice, hatred, strife and all evil from their hearts, and their whole desire will be to do good, bring forth righteousness, and build up the kingdom of God."

Conference Report, April 1944, pp. 140–41.

THE SPOT FOR
THE SALT LAKE TEMPLE

BRIGHAM YOUNG

Does the Lord require the building of a temple at our hands? I can say that he requires it just as much as ever he required one to be built elsewhere. If you should ask, "Brother Brigham, have you any knowledge concerning this; have you ever had a revelation from heaven upon it?" I can answer truly, it is before me all the time, not only today, but it was almost five years ago, when we were on this ground, looking for locations, sending our scouting parties through the country, to the right and to the left, to the north and the south, to the east and the west; before we had any returns from any of them, I knew, just as well as I now know, that this was the ground on which to erect a temple—it was before me.

Journal of Discourses, 26 vols. (London: Latter-day Saints' Book Depot, 1854–86), 1:277.

THE SIGNERS OF THE DECLARATION OF INDEPENDENCE

W I L F O R D   W O O D R U F F

I will here say . . . that two weeks before I left St. George, the spirits of the dead gathered around me, wanting to know why we did not redeem them. Said they, "You have had the use of the Endowment House for a number of years, and yet nothing has ever been done for us. We laid the foundation of the government you now enjoy, and we never apostatized from it, but we remained true to it and were faithful to God."

These were the signers of the Declaration of Independence, and they waited on me for two days and two nights. I thought it very singular, that notwithstanding so much work had been done, and yet nothing had been done for them. The thought never entered my heart, from the fact, I suppose, that heretofore our minds were reaching after our more immediate friends and relatives.

I straightway went into the baptismal font and called upon Brother McAllister to baptize me for the signers of the Declaration of Independence, and fifty other eminent men, making one hundred in all, including John Wesley, Columbus, and others. I then baptized him for every President of the United States, except three; and when their cause is just, somebody will do the work for them.

Journal of Discourses, 26 vols. (London: Latter-day Saints' Book Depot, 1854–86), 19:229.

DEATH BY APPOINTMENT

WILFORD WOODRUFF

The Prophet Joseph Smith held the keys of this dispensation on this side of the veil, and he will hold them throughout the countless ages of eternity. He went into the spirit world to unlock the prison doors and to preach the Gospel to the millions of spirits who are in darkness, and every Apostle, every Seventy, every Elder, etc., who has died in the faith as soon as he passes to the other side of the veil, enters into the work of the ministry, and there is a thousand times more to preach there than there is here. I have felt of late as if our brethren on the other side of the veil had held a council, and that they had said to this one, and that one, "Cease thy work on earth, come hence, we need help," and they have called this man and that man. It has appeared so to me in seeing the many men who have been called from our midst lately.

Perhaps I may be permitted to relate a circumstance with which I am acquainted in relation to Bishop Roskelley, of Smithfield, Cache Valley. On one occasion he was suddenly taken very sick—near to death's door. While he lay in this condition, President Peter Maughan, who was dead, came to him and said: "Brother Roskelley, we held a council on the other side of the veil. I have had a great deal to do, and I have the privilege of coming here to appoint one man to come and help. I have had three names given to me in council, and you are one of them. I want to inquire into your circumstances."

The Bishop told him what he had to do, and they conversed together as one man would converse with another. President Maughan then said to him: "I think I will not call you. I think you are wanted here more than perhaps one of the others." Bishop Roskelley got well from that hour.

Very soon after, the second man was taken sick, but not being able to exercise sufficient faith, Brother Roskelley did not go to him. By and by this man recovered, and on meeting Brother Roskelley he said: "Brother Maughan came to me the other night and told me he was sent to call one man from the ward," and he named two men as had been done to Brother Roskelley. A few days afterwards the third man was taken sick and died.

Now, I name this to show a principle. They have work on the other side of the veil; and they want men, and they call them. And that was my view in regard to Brother George A. Smith. When he was almost at death's door, Brother Cannon administered to him, and in thirty minutes he was up and ate breakfast with his family. We labored with him in this way, but ultimately, as you know, he died. But it taught me a lesson. I felt that man was wanted behind the veil. We labored also with Brother Pratt; he, too, was wanted behind the veil.

Now, my brethren and sisters, those of us who are left here have a great work to do. We have been raised up of the Lord to take this kingdom and bear it off. This is our duty; but if we neglect our duty and set our hearts upon the things of this world, we will be sorry for it. We ought to understand the responsibility that rests upon us. We should gird up our loins and put on the whole armor of God. We should rear temples to the name of the Most High God, that we may redeem the dead.

Journal of Discourses, 26 vols. (London: Latter-day Saints' Book Depot, 1854–86), 22:333–34.

JESUS CHRIST APPEARS TO LORENZO SNOW

LEROI C. SNOW

For some time President Woodruff's health had been failing. Nearly every evening President Lorenzo Snow visited him at his home. This particular evening the doctors said that President Woodruff could not live much longer, that he was becoming weaker every day. President Snow was greatly worried. . . .

[President Snow] went in his room in the Salt Lake Temple, dressed in his robes of the priesthood, knelt at the sacred altar in the Holy of Holies in the House of the Lord, and there plead to the Lord to spare President Woodruff's life, that President

Woodruff might outlive him, and that the great responsibility of Church leadership would not fall upon his shoulders. Yet he promised the Lord that he would devotedly perform any duty required at his hands. At this time he was in his eighty-sixth year.

Soon after this President Woodruff was taken to California, where he died Friday morning at 6:40 o'clock, September 2, 1898. President George Q. Cannon at once wired the information to the President's office in Salt Lake City. Word was forwarded to President Snow who was in Brigham City. The telegram was delivered to him on the street in Brigham. He read it to President Rudger Clawson, then president of Box Elder Stake, who was with him, went to the telegraph office, and replied that he would leave on the train about 5:30 that evening. He reached Salt Lake City about 7:15, proceeded to the President's office, gave some instructions, and then went to his private room in the Salt Lake Temple.

President Snow put on his holy temple robes, repaired again to the same sacred altar, offered up the signs of the Priesthood, and poured out his heart to the Lord. He reminded the Lord how he plead for President Woodruff's life to be spared, that President Woodruff's days would be lengthened beyond his own that he might never be called upon to bear the heavy burdens and responsibilities of the Church. "Nevertheless," he said, "Thy will be done. I have not sought this responsibility, but if it be Thy will, I now present myself before Thee for Thy guidance and instruction. I ask that Thou show me what Thou wouldst have me do."

After finishing his prayer he expected a reply, some special manifestation from the Lord. So he waited—and waited—and waited. There was no reply, no voice, no visitation, no manifestation. He left the altar and the room in great disappointment. Passing through the Celestial room and out into the large corridor, a glorious manifestation was given President Snow which I relate in the words of his granddaughter, Allie Young Pond:

"One evening while I was visiting Grandpa Snow in his room

in the Salt Lake Temple, I remained until the door keepers had gone and the night-watchmen had not yet come in, so grandpa said he would take me to the main front entrance and let me out that way. He got his bunch of keys from his dresser. After we left his room, and while we were still in the large corridor leading into the celestial room, I was walking several steps ahead of grandpa when he stopped me and said: 'Wait a moment, Allie, I want to tell you something. It was right here that the Lord Jesus Christ appeared to me at the time of the death of President Woodruff. He instructed me to go right ahead and reorganize the First Presidency of the Church at once and not wait as had been done after the death of the previous presidents, and that I was to succeed President Woodruff.'

"Then grandpa came a step nearer and held out his left hand and said: 'He stood right here, about three feet above the floor. It looked as though He stood on a plate of solid gold.'

"Grandpa told me what a glorious personage the Savior is and described His hands, feet, countenance and beautiful white robes, all of which were of such a glory of whiteness and brightness that he could hardly gaze upon Him.

"Then he came another step nearer and put his right hand on my head and said: 'Now granddaughter, I want you to remember that this is the testimony of your grandfather, that he told you with his own lips that he actually saw the Savior, here in the Temple, and talked with him face to face.'"

Improvement Era, September 1933, p. 677.

DROUGHT AND TITHING
IN ST. GEORGE

LEROI C. SNOW

President Snow, after his call to the Presidency, humbly admitted that he did not know just what he would do; but he was confident that the Lord would show him, and he placed such dependence upon the promptings of God's spirit, and was so sure that he would follow those instructions that he said: "My administration will not be known as mine, but as God's administration through me."

The day after President John Taylor's funeral, proceedings for the confiscation of Church property were begun in the United States Court (because of plural marriage in the Church). All the property of the Church was seized, and for nearly ten years tedious and expensive litigation continued. Then, too, for several years the General Authorities had been compelled, by prosecution under the Edmunds-Tucker Law, to remain from home. Therefore, during this period, the business interests of the Church suffered greatly.

These are but two of the several contributing causes which brought about serious financial distress. . . . I well remember my father's approaching his personal clerk, James Jack, with the warning, "Brother Jack, we must raise some money. Go through all the securities we have and see if you can find something we can sell to make some money." . . .

One prominent businessman presented a plan to solicit contributions from the entire Church membership. He suggested a "one thousand dollar club" to include all who would contribute one thousand dollars each, a "five hundred dollar club," etc., but President Snow shook his head and said: "No, that is not the Lord's plan." The Lord had not yet shown his servant just how the problem was to be solved, but he revealed the plan a little later.

One morning my father said he was going to St. George in Southern Utah. I was much surprised at the thought of his making this long and hard trip. Mother expressed considerable surprise, but asked no questions.

Upon entering the President's office, father informed Secretary George F. Gibbs of the contemplated trip to St. George. Brother Gibbs at once asked how soon President Snow expected to leave and who would be in the party. The reply was that he would leave just as soon as arrangements could be made, and that he would take as many of the General Authorities as could be spared from the important work at home. . . .

President Snow stood the trip exceptionally well, but was very tired on reaching St. George. . . .

He had the most painful and anxious expression on his face that I had ever seen, and he must have been going through intense mental suffering. After pacing up and down the floor several times, he commenced talking aloud as follows: "Why have I come to St. George, and why have I brought so many of the Church authorities, when we are so much needed at home to look after the important affairs of the Church? Haven't I made a mistake? Why have I come here?"

When the Lord instructed his servant to go to St. George, the purpose of the journey was withheld. President Snow answered the call to go, and then wondered and worried until further light was given.

He finally went to bed and rested very well during the night, appearing to feel very much better the following morning. It was Wednesday, May 17, the day on which the special conference opened in the tabernacle in St. George. It was during one of these meetings that President Snow received the revelation on tithing. I was sitting at a table on the stand, recording the proceedings, when all at once father paused in his discourse.

Complete stillness filled the room. I shall never forget the thrill as long as I live. When he commenced to speak again his voice strengthened, and the inspiration of God seemed to come over him, as well as over the entire assembly. His eyes seemed to brighten and his countenance to shine. He was filled with unusual power. Then he revealed to the Latter-day Saints the vision that was before him.

God manifested to him there and then not only the purpose of the call to visit the Saints in the South, but also Lorenzo Snow's special mission, the great work for which God had prepared and preserved him. And he unveiled the vision to the people. He told them that he could see, as he had never realized before, how the law of tithing had been neglected by the people; also that the Saints, themselves, were heavily in debt, as well as the Church. And now through strict obedience to this law—the paying of a full and honest tithing—not only would the Church be relieved of its great indebtedness, but through the blessings of the Lord this would also be the means of freeing the Latter-day Saints from their individual obligations. And they would become a prosperous people.

Directly on tithing President Snow said:

"The word of the Lord is: The time has now come for every Latter-day Saint, who calculates to be prepared for the future and to hold his feet strong upon a proper foundation, to do the will of the Lord and to pay his tithing in full. That is the word of the Lord to you, and it will be the word of the Lord to every settlement throughout the land of Zion."

President Snow then referred to the terrible drought which had continued so severely for three years in the South. The Virgin River and all its tributaries were virtually dry. . . .

President Snow said . . . :

"All through Dixie we found everything dying out. The stock were dying by hundreds; we could see them as we traveled along, many of them being nothing but skin and bones, and many lying down never, I suppose, to get up again."

In speaking of these serious drought conditions President Snow told the people that if they would observe the law of tithing from then on, and pay a full and honest tithing, that they might go ahead, plough their land and plant the seed. And he promised them, in the name of the Lord, that the clouds would gather, the rains from heaven descend, their lands would be drenched, and the rivers and ditches filled, and they would reap a bounteous harvest that very season.

Many of the people had become so discouraged that they were not willing to risk the seeds of another planting, and many had not even ploughed their fields. Cattle everywhere were dying, and the country was parched. It was now getting very late in the planting season in that southern country, and here the prophet of the Lord made this wonderful prediction. Everyone present in that vast congregation knew that he was speaking under the inspiration of the Holy Spirit.

That evening, father, mother, and I were again in the room together and father walked up and down the floor as he had done the previous night, but there was a sweet expression of happiness and joy on his face. He talked aloud again, as he did the night before, and this is what he said:

"Now I know why I came to St. George. The Lord sent me here, and he has a great work for me to perform. There is no mistake about it. I can see the great future for the Church, and I can hardly wait to get back to Salt Lake City to commence the great work."

When the returning party reached Nephi, where we were to take train for home, President Snow called the members all together in a meeting which will never be forgotten by those who were present. He commissioned every one present to be his special witness to the fact that the Lord had given this revelation to him. He put all the party under covenant and promise not only to obey the law of tithing themselves, but also that each would bear witness to this special manifestation and would spread the tithing message at every opportunity. He made wonderful promises to those who would be faithful to these admonitions. He was filled with great power and inspiration and spoke with such feeling that Elder Francis M. Lyman says in his journal: "I was almost overcome, could hardly control my feelings. . . ."

President Snow, with his party, returned to Salt Lake City, Saturday, May 27, 1899. During his absence of eleven days, he visited sixteen settlements, held twenty-four meetings, delivered twenty-six addresses. . . .

President Snow gathered and compiled data regarding the tithes being paid by the people, but kept especially in mind the Saints in the south. He called for a daily report showing the exact amount of tithing received from those settlements. I well remember handing him one of these reports. After looking it over carefully he said, "Wonderful, wonderful. The good people in Dixie are not only paying one-tenth of their income, but they must be giving all they have to the Lord's work!"

But the rains did not come, and the drought was not broken. President Snow had the daily weather report placed on his desk, which he carefully looked over, but there was no indication of any storms moving in the direction of southern Utah. Week after week passed, and the only word was that southern Utah was burning up under the hot weather, and there seemed to be no prospect of any change.

One morning, as I was going up the stairway leading to father's bedroom, I was surprised to hear him talking to someone. I did not know that anyone had preceded me to the room that morning, but not wanting to disturb him, I walked quietly up the heavily carpeted stairway leading to his room. The door was open, and as I reached it, there I saw this aged, gray-haired prophet, down on his knees before his bedside, in the manner of praying, but seeming to talk to the Lord as if he might have been right in His very presence. He was pouring out his heart and pleading for the Saints in the south. I stood at the open door for a few moments and heard him say:

"Oh Lord, why didst thou make those promises to the good people in St. George if they are not to be fulfilled? Thou didst promise them, if they would accept the command to obey the law of tithing, thou wouldst send the rains from heaven and bless them with a bounteous harvest. These good people accepted thy word and are not only paying a tenth of their income, but they are offering all they have to thee. Do keep thy promise and vindicate the words of thy servant through whom thou didst speak."

I could not bear to hear any more. I turned from the door with my heart bleeding and went down the stairs.

When father came into his office that morning, I noticed that he looked discouraged and seemed to have little interest in his work. [There was] still no report of rain in St. George. Several days passed. One day there was a knock at the door. Brother Gibbs, the secretary, being out, I answered the call. It was a messenger boy with a telegram. I signed for it, opened the telegram, and as I was approaching father's desk I could see on the face of the telegram: "Rain in St. George." I was so happy I could not wait, but cried out: "Father, they have had rain in St. George."

"Read it, my boy, read it," he said, and I read the telegram telling of a great rain that had come to the people there, filling the river and its tributaries and the canals and reaching the entire country. . . .

Father took the telegram from my hand, read it very slowly, and after a few moments, got up from his desk and left the office.

A little while afterwards I followed him into the house and asked mother where he was. When she told me she had not seen him, I knew he must have gone to his room. I walked quietly up the stairway and before reaching the top I heard him talking, as I had on the other occasion. I went to his room and there he was again, down on his knees pouring out his heart in gratitude and thanksgiving to the Lord. He said:

"Father, what can I do to show my appreciation for the blessing which thou hast given to the good people in St. George? Thou hast fulfilled thy promise to them and vindicated the words spoken through thy servant. Do show me some special thing I can do to prove my love for thee."

This faithful servant of the Lord, who had devoted all his long life in beautiful and unwavering service to God, felt that he had not done enough and wanted to do more. There he was in the presence of his Heavenly Father, overcome with joy and happiness. The last words I heard, as I was returning down the stairs, were: "Thou canst not ask anything of me that I am not willing to do, even though it be the offering of my life, to prove my love for thee."

When father returned to his office, his face was filled with happiness, and I am very sure that his heart was lightened and his difficult task made much easier. . . .

During the MIA conference in 1899, at one of the officers' meetings, President Snow spoke on tithing. At the conclusion of his address the following resolution was presented by Elder B. H. Roberts:

"Resolved: That we accept the doctrine of tithing, as now presented by President Snow, as the present word and will of the Lord unto us, and we do accept it with all our hearts; we will ourselves observe it, and we will do all in our power to get the Latter-day Saints to do likewise."

Improvement Era, July 1938, pp. 400–401, 439–42.

"I AM CLEAN"

⌒

JOSEPH F. SMITH

I was very much oppressed, once, on a mission. I was almost naked and entirely friendless, except the friendship of a poor, benighted, degraded people. I felt as if I was so debased in my condition of poverty, lack of intelligence and knowledge, just a boy, that I hardly dared look a . . . man in the face.

While in that condition I dreamed that I was on a journey, and I was impressed that I ought to hurry—hurry with all my might, for fear I might be too late. I rushed on my way as fast as I possibly could, and I was only conscious of having just a little bundle, a handkerchief with a small bundle wrapped in it. I did not realize just what it was, when I was hurrying as fast as I could; but finally I came to a wonderful mansion, if it could be called a mansion. It seemed too large, too great to have been made by hand, but I thought I knew that was my destination. As I passed towards it, as fast as I could, I saw a notice, "Bath." I turned aside quickly and went into the bath and washed myself clean. I opened up this little bundle that I had, and there was a pair of white, clean garments, a thing I had not seen for a long time, because the people I was with did not think very much of making things exceedingly clean. But my garments were clean, and I put them on. Then I rushed to what appeared to be a great opening, or door. I knocked and the door opened, and the man who stood there was the Prophet Joseph Smith. He looked at me a little reprovingly, and the first words he said: "Joseph, you are late." Yet I took confidence and said:

"Yes, but I am clean—I am clean!"

He clasped my hand and drew me in, then closed the great door. I felt his hand just as tangible as I ever felt the hand of man. I knew him, and when I entered I saw my father, and Brigham and Heber, and Willard, and other good men that I had known, standing in a row. I looked as if it were across this valley, and it seemed to be filled with a vast multitude of people, but on the stage were all the people that I had known. My mother was there, and she sat with a child in her lap; and I could name over as many as I remember of their names, who sat there, who seemed to be among the chosen, among the exalted.

The Prophet said to me, "Joseph," then pointing to my mother, he said: "Bring me that child."

I went to my mother and picked up the child, and thought it was a fine baby boy. I carried it to the Prophet, and as I handed it to him I purposely thrust my hands up against his breast. I felt the warmth—I was alone on a mat, away up in the mountains of Hawaii—no one was with me. But in this vision I pressed my hand up against the Prophet, and I saw a smile cross his countenance. I handed him the child and stepped back. President Young stepped around two steps, my father one step, and they formed a triangle. Then Joseph blessed that baby, and when he finished blessing it they stepped back in line; that is, Brigham and father stepped back in line. Joseph handed me the baby, wanted me to come and take the baby again; and this time I was determined to test whether this was a dream or a reality. I wanted to know what it meant. So I purposely thrust myself up against the Prophet. I felt the warmth of his stomach. He smiled at me, as if he comprehended my purpose. He delivered the child to me and I returned it to my mother, laid it on her lap.

When I awoke that morning I was a man, although only a boy. There was not anything in the world that I feared. I could meet any man or woman or child and look them in the face, feeling in my soul that I was a man every whit. That vision, that manifestation and witness that I enjoyed at that time has made me what I am, if I am anything that is good, or clean, or upright before the Lord, if there is anything good in me. That has helped me out in every trial and through every difficulty.

Now, I suppose that is only a dream? To me it is a reality. There never could be anything more real to me. I felt the hand of Joseph Smith. I felt the warmth of his stomach, when I put my hand against him. I saw the smile upon his face. I did my duty as he required me to do it, and when I woke up I felt as if I had been lifted out of a slum, out of a despair, out of the wretched condition that I was in; and naked as I was, or as nearly as I was, I was not afraid of . . . anyone . . . , and I have not been very much afraid of anybody else since that time. I know that that was a reality, to show me my duty, to teach me something, and to impress upon me something that I cannot forget. I hope it never can be banished from my mind.

Joseph F. Smith, *Gospel Doctrine,* 5th ed. (Salt Lake City: Deseret Book Co., 1939), pp. 542–43.

"WHAT HAVE YOU DONE
WITH MY NAME?"

~~~

GEORGE ALBERT SMITH

A number of years ago I was seriously ill. In fact, I think everyone gave me up but my wife. With my family I went to St. George, Utah, to see if it would improve my health. We went as far as we could by train, and then continued the journey in a wagon, in the bottom of which a bed had been made for me.

In St. George we arranged for a tent for my health and comfort, with a built-in floor raised about a foot above the ground, and we could roll up the south side of the tent to make the sunshine and fresh air available. I became so weak as to be scarcely able to move. It was a slow and exhausting effort for me even to turn over in bed.

One day, under these conditions, I lost consciousness of my surroundings and thought I had passed to the Other Side. I found myself standing with my back to a large and beautiful lake, facing a great forest of trees. There was no one in sight, and there was no boat upon the lake or any other visible means to indicate how I might have arrived there. I realized, or seemed to realize, that I had finished my work in mortality and had gone home. I began to look around, to see if I could not find someone. There was no evidence of anyone living there, just those great, beautiful trees in front of me and the wonderful lake behind me.

I began to explore, and soon I found a trail through the woods which seemed to have been used very little, and which was almost obscured by grass. I followed this trail, and after I had walked for some time and had traveled a considerable distance through the forest, I saw a man coming towards me. I became aware that he was a very large man, and I hurried my steps to reach him, because I recognized him as my grandfather [George A. Smith]. In mortality he weighed over three hundred pounds, so you may know he was a large man. I remember how happy I was to see him coming. I had been given his name and had always been proud of it.

When Grandfather came within a few feet of me, he stopped. His stopping was an invitation for me to stop. Then . . . he looked at me very earnestly and said:

"I would like to know what you have done with my name."

Everything I had ever done passed before me as though it were a flying picture on a screen—everything I had done. Quickly this vivid retrospect came down to the very time I was standing there. My whole life had passed before me. I smiled and looked at my grandfather and said:

"I have never done anything with your name of which you need be ashamed."

He stepped forward and took me in his arms, and as he did so, I became conscious again of my earthly surroundings. My pillow was as wet as though water had been poured on it—wet with tears of gratitude that I could answer unashamed.

I have thought of this many times, and I want to tell you that I have been trying, more than ever since that time, to take care of that name. So I want to say . . . : Honor your fathers and your mothers. Honor the names that you bear, because some day you will have the privilege and the obligation of reporting to them (and to your Father in heaven) what you have done with their name.

George Albert Smith, *Sharing the Gospel with Others,* selected and compiled by Preston Nibley (Salt Lake City: Deseret Book Co., 1948), pp. 111–12.

"TAKE THIS TO YOUR FATHER"

MELVIN J. BALLARD

I recall an incident in my own father's experience. How we looked forward to the completion of the Logan Temple. It was about to be dedicated. My father had labored on that house from its very beginning, and my earliest recollection was carrying his dinner each day as he brought the rock down from the quarry. How we looked forward to that great event! I remember how in the meantime father made every effort to obtain all the data and information he could concerning his relatives. It was the theme of his prayer night and morning that the Lord would open up the way whereby he could get information concerning his dead.

The day before the dedication while writing recommends to the members of his ward who were to be present at the first service, two elderly gentlemen walked down the streets of Logan, approached my two young sisters, and, coming to the older one of the two placed in her hands a newspaper and said:

"Take this to your father. Give it to no one else. Go quickly with it. Don't lose it."

The child responded and when she met her mother, her mother wanted the paper. The child said, "No. I must give it to father and to no one else."

She was admitted into the room and told her story. We looked in vain for these travelers. They were not to be seen. No one else saw them. Then we turned to the paper.

The newspaper, *The Newbury Weekly News*, was printed in my father's old English home, Thursday, May 15th, 1884, and reached our hands May 18, 1884, three days after its publication. We were astonished, for by no earthly means could it have reached us, so that our curiosity increased as we examined it. Then we discovered one page devoted to the writings of a reporter of the paper, who had gone on his vacation, and among other places had visited an old cemetery. The curious inscriptions led him to write what he found on the tombstones, including the verses. He also added the names, date of birth, death, etc., filling nearly an entire page.

It was the old cemetery where the Ballard family had been buried for generations, and very many of my father's immediate relatives and other intimate friends were mentioned.

When the matter was presented to President Merrill of the Logan Temple he said, "You are authorized to do the work for those, because you received it through messengers of the Lord."

There is no doubt but that the dead who had received the Gospel in the spirit world had put it into the heart of that reporter to write these things, and thus the way was prepared for my father to obtain the information he sought.

Melvin J. Ballard, *Three Degrees of Glory* (Salt Lake City: Magazine Printing Co., 1922).

"TWENTY-FIVE THOUSAND DOLLARS' WORTH OF GENEALOGY"

GEORGE ALBERT SMITH

In Chicago a number of years ago, during the Century of Progress Exposition, I went into our Church booth one day and inquired of the missionaries as to who had charge of that great cultural and scientific fair.

They told me the man's name was Dawes, and I asked "Is he the brother of Charles G. Dawes, who was vice president of the United States and also ambassador to Great Britain?"

And they answered, "Yes."

"Well," I said, "I am delighted to know that. I happen to know him."

I said to myself, "I think I will go and call on him. He will be Henry Dawes." I knew Henry Dawes, so I went to the telephone and called his office. His secretary answered and I inquired, "Is Mr. Dawes there?"

She said, "Yes, sir."

"May I come over and see him?" I said.

She said, "There are already a hundred people ahead of you, and they all want a job."

I smiled to myself, and said, "Well that may be true, but I am probably the one man he would like to see, because I have a job."

"Do you know him?"

"Yes," I said, "I am from Salt Lake City. I just want to pay my respects."

She said, "Just a minute."

She told Mr. Dawes that George Albert Smith of Salt Lake City was there and wanted to meet him, and he told her to have me come over. So, instead of running me behind a hundred people to wait my turn, she took me to a side door, and there stood before me a tall man whom I had never seen before in my life.

He said, "I am Mr. Dawes."

He was very pleasant, but you can imagine how embarrassed I was. He was Mr. Dawes, and he was Ambassador Dawes' brother, but he was Rufus Dawes. I did not know there was a Rufus Dawes in the world.

"Well," I said, "I have only come to tell you that this is a wonderful fair, and to express to you my appreciation for what you have done in organizing and seeing it through. It is marvelous what has been accomplished, and what an education it is to so many people. Now, I understand that you are a busy man, and that is all I wanted to come and say, and to congratulate you and thank you."

"That is very considerate," he said. "Come in."

"No, that is all I came to say," I replied.

He said, "Come right in."

I said, "No, there are a hundred people waiting to see you."

"None of them will say anything as nice as what you have said."

So I went in, out of ideas and out of breath, almost. He insisted on my sitting down, and the next thing I said was: "By the way, Mr. Dawes, where do your people come from?"

"Do you mean in America?" he asked.

"I mean anywhere."

He said, "Are you interested in genealogy?"

"I certainly am," I answered. "We have one of the finest genealogical libraries in Salt Lake City to be found anywhere."

He said, "Excuse me just a moment," and walked out of his office and came back with a carton about the size of an old family Bible. He took his knife, opened the carton, and took out a package wrapped in white tissue paper. He took the tissue paper off and put on the table one of the most beautifully bound books I have ever seen. It was well printed and profusely illustrated, and the cover was elegantly embossed with gold.

As I looked it over, I said, "Mr. Dawes, that is a beautiful piece of work."

"It ought to be. It cost me twenty-five thousand dollars."

"Well," I said, "it is worth it."

He said, "Is it worth anything to you?"

I said, "It would be if I had it."

He said, "All right, you may have it!"—twenty-five thousand dollars worth of genealogy placed in my hand by a man whom I had met only five minutes before! Well, I was amazed. Our visit continued but a short while longer. I told him how delighted I was to have it and that I would place it in the genealogical library in Salt Lake City.

Before I left the room, he said, "Mr. Smith, this is my mother's genealogy, the Gates' genealogy. We are also preparing my father's genealogy—the Dawes' family. It will be one just like this. When it is finished, I would like to send you a copy of that also."

Fifty thousand dollars worth of genealogy!—and just because I tried to be polite to someone.

I do not think that was an accident. The Dawes family is one of the most prominent families in the United States; and in that line is the Gates family, including Jacob Gates. Other Church families also run through these books.

This man Rufus Dawes died before the second volume was finished. He left word with Charles G. Dawes, his elder brother, to be sure to send me a copy of that book when it was finished. Well, I was afraid that Charles G. Dawes didn't know anything about it, so about a year later I called on him and told him how I had obtained the other volume. He said, "I know all about it, and we will have another of my father's line for you as soon as it is completed." And this second volume, according to promise, also came to me.

The Lord is helping us; it is marvelous how the way is opened and how other people frequently are prompted to prepare their genealogies. But sometimes we fail to take advantage of our opportunities to prepare our genealogies, notwithstanding the Lord has very pointedly said that unless we take care of our temple work we will be rejected with our dead. This is a very serious thing. This is something that we cannot change, if we have wasted our opportunities until life passes.

There may be other such men—there may be a Charles G. Dawes or Rufus Dawes in your line, or mine, someone who is prompted by the Lord to gather these wonderful records. And if there is, we shall have been greatly blessed—if we use such findings for the purpose for which they have been given us, but we cannot expect others to do this work for us.

So the Lord, in one way or another, encourages, advises, and counsels us to do our work. Some families who can't do the work themselves have someone else working all the time on their temple genealogy, and records.

If we do our part, our genealogies will be unfolded to us— sometimes in one way, sometimes in another. So I want to suggest to you, my brethren and sisters: let us do our part.

George Albert Smith, *Sharing the Gospel with Others*, selected and compiled by Preston Nibley (Salt Lake City: Deseret Book Co., 1948), pp. 175–80.

CALL TO THE QUORUM
OF THE TWELVE

<img>~~~</img>

HEBER J. GRANT

Forty years ago this October conference [1922], I met the late Elder George Teasdale at the south gate of the Tabernacle grounds. He shook hands with me and said: "Brother Grant, I am delighted to see you. You and I are going to be—" and he stopped suddenly and his face turned red. But the Lord gave me the balance of the sentence. Four times in my life I have been permitted to read the thoughts of people. The balance of Brother Teasdale's sentence was—"sustained this afternoon as apostles of the Lord Jesus Christ to fill the vacancies in the Quorum." And that went through me like a shock of electricity.

I came to the Sunday afternoon meeting of the conference, because of this partial sentence, and the balance that was given to me, with the assurance in my heart that Brother Teasdale and myself would be sustained as apostles. Those of you who were at that conference remember that it adjourned without filling those vacancies. I do not believe that any mortal man ever more humbly supplicated God during the next few days to forgive him for his egotism than I did for thinking I was to be chosen as an apostle. As you are aware, within a week a revelation came to John Taylor calling Brother Teasdale and myself to those positions.

It has never ceased to be a wonder to me that I do represent the Lord here upon the earth. My association from childhood with the remarkable and wonderful men that have preceded me has made it almost overwhelming to think of being in the same class with them.

The last words uttered by President Joseph F. Smith were to the effect that, when he shook hands with me—he died that night—"The Lord bless you, my boy, the Lord bless you; you have got a great responsibility. Always remember this is the Lord's work and not man's. The Lord is greater than any man. He knows whom He wants to lead His Church, and never makes any mistake. The Lord bless you."

I have felt my own lack of ability. In fact when I was called as one of the apostles I arose to my feet to say it was beyond anything I was worthy of, and as I was rising the thought came to me, "You know as you know that you live that John Taylor is a prophet of God, and to decline this office when he had received a revelation is equivalent to repudiating the prophet." I said, "I will accept the office and do my best." I remember that it was with difficulty that I took my seat without fainting.

There are two spirits striving with us always, one telling us to continue our labor for good, and one telling us that with the faults and failings of our nature we are unworthy. I can truthfully say that from October, 1882, until February, 1883, that spirit followed me day and night, telling me that I was unworthy to be an apostle of the Church and that I ought to resign. When I would testify of my knowledge that Jesus is the Christ, the Son of the living God, the Redeemer of mankind, it seemed as though a voice would say to me: "You lie! You lie! You have never seen Him."

While on the Navajo Indian reservation with Brigham Young, Jr., and a number of others, six or eight on horseback, and several others in "white tops"—I was riding along with Lot Smith at the rear of that procession. Suddenly the road veered to the left almost straight, but there was a well-beaten path leading ahead. I said: "Stop, Lot, stop. Where does this trail lead? There are plenty of footmarks and plenty of horses' hoof marks here." He said, "It leads to an immense gully just a short distance ahead, that it is impossible to cross with a wagon. We have made a regular 'Muleshoe' of miles here to get on the other side of the gully."

I had visited the day before the spot where a Navajo Indian had asked George A. Smith, Jr., to let him look at his pistol. George A. handed it to him, and the Navajo shot him.

I said, "Lot, is there any danger from Indians here?"

"None at all."

"I want to be all alone. Go ahead and follow the crowd." I first asked him if I allowed the animal I was riding to walk if I would reach the road on the other side of the gully before the horsemen and the wagons, and he said, "Yes."

As I was riding along to meet them on the other side, I seemed to see, and I seemed to hear, what to me is one of the most real things in all my life. I seemed to hear the words that were spoken. I listened to the discussion with a great deal of interest. The First Presidency and the Quorum of the Twelve Apostles had not been able to agree on two men to fill the vacancies in the Quorum of the Twelve. There had been a vacancy of one for two years, and a vacancy of two for one year, and the conferences had adjourned without the vacancies being filled. In this council the Savior was present, my father was there, and the Prophet Joseph Smith was there. They discussed the question that a mistake had been made in not filling those two vacancies and that in all probability it would be another six months before the Quorum would be completed. And they discussed as to whom they wanted to occupy those positions, and decided that the way to remedy the mistake that had been made in not filling these vacancies was to send a revelation. It was given to me that the Prophet Joseph Smith and my father mentioned me and requested that I be called to that position. I sat there and wept for joy. It was given to me that I had done nothing to entitle me to that exalted position, except that I had lived a clean, sweet life. It was given to me that because of my

261

father's having practically sacrificed his life in what was known as the great reformation, so to speak, of the people in early days, having been practically a martyr, that the Prophet Joseph and my father desired me to have that position, and it was because of their faithful labors that I was called, and not because of anything I had done of myself or any great thing that I had accomplished. It was also given to me that that was all these men, the Prophet and my father, could do for me. From that day it depended upon me and upon me alone as to whether I made a success of my life or a failure.

"There is a law, irrevocably decreed in heaven before the foundations of this world, upon which all blessings are predicated— And when we obtain any blessing from God, it is by obedience to that law upon which it is predicated" (D&C 130:20–21).

It was given to me, as I say, that it now depended upon me.

No man could have been more unhappy than I was from October, 1882, until February, 1883, but from that day I have never been bothered, night or day, with the idea that I was not worthy to stand as an apostle, and I have not been worried since the last words uttered by Joseph F. Smith to me: "The Lord bless you, my boy, the Lord bless you; you have got a great responsibility. Always remember this is the Lord's work and not man's. The Lord is greater than any man. He knows whom He wants to lead His Church, and never makes any mistake. The Lord bless you."

I have been happy during the twenty-two years that it has fallen to my lot to stand at the head of this Church. I have felt the inspiration of the living God directing me in my labors. From the day that I chose a comparative stranger to be one of the apostles, instead of my lifelong and dearest living friend, I have known as I know that I live, that I am entitled to the light and the inspiration and the guidance of God in directing His work here upon this earth. And I know, as I know that I live, that it is God's work, and that Jesus Christ is the Son of the living God, the Redeemer of the world and that He came to this earth with a divine mission to die upon the cross as the Redeemer of mankind, atoning for the sins of the world.

Heber J. Grant, *Gospel Standards,* compiled by G. Homer Durham (Salt Lake City: Improvement Era, 1969), pp. 193–97.

MY BROTHER'S CONVERSION

HEBER J. GRANT

As I stand here today, I remember what to me was the greatest of all the great incidents in my life, in this tabernacle. I saw for the first time, in the audience, my brother who had been careless, indifferent, and wayward, who had evinced no interest in the gospel of Jesus Christ.

As I saw him for the first time in this building, and as I realized that he was seeking God for light and knowledge regarding the divinity of this work, I bowed my head and I prayed God that if I were requested to address the audience, that the Lord would inspire me by the revelations of His Spirit, by that Holy Spirit in whom every true Latter-day Saint believes, that my brother would have to acknowledge to me that I had spoken beyond my natural ability, that I had been inspired of the Lord.

I realized that if he made that confession, then I should be able to point out to him that God had given him a testimony of the divinity of this work.

Brother Milton Bennion was sitting on the stand that day, and he had been asked to address the congregation. President Angus M. Cannon came to me and said, "Before you entered the building, Brother Grant, I had invited Brother Milton Bennion to speak, but he can come some other day."

I said, "Let him speak."

Brother Cannon said, "Well, I will ask him to speak briefly, and you will please follow him."

Brother Bennion told of his visit around the world; among other things, of visiting the sepulcher of Jesus.

I took out of my pocket a book that I always carried, called a *Ready Reference,* and I laid it down on the stand in front of me, when I stood up to speak. It was opened at the passages that tell of the vicarious work for the dead, of the announcement that Jesus went and preached to the spirits in prison, and proclaimed the gospel of Jesus Christ to them. I intended to read about the baptism for the dead, and I intended to preach upon the fact that the Savior of the world had not only brought the gospel to every soul upon the earth, but also that it reached back to all those who had died without a knowledge of it, or in their sins, that they would have the privilege of hearing it; that, as I understood and had read in the Doctrine and Covenants, Jesus came into the world to be crucified for the world and to die for the sins of the world and that he saved all except only those who denied the Son after the Father had revealed Him—those who had lived and those who had died.

I remember standing there feeling that this was perhaps the greatest of all the great themes that we as Latter-day Saints had to proclaim to the world. I laid the book down, opened at that page; I prayed for the inspiration of the Lord, and the faith of the Latter-day Saints, and I never thought of the book from that minute until I sat down, at the end of a thirty-minute address. I closed my remarks at twelve minutes after three o'clock, expecting that President George Q. Cannon would follow me. Brother Angus came to the upper stand, and said, "George, please occupy the balance of the time."

He said, "No, I do not wish to speak." But Brother Angus refused to take "No" for an answer.

Brother Cannon said, finally: "All right, go take your seat, and I will say something." And he arose and said in substance:

"There are times when the Lord Almighty inspires some speaker by the revelations of His Spirit, and he is so abundantly blessed by the inspiration of the living God that it is a mistake for anybody else to speak following him, and one of those occasions has been today, and I desire that this meeting be dismissed without further remarks," and he sat down.

I devoted the thirty minutes of my speech almost exclusively to a testimony of my knowledge that God lives, that Jesus is the Christ, and to the wonderful and marvelous labors of the Prophet Joseph Smith, and bearing witness to the knowledge God had given me that Joseph was in very deed a prophet of the true and living God.

The next morning my brother came into my office and said, "Heber, I was at a meeting yesterday and heard you preach."

I said, "The first time you ever heard your brother preach, I guess?"

"Oh, no," he said, "I have heard you many times."

I said, "I never saw you in meeting before."

He said, "I generally come in late and go into the gallery. I often go out before the meeting is over. But you never spoke as you did yesterday. You spoke beyond your natural ability. You were inspired of the Lord." The identical words I had uttered the day before, in my prayer to the Lord!

When I heard George Q. Cannon, after I sat down, and before his brother spoke to him, say to himself, "Thank God for the power of that testimony," the tears gushed from my eyes like rain and I rested my elbows on my knees and put my hands over my face, so that the people by me would not see that I was weeping like a child. I knew when I heard those words of George Q. Cannon, that God had heard and answered my prayer. I knew that my brother's heart was touched, the next day when he came and repeated my words, I said to him, "Are you still praying for a testimony of the gospel?"

He said, "Yes, and I am going nearly wild."

I asked, "What did I preach about yesterday?"

He replied, "You know what you preached about."

I said, "Well, you tell me."

"You preached upon the divine mission of the Prophet Joseph Smith."

I answered, "And I was inspired beyond my natural ability; and I never spoke before—at any time you have heard me, as I spoke yesterday. Do you expect the Lord to get a club and knock you down? What more testimony do you want of the gospel of Jesus Christ than that a man speaks beyond his natural ability and under the inspiration of God, when he testifies of the divine mission of the Prophet Joseph Smith?"

The next Sabbath he applied to me for baptism.

Conference Report, October 1922, pp. 188–90.

"THE WILL OF THE LORD"

MARBA C. JOSEPHSON

Faith has always been the fundamental characteristic of Lucy ["Lutie"] G. Cannon. From the earliest childhood, the Lord has manifested himself in her behalf. When she was about twelve years of age, her mother died. When her father [President Heber J. Grant] told Lucy that her mother was dying, Lucy would not believe him. She hurried from the room and returned with a bottle of consecrated oil and implored him to bless her mother. [President Grant] blessed his wife, dedicating her to the Lord. As the children left the room, he fell on his knees and prayed that his wife's death might not affect the faith of their children in the ordinances of the Gospel. "Lutie" herself ran from the house feeling very bad, as she expressed in the following words:

"I was stunned and shocked and felt my father had not sufficient faith. I went behind the house and knelt down and prayed for the restoration of my mother. Instantly a voice, not an audible one, but one that seemed to speak to my whole being, said, 'In the death of your mother the will of the Lord will be done.' Immediately I was a changed child. I felt reconciled and happy."

Improvement Era, December 1937, p. 790.

"WHO WAS THAT OTHER MAN IN THERE?"

ELI H. PEIRCE

I... was called in to administer to the youngest child of one of the branch presidents. The mother, an apostate, seriously objected to anything of the kind in her presence, and she refused to leave the bedside of the dying child.

Not wishing to intrude, we retired to an upper room to pray, and she, designing our motives, sent her little girl to spy upon us. In a secluded chamber we knelt down and prayed, earnestly and fervently, until we felt that the child would live and knew that our prayers had been heard and answered.

Turning round, we saw the little girl standing in the half open door gazing intently into the room, but not heeding our movements. She stood as if entranced for some seconds, her eyes fixed immovably upon a certain spot, and did not stir until her father spoke. She then said, "Papa, who was that other man in there?"

He answered, "Brother Peirce."

She said, "No, I mean that *other* man."

He replied, "There was no other, darling, except Brother Peirce and myself; we were praying for baby."

She shook her head, and, with perfect composure, said, "Oh, yes, there was; I saw him standing between you and Mr. Peirce, and he was all dressed in white."

This was repeated to the mother, who tried every means in her power to persuade the child that it was a mere delusion, but all to no purpose. Entreaties, bribes, threats and expostulations were

268

alike unavailing. She knew what she had seen and nothing could shake that conviction.

The baby was speedily restored to perfect health.

Eliza R. Snow, *Biography and Family Record of Lorenzo Snow* (Salt Lake City: Deseret News Co., 1884), p. 413.

"MY PROPHECY WAS FULFILLED"

HEBER J. GRANT

Never but once in all my life have I stood up in a meeting and prophesied in the name of the Lord Jesus Christ, and that once was many, many years ago up in Idaho, at Paris. I was preaching that we should judge things not by the exception but by the general average, and that the most prosperous, the most successful, the best financial men were those that were honest with God. And it seemed as though a voice said to me: "You lie, you lie; You will never live to pay your debts, although you have been an honest tithe-payer." If I had had a bucket of cold water poured over me, it could not have made a greater impression.

I stopped a moment, then I said, "I prophesy in the name of the Lord Jesus Christ that what I have said to you people is true, and that the Lord rewards us when we do our duty, and I prophesy that although I am a ruined man in the estimation of many men, I will yet live to pay my debts." And I was just $91,000 worse off than nothing, had two wives to support and the children of a dead wife. But from that very day my prophecy was fulfilled. The Lord blessed everything I touched, and in only three short years I was even with the world, financially speaking.

Conference Report, April 1941, p. 130.

THE DEATH OF MY LAST SON

HEBER J. GRANT

I have been blessed with only two sons. One of them died at five years of age and the other at seven.

My last son died of a hip disease. I had built great hopes that he would live to spread the gospel at home and abroad and be an honor to me. About an hour before he died I had a dream that his mother, who was dead, came for him, and that she brought with her a messenger, and she told this messenger to take the boy while I was asleep. In the dream I thought I awoke and I seized my son and fought for him and finally succeeded in getting him away from the messenger who had come to take him, and in so doing I dreamed that I stumbled and fell upon him.

I dreamed that I fell upon his sore hip, and the terrible cries and anguish of the child drove me nearly wild. I could not stand it, and I jumped up and ran out of the house so as not to hear his distress. I dreamed that after running out of the house I met Brother Joseph E. Taylor and told him of these things.

He said: "Well, Heber, do you know what I would do if my wife came for one of her children—I would not struggle for that child; I would not oppose her taking that child away. If a mother who had been faithful had passed beyond the veil, she would know of the suffering and the anguish her child may have to suffer. She would know whether that child might go through life as a cripple and whether it would be better or wiser for that child to be relieved from the torture of life. And when you stop to think, Brother Grant, that the mother of that boy went down into the shadow of death to give him life, she is the one who ought to have the right to take him or leave him."

I said, "I believe you are right, Brother Taylor, and if she comes again, she shall have the boy without any protest on my part."

After coming to that conclusion, I was waked by my brother, B. F. Grant, who was staying that night with us.

He called me into the room and told me that my child was dying.

I went in the front room and sat down. There was a vacant chair between me and my wife who is now living, and I felt the presence of that boy's deceased mother, sitting in that chair. I did not tell anybody what I felt, but I turned to my living wife and said: "Do you feel anything strange?" She said: "Yes, I feel assured that Heber's mother is sitting between us, waiting to take him away."

Now, I am naturally, I believe, a sympathetic man. I was raised as an only child with all the affection that a mother could lavish upon a boy. I believe that I am naturally affectionate and sympathetic and that I shed tears for my friends—tears of joy for their success and tears of sorrow for their misfortunes. But I sat by the deathbed of my little boy and saw him die, without shedding a tear. My living wife, my brother, and I, upon that occasion experienced a sweet, peaceful, and heavenly influence in my home, as great as I have ever experienced in my life. And no person can tell me that every other Latter-day Saint that has a knowledge of the gospel in his heart and soul, can really mourn for his loved ones; only in the loss of their society here in this life.

I never think of my wives and my dear mother and my two boys, my daughter, and my departed friends, and beloved associates being in the graveyard. I think only of the joy and the happiness and the peace and satisfaction that my mother is having in meeting with the Prophet and the Patriarch and Brigham Young and my father and the beloved friends that she knew from the days of Nauvoo to the day that she died. I think only of the joy they have in meeting with father and mother and loved ones who have been true and faithful to the gospel of the Lord Jesus Christ. My mind reaches out to the wonderful joy and satisfaction and happiness that they are having, and it robs the grave of its sting.

Heber J. Grant, *Gospel Standards,* compiled by G. Homer Durham (Salt Lake City: Improvement Era, 1969), pp. 364–66.

"HER SON APPEARED TO HER"

DAVID O. MCKAY

One day in Salt Lake City a son kissed his mother good morning, took his dinner bucket, and went to City Creek Canyon where he worked. He was a switchman on the train that was carrying logs out of the canyon. Before noon his body was brought back lifeless. The mother was inconsolable. She could not be reconciled to that tragedy—her boy just in his early twenties so suddenly taken away. The funeral was held, and words of consolation were spoken, but she was not consoled. She couldn't understand it.

One forenoon, . . . after her husband had gone to his office to attend to his duties as a member of the Presiding Bishopric, she lay in a relaxed state on the bed, still yearning and praying for some consolation. She said that her son appeared and said, "Mother, you needn't worry. That was merely an accident. I gave the signal to the engineer to move on, and as the train started, I jumped for the handle of the freight car, and my foot got caught in a sagebrush, and I fell under the wheel. I went to father soon after that, but he was so busy in the office I couldn't influence him—I couldn't make any impression upon him, and I tried again. Today I come to you to give you that comfort and tell you that I am happy."

Well, you may not believe it. You may think she imagined it, but you can't make her think so, and you can't make that boy's father think it. I cite it today as an instance of the reality of the existence of intelligence and environment to which you and I are "dead," so to speak, as was this boy's father.

David O. McKay, *Gospel Ideals* (Salt Lake City: Improvement Era, 1953), pp. 525–26.

"NOTHING WILL HURT YOU"

DAVID O. MCKAY

Since childhood it has been very easy for me to believe in the reality of the visions of the Prophet Joseph Smith. What I am going to say may seem very simple to you, but to me it is a heart petal.

When a very young child in the home of my youth, I was fearful at night. I traced it back to a vivid dream in which two Indians came into the yard. I ran to the house for protection, and one of them shot an arrow and hit me in the back. Only a dream, but I felt that blow, and I was very much frightened, for in the dream they entered [the house], . . . a tall one, and a smaller one, and sneered and frightened Mother.

I never got over it. Added to that were the fears of my mother, for when Father was away with the herd, or on some mission, Mother would never retire without looking under the bed; so burglars or men who might enter the house and try to take advantage of Mother and the young children were real to me.

Whatever the conditions, I was very much frightened. One night I could not sleep, and I fancied I heard noises around the house. Mother was away in another room. Thomas E. by my side was sleeping soundly. I became terribly wrought in my feeling, and I decided to pray as my parents had taught me.

I thought I could pray only by getting out of bed and kneeling, and that was a terrible test. But I did finally bring myself to get out of bed and kneel and pray to God to protect Mother and the family. And a voice, [speaking] as clearly to me as mine is to you, said, "Don't be afraid. Nothing will hurt you." Where it came from, what it was, I am not saying. You may judge. To me it was a direct answer.

———————

Conference Report, October 1951, p. 182.

"THE MOST GLORIOUS BEING"

MELVIN J. BALLARD

Melvin J. Ballard related this experience on January 7, 1919, at a temple meeting of the First Presidency and the Council of the Twelve.]

Two years ago, about this time, I had been on the Fort Peck Reservation for several days with the brethren, solving the problems connected with our work among the Lamanites. . . . There was no precedent for us to follow, and we just had to go to the Lord and tell Him our troubles, and get inspiration and help from Him. On this occasion I had sought the Lord, under such circumstances, and that night I received a wonderful manifestation and impression which has never left me. I was carried to this place—into this room. I saw myself here with you. I was told there was another privilege that was to be mine; and I was led into a room where I was informed I was to meet someone. As I entered the room I saw, seated on a raised platform, the most glorious being I have ever conceived of, and was taken forward to be introduced to Him. As I approached He smiled, called my name, and stretched out His hands toward me. If I live to be a million years old I shall never forget that smile. He put His arms around me and kissed me, as He took me into His bosom, and He blessed me until my whole being was thrilled. As He finished I fell at His feet, and there saw the marks of the nails; and as I kissed them, with deep joy swelling through my whole being, I felt that I was in heaven indeed. The feeling that came to my heart then was: Oh! if I could live worthy, though it would require four-score years, so that in the end when I have finished I could go into His presence and receive the feeling that I *then* had in His presence, I would give everything that I am and ever hope to be!

Melvin J. Ballard, *Crusader for Righteousness* (Salt Lake City: Bookcraft, 1968), pp. 65–66.

"MIRACLES AS A MATTER OF COURSE"

MATTHEW COWLEY

These natives [of Polynesia] live close to God. They have some kind of power. I guess it's just because they accept miracles as a matter of course. They never doubt anything. They used to scare me. Someone would come up and say, "Brother Cowley, I've had a dream about you."

I'd say, "Don't tell me. I don't want to hear about it."

"Oh, it was a good one."

"All right. Tell me."

And they'd tell me something. Now I remember when President Rufus K. Hardy of the First Council of the Seventy passed away. I was walking along the street of one of the cities in New Zealand, and one of our native members came up—a lady.

She said to me, "President Hardy is dead."

I said, "Is that so? Have you received a wire?"

She said, "No. I received a message, but I haven't received any wire." She repeated, "He's dead. I know."

Well, I always believed them when they told me those things. When I got back to headquarters, I wasn't there long when here came a cablegram which said that President Hardy had passed away the night before. But she knew that without any cablegram. She told me about it.

I got out of my car once in a city. I got out to do some window-shopping to get a little rest from driving. I walked around, and finally I went around a corner, and there stood a native woman and her daughter. The mother said to the daughter, "What did I tell you?"

I said, "What's going on here?"

The daughter said, "Mother said if we'd stand here for fifteen minutes you'd come around the corner." Now she didn't have any radio set with her, just one in her heart where she received the impression.

Matthew Cowley, *Matthew Cowley Speaks* (Salt Lake City: Deseret Book Co., 1954), pp. 243–45.

PROPHECY AT A MEMORIAL SERVICE

MATTHEW COWLEY

After President Hardy died, we had a memorial service for him. I'll never forget the native who was up speaking, saying what a calamity it was to the mission to lose this great New Zealand missionary who could do so much for them as one of the Authorities of the Church. He was talking along that line, and all of a sudden he stopped and looked around at me and said, "Wait a minute. There's nothing to worry about. When President Cowley gets home, he'll fill the first vacancy in the Council of the Twelve Apostles, and we'll still have a representative among the Authorities of the Church." Then he went on talking about President Hardy. When I arrived home the following September, I filled the first vacancy in the Quorum of the Twelve. Now did that just happen by chance? Oh, I might have thought so if it had been one of you white Gentiles that had prophesied that, but not from the blood of Israel. Oh, no, I could not deny, I couldn't doubt it.

Matthew Cowley, *Matthew Cowley Speaks* (Salt Lake City: Deseret Book Co., 1954), pp. 244–45.

"HE DOES SPEAK"

HUGH B. BROWN

I should like to give some reasons for [my] faith and attempt to justify my allegiance to the Church. Perhaps I can do this best by referring again to an interview I had in London, England, in 1939, just before the outbreak of World War II.

I had met a very prominent English gentleman, a member of the House of Commons and formerly one of the justices of the supreme court of Britain. In a series of conversations on various subjects, "vexations of the soul," he called them, we talked about business and law; about politics, international relations, and war; and we frequently discussed religion.

He called me on the phone one day and asked if I would meet him at his office and explain some phases of my faith. He said, "There is going to be a war, and you will have to return to America, and we may not meet again." His statement regarding the imminence of war and the possibility that we would not meet again proved to be prophetic.

When I went to his office, he said he had been intrigued by some things I had told about my church. He asked me if I would prepare a brief on Mormonism and discuss it with him as I would discuss a legal problem. He said, "You have told me that you believe that Joseph Smith was a prophet and that you believe that God the Father and Jesus of Nazareth appeared to him in vision.

"I cannot understand," he said, "how a barrister and solicitor from Canada, a man trained in logic and evidence and unemotional cold fact, could accept such absurd statements. What you tell me about Joseph Smith seems fantastic, but I wish you would take three days at least to prepare a brief and permit me to examine it and question you on it."

I suggested that, as I had been working on such a brief for more than 50 years, we proceed at once to have an examination for discovery, which is, briefly, a meeting of the opposing sides in a lawsuit where the plaintiff and defendant, with their attorneys, meet to examine each other's claims and see whether they can find some area of agreement and thus save the time of the court later on.

I said perhaps we could find some common ground from which we could discuss my "fantastic ideas." He agreed, and we proceeded with our "examination for discovery."

Because of time limitations, I can only give a condensed or abbreviated synopsis of the three-hour conversation that followed. I began by asking, "May I proceed, sir, on the assumption that you are a Christian?"

"I am."

"I assume that you believe in the Bible—the Old and New Testaments?"

"I do!"

"Do you believe in prayer?"

"I do!"

"You say that my belief that God spoke to a man in this age is fantastic and absurd?"

"To me it is."

"Do you believe that God ever did speak to anyone?"

"Certainly, all through the Bible we have evidence of that."

"Did he speak to Adam?"

"Yes."

"To Enoch, Noah, Abraham, Moses, Jacob, and to others of the prophets?"

"I believe he spoke to each of them."

"Do you believe that contact between God and man ceased when Jesus appeared on the earth?"

"Certainly not. Such communication reached its climax, its apex at that time."

"Do you believe that Jesus of Nazareth was the Son of God?"

"He was."

"Do you believe, sir, that after the resurrection of Christ, God ever spoke to any man?"

He thought for a moment and then said, "I remember one Saul of Tarsus who was going down to Damascus to persecute the saints and who had a vision, was stricken blind, in fact, and heard a voice."

"Whose voice did he hear?"

"Well," he said, "the voice said 'I am Jesus whom thou persecutest: it is hard for thee to kick against the pricks.'"

"Do you believe that actually took place?"

"I do."

"Then, my Lord"—that is the way we address judges in the British commonwealth—"my Lord, I am submitting to you in all seriousness that it was standard procedure in Bible times for God to talk to men."

"I think I will admit that, but it stopped shortly after the first century of the Christian era."

"Why do you think it stopped?"

"I can't say."

"You think that God hasn't spoken since then?"

"Not to my knowledge."

"May I suggest some possible reasons why he has not spoken. Perhaps it is because he cannot. He has lost the power."

He said, "Of course that would be blasphemous."

"Well, then, if you don't accept that, perhaps he doesn't speak to men because he doesn't love us anymore. He is no longer interested in the affairs of men."

"No," he said, "God loves all men, and he is no respecter of persons."

"Well, then, if you don't accept that he loves us, then the only other possible answer as I see it is that we don't need him. We have made such rapid strides in education and science that we don't need God any more."

And then he said, and his voice trembled as he thought of impending war, "Mr. Brown, there never was a time in the history of the world when the voice of God was needed as it is needed now. Perhaps you can tell me why he doesn't speak."

My answer was, "He does speak, he has spoken; but men need faith to hear him."

Conference Report, October 1967, pp. 117–18.

"BROTHER McKAY, THEY GOT YOUR MESSAGE!"

DAVID O. MCKAY

The occasion was a conference held at Huntly, New Zealand, a thousand people assembled. Before that time I had spoken through interpreters in China, Hawaii, Holland, and other places, but I felt impressed on that occasion to speak in the English language. In substance I said, "I have never been much of an advocate of the necessity of tongues in our

Church, but today I wish I had that gift. But I haven't. However, I am going to speak to you, my brothers and sisters, in my native tongue and pray that you may have the gift of interpretation of tongues. We will ask Brother Stuart Meha who is going to interpret for me, to make notes, and if necessary he may give us a summary of my talk afterwards."

Well, the outpouring of the gift of tongues on that occasion was most remarkable. Following the end of my sermon Brother Sid Christy, who was a student of Brigham Young University, a Maori, who had returned to New Zealand, rushed up and said, "Brother McKay, they got your message!"

Well, I knew they had by the attention and the nodding of their heads during the talk. I said, "I think they have but for the benefit of those who may not have understood or had that gift, we shall have the sermon interpreted."

While Brother Meha was interpreting that or giving a summary of it in the Maori language some of the natives, who had understood it, but who did not understand English, arose and corrected him in his interpretations.

President George Albert Smith and Brother Rufus K. Hardy visited New Zealand several years after that event, and Brother Hardy, hearing of the event, brought home testimonies of those who were present, and he took the occasion to have those testimonies notarized. So it is the gift of interpretation rather than the gift of tongues, that was remarkable.

David O. McKay, *Gospel Ideals* (Salt Lake City: Improvement Era, 1953), p. 552.

"IT WAS THE CITY ETERNAL"

⌒〜⌒

DAVID O. MCKAY

On Tuesday, May 10, 1921, we sailed all day on the smoothest seat of our entire trip. The slightly undulating waves had been so free from even signs of unrest that the slight ripples discernible appeared on the surface like millions of little squares—like plaited cloth with the rich design of the same deep blue material as the body.

Nearing Savaii, we could see with the aid of field glasses the "Spouting Horns," which looked like geysers. On our right we caught a glimpse of the little village nestling safely in the mouth of an extinct volcano on the little island of Apolima.

Towards evening, the reflection of the afterglow of a beautiful sunset was most splendid! The sky was tinged with pink, and the clouds lingering around the horizon were fringed with various hues of crimson and orange, while the heavy cloud farther to the west was somber purple and black. These various colors cast varying shadows on the peaceful surface of the water. Those from the clouds were long and dark, those from the crimson-tinged sky, clear but rose-tinted and fading into a faint pink that merged into the clear blue of the ocean. Gradually, the shadows became deeper and heavier, and then all merged into a beautiful calm twilight that made the sea look like a great mirror upon which fell the faint light of the crescent moon!

Pondering still upon this beautiful scene, I lay in my berth at ten o'clock that night, and thought to myself: Charming as it is, it doesn't stir my soul with emotion as do the innocent lives of children, and the sublime characters of loved ones and friends. Their beauty, unselfishness, and heroism are after all the most glorious!

I then fell asleep, and beheld in vision something infinitely sublime. In the distance I beheld a beautiful white city. Though far away, yet I seemed to realize that trees with luscious fruit, shrubbery with gorgeously-tinted leaves, and flowers in perfect bloom abounded everywhere. The clear sky above seemed to reflect these beautiful shades of color. I then saw a great concourse of people approaching the city. Each one wore a white flowing robe and a white headdress. Instantly my attention seemed centered upon their leader, and though I could see only the profile of his features and his body, I recognized him at once as my Savior! The tint and radiance of his countenance were glorious to behold! There was a peace about him which seemed sublime—it was divine!

The city, I understood, was his. It was the City Eternal; and the people following him were to abide there in peace and eternal happiness.

But who were they?

As if the Savior read my thoughts, he answered by pointing to a semicircle that then appeared above them, and on which was written in gold the words:

"These Are They Who Have Overcome the World—Who Have Truly Been Born Again!"

When I awoke, it was breaking day over Apia harbor.

David O. McKay, *Cherished Experiences from the Writings of President David O. McKay*, compiled by Clare Middlemiss (Salt Lake City: Deseret Book Co., 1955), pp. 101–2.

CALLED TO SERVE

SPENCER W. KIMBALL

It was [nearly a week since I had been called to serve in the Quorum of the Twelve]. . . . No peace had yet come, though I had prayed for it almost unceasingly these six days and nights. I had no plan or destination. I only knew I must get out in the open, apart, away. I dressed quietly and without disturbing the family, I slipped out of the house. I turned toward the hills. I had no objective. I wanted only to be alone. I had begun a fast.

The way was rough, I wandered aimlessly and finally came to the top of the hill. I nearly stepped on a snake coiled on my path. An unexplainable sudden strength sent me into a high jump over his striking head. Could this be symbolic of my other worries and problems? I stopped to rest, thinking that here I was alone, but cows were near and people stirring in the homes below. Over the little ridge was a sloping little valley and on the other side the high mountain rose rapidly and farther up almost precipitously to a high peak far above. Without thought I found my way down and started up again on the other side. The grass was ankle high and the seeds fell into my shoes. The lower reaches had been pastured by cattle when it was wet and it was pitted with deep hoofprints. The rocks on the hillside increased in quantity and size.

My weakness overcame me again. Hot tears came flooding down my cheeks as I made no effort to mop them up. I was accusing myself, and condemning myself and upbraiding myself. I was praying aloud for special blessings from the Lord. I was telling Him that I had not asked for this position, that I was incapable of doing the work, that I was imperfect and weak and human, that I

286

was unworthy of so noble a calling, though I had tried hard and my heart had been right. I knew that I must have been at least partly responsible for offenses and misunderstandings which a few people fancied they had suffered at my hands. I realized that I had been petty and small many times. I did not spare myself. A thousand things passed through my mind. Was I called by revelation? Or, had the Brethren been impressed by the recent contacts in my home and stake when they had visited us, or by the accounts of my work in the flood rehabilitation which reports I knew had been greatly exaggerated in my favor? Had I been called because of my relationship to one of the First Presidency?

If I could only have the assurance that my call had been inspired most of my other worries would be dissipated. I knew if the Lord had revealed to the Brethren that I was to be one of His leaders, that He would forgive all my weaknesses and make me strong. I knew full well that He knew all the imperfections of my life and He knew my heart. And I knew that I must have His acceptance before I could go on. I stumbled up the hill and onto the mountain, as the way became rough. I faltered some as the way became steep. No paths were there to follow; I climbed on and on. Never had I prayed before as I now prayed. What I wanted and felt I must have was an assurance that I was acceptable to the Lord. I told Him that I neither wanted nor was worthy of a vision or appearance of angels or any special manifestation. I wanted only the calm peaceful assurance that my offering was accepted. Never before had I been tortured as I was now being tortured. And the assurance did not come.

I was getting higher and the air was thinner and I was reaching some cliffs and jagged rocky points. I came to a steep slide area and it was almost impossible to make the grade. I stumbled over an old oak stick which I picked up. I broke off one end and it was exactly the right length for a cane. It was rough and a little crooked and worm-eaten in places, but it helped me climb. I stopped to catch my breath in a protected cove behind some large rocks but unsatisfied I continued to climb, up steep jagged rocks made the more difficult of scaling by my tear-filled eyes.

As I rounded a promontory I saw immediately above me the peak of the mountain and on the peak a huge cross with its arms silhouetted against the blue sky beyond. It was just an ordinary cross made of two large heavy limbs of a tree, but in my frame of mind, and coming on it so unexpectedly, it seemed a sacred omen. It seemed to promise that here on this cross, on this peak, I might get the answer for which I had been praying intermittently for six days and nights and constantly and with all the power at my command these hours of final torture. I threw myself on the ground and wept and prayed and pleaded with the Lord to let me know where I stood. I thought of my Father and Mother and my Grandfather, Heber C. Kimball, and my other relatives that had been passed from the earth for long years and wondered what part they had had, if any, in this call, and if they approved of me and felt that I would qualify. I wondered if they had influenced, in any way, the decision that I should be called, I felt strangely near them, nearer than ever in my life.

I mentally beat myself and chastised myself and accused myself. As the sun came up and moved in the sky I moved with it, lying in the sun, and still I received no relief. I sat upon the cliff and strange thoughts came to me: all this anguish and suffering could be ended so easily from this high cliff and then came to my mind the temptations of the Master when he was tempted to cast Himself down—then I was ashamed for having placed myself in a comparable position and trying to be dramatic. I looked out over the beautiful world below, stretching out to the horizon, with its lovely homes, fertile fields and prosperous businesses and I was reminded that I had had a small part of that world and was in a position that I could get more and more of it, and that I was asked to give up a part of it; then I was filled with remorse because I had permitted myself to place myself again in a position comparable, in a small degree, to the position the Saviour found Himself in when He was tempted, and I was filled with remorse because I felt I had cheapened the experiences of the Lord, having compared mine with His. Again I challenged myself and told myself that I was only trying to be dramatic and sorry for myself.

Again I lay on the cool earth. The thought came that I might take cold, but what did it matter now. There was one great desire, to get a testimony of my calling, to know that it was not human and inspired by ulterior motives, kindly as they might be. How I prayed! How I suffered! How I wept! How I struggled!

Was it a dream which came to me? I was weary and I think I went to sleep for a little. It seemed that in a dream I saw my grandfather and became conscious of the great work he had done. I cannot say that it was a vision, but I do know that with this new experience came a calm like the dying wind, the quieting wave after the storm is passed. I got up, walked to the rocky point and sat on the same ledge. My tears were dry, my soul was at peace. A calm feeling of assurance came over me, doubt and questionings subdued. It was as though a great burden had been lifted. I sat in tranquil silence surveying the beautiful valley, thanking the Lord for the satisfaction and the reassuring answer to my prayers. Long I meditated here in peaceful quietude, apart, and I felt nearer my Lord than ever at any time in my life.

I finally looked at my wrist watch and discovered that it would soon be time to leave for Salt Lake. With my cane, which now seemed an important part of my spiritual experience, I went down the mountain, not down the steep difficult precipitous way, but down the other side which was easy and gradual. I had found a path that was easy to follow. I felt I knew my way, now, physically and spiritually, and knew where I was going.

Edward L. Kimball and Andrew E. Kimball Jr., *Spencer W. Kimball* (Salt Lake City: Bookcraft, 1977), pp. 192–95.

"DO YOU EVER CRY WHEN YOU READ THE BOOK OF MORMON?"

MARION G. ROMNEY

I urge you to get acquainted with this great book [the Book of Mormon]. Read it to your children; they are not too young to understand it. I remember reading it with one of my lads when he was very young. On one occasion I lay in the lower bunk and he in the upper bunk. We were each reading aloud alternate paragraphs of those last three marvelous chapters of Second Nephi. I heard his voice breaking and thought he had a cold, but we went on to the end of the three chapters. As we finished he said to me, "Daddy, do you ever cry when you read the Book of Mormon?"

"Yes, Son," I answered "'Sometimes the Spirit of the Lord so witnesses to my soul that the Book of Mormon is true that I do cry."

"Well," he said, "that is what happened to me tonight."

Conference Report, April 1949, p. 41.

A LIVING PROPHET

H A R O L D   B .   L E E

I t is very interesting to see the reaction of people. Soon after President David O. McKay announced to the Church that members of the First Council of the Seventy were being ordained high priests in order to extend their usefulness and to give them authority to act when no other General Authority could be present, a seventy I met in Phoenix, Arizona, was very much disturbed. He said to me, "Didn't the Prophet Joseph Smith say that this was contrary to the order of heaven to name high priests as presidents of the First Council of the Seventy?"

And I said, "Well, I have understood that he did, but have you ever thought that what was contrary to the order of heaven in 1840 might not be contrary to the order of heaven in 1960?" He had not thought of that. He . . . was following a dead prophet, and he was forgetting that there is a living prophet today. Hence the importance of our stressing that word *living*.

Harold B. Lee, *Stand Ye in Holy Places* (Salt Lake City: Deseret Book Co., 1974), pp. 152–53.

"HOW CAN I KNOW
THE LORD HAS FORGIVEN ME?"

HAROLD B. LEE

Some years ago, President Marion G. Romney and I were sitting in my office. The door opened and a fine young man came in with a troubled look on his face, and he said, "Brethren, I am going to the temple for the first time tomorrow. I have made some mistakes in the past, and I have gone to my bishop and my stake president, and I have made a clean disclosure of it all; and after a period of repentance and assurance that I have not returned again to those mistakes, they have now adjudged me ready to go to the temple. But, brethren, that is not enough. I want to know, and how can I know, that the Lord has forgiven me also."

What would you answer one who might come to you asking that question? As we pondered for a moment, we remembered King Benjamin's address contained in the book of Mosiah. Here was a group of people asking for baptism, and they said they viewed themselves in their carnal state:

. . . And they all cried aloud with one voice, saying: O have mercy, and apply the atoning blood of Christ that we may receive forgiveness of our sins, and our hearts may be purified; . . .

. . . after they had spoken these words the Spirit of the Lord came upon them, and they were filled with joy, having received a remission of their sins, and having peace of conscience . . . (Mosiah 4:2–3).

There was the answer.

Harold B. Lee, *Stand Ye in Holy Places* (Salt Lake City: Deseret Book Co., 1974), pp. 184–85.

PROTECTION

"WE PASSED ON
WITHOUT INTERRUPTION"

JOSEPH SMITH

Towards the latter end of August, in company with John and David Whitmer, and my brother Hyrum Smith, I visited the Church at Colesville, New York. Well knowing the determined hostility of our enemies in that quarter, and also knowing that it was our duty to visit the Church, we had called upon our Heavenly Father, in mighty prayer, that he would grant us an opportunity of meeting with them, that he would blind the eyes of our enemies so that they would not know us, and that we might on this occasion return unmolested. Our prayers were not in vain, for when within a little distance of Mr. Knight's place, we encountered a large company at work upon the public road, amongst whom were several of our most bitter enemies. They looked earnestly at us, but not knowing us, we passed on without interruption. That evening we assembled the Church, and confirmed them, partook of the Sacrament, and held a happy meeting, having much reason to rejoice in the God of our salvation and sing hosannas to His holy name. Next morning we set out on our return home, and although our enemies had offered a reward of five dollars to any one who would give them information of our arrival, yet did we get out of the neighborhood, without the least annoyance, and arrived home in safety. Some few days afterwards, however, Newel Knight came to my place, and from him we learned that, very shortly after our departure, the mob came to know of our having been there, when they immediately collected

together, and threatened the brethren, and very much annoyed
them during all that day.

Joseph Smith, *History of The Church of Jesus Christ of Latter-day Saints,* 7 vols., 2d ed. rev.,
edited by B. H. Roberts (Salt Lake City: The Church of Jesus Christ of Latter-day Saints,
1932–51), 1:108–9.

THE STORM KEPT BACK THE MOB

JOSEPH SMITH

This night we camped on an elevated piece of land between
Little Fishing and Big Fishing rivers, which streams were
formed by seven small streams or branches.

As we halted and were making preparations for the night, five
men armed with guns rode into our camp, and told us we should
"see hell before morning;" and their accompanying oaths partook
of all the malice of demons. They told us that sixty men were coming from Richmond, Ray county, and seventy more from Clay
county, to join the Jackson county mob, who had sworn our utter
destruction.

During this day, the Jackson county mob, to the number of
about two hundred, made arrangements to cross the Missouri
river, above the mouth of Fishing river, at Williams' ferry, into Clay
county, and be ready to meet the Richmond mob near Fishing
river ford for our utter destruction; but after the first scow load of
about forty had been set over the river, the scow in returning was

296

met by a squall, and had great difficulty in reaching the Jackson side by dark.

When these five men were in our camp, swearing vengeance, the wind, thunder, and rising cloud indicated an approaching storm, and in a short time after they left the rain and hail began to fall. The storm was tremendous; wind and rain, hail and thunder met them in great wrath, and soon softened their direful courage, and frustrated all their designs to "kill Joe Smith and his army." Instead of continuing a cannonading which they commenced when the sun was about one hour high, they crawled under wagons, into hollow trees, and filled one old shanty, till the storm was over, when their ammunition was soaked, and the forty in Clay county were extremely anxious in the morning to return to Jackson, having experienced the pitiless pelting of the storm all night. . . .

Very little hail fell in our camp, but from half a mile to a mile around, the stones or lumps of ice cut down the crops of corn and vegetation generally, even cutting limbs from trees, while the trees, themselves were twisted into withes by the wind. The lightning flashed incessantly, which caused it to be so light in our camp through the night, that we could discern the most minute objects; and the roaring of the thunder was tremendous. The earth trembled and quaked, the rain fell in torrents, and, united, it seemed as if the mandate of vengeance had gone forth from the God of battles, to protect His servants from the destruction of their enemies, for the hail fell on them and not on us, and we suffered no harm, except the blowing down of some of our tents, and getting wet; while our enemies had holes made in their hats, and otherwise received damage, even the breaking of their rifle stocks, and the fleeing of their horses through fear and pain.

Many of my little band sheltered in an old meetinghouse through this night, and in the morning the water in Big Fishing river was about forty feet deep, where, the previous evening, it was no more than to our ankles, and our enemies swore that the water rose thirty feet in thirty minutes in the Little Fishing river. They reported that one of their men was killed by lightning, and that another had his hand torn off by his horse drawing his hand between the logs of a corn crib while he was holding him on the inside. They declared that if that was the way God fought for the Mormons, they might as well go about their business.

Joseph Smith, *History of The Church of Jesus Christ of Latter-day Saints,* 7 vols., 2d ed. rev., edited by B. H. Roberts (Salt Lake City: The Church of Jesus Christ of Latter-day Saints, 1932–51), 2:103–5.

"AN ALMIGHTY POWER PROTECTS THIS PEOPLE"

JOSEPH SMITH

Colonel Sconce, with two other leading men from Ray county, came to see us, desiring to know what our intentions were; "for," said he, "I see that there is an Almighty power that protects this people, for I started from Richmond, Ray county, with a company of armed men, having a fixed determination to destroy you, but was kept back by the storm, and was not able to reach you." When he entered our camp he was seized with such a trembling that he was obliged to sit down to compose himself; and when he had made known the object of their visit, I arose, and, addressing them, gave a relation of the sufferings of the Saints in Jackson county, and also our persecutions generally, and what we had suffered by our enemies for our religion; and that we had come one thousand miles to assist our brethren, to bring them clothing, etc., and to reinstate them upon their own lands; and that we had no intention to molest or injure any people, but only to administer to the wants of our afflicted friends; and that the evil reports circulated about us were false, and got up by our enemies to procure our destruction. When I had closed a lengthy speech, the spirit of which melted them into compassion, they arose and offered me their hands, and said they would use their influence to allay the excitement which everywhere prevailed against us; and they wept when they heard of our afflictions and persecutions, and learned that our intentions were good. Accordingly they went forth among the people, and made unwearied exertions to allay the excitement.

Joseph Smith, *History of The Church of Jesus Christ of Latter-day Saints,* 7 vols., 2d ed. rev., edited by B. H. Roberts (Salt Lake City: The Church of Jesus Christ of Latter-day Saints, 1932–51), 2:105–6.

ESCAPING THE MOB

MARY FIELDING SMITH

I felt much pleased to see Sisters Walton and Snider who arrived here on Saturday about noon, having left Brother Joseph Smith and Rigdon about twenty miles from Fairport [Ohio] to evade the mobbers. They were to come home in Dr. [Sampson] Avards carriage and expected to arrive about

10 o'clock at night but to their great disappointment they were prevented in a most grievous manner. They had got within four miles of home after a very fatiguing journey, much pleased with their visit to Canada and greatly anticipating the pleasure of seeing their homes and families, when they were surrounded with a mob and taken back to Painesville and secured as was supposed in a tavern where they intended to hold a mock trial. But to the disappointment of the wretches the housekeeper was a member of the church who assisted our beloved brethren in making their escape, but as Brother Joseph Smith says not by a basket let down through a window, but by the kitchen door.

No doubt the hand of the Lord was in it or it could not have been effected. The day had been extremely wet and the night was unusually dark and you may try if you can to conceive what their situation was. They hardly knew which way to steer, as it had by that time got to be about 10 o'clock. The first step they took was to find the woods as quick as possible where they thought they should be safe. But in order to reach thereto they had to lay down in a swamp or by an old log just where they happened to be, so determinedly were they pursued by their mad enemies in every direction, sometimes so closely that Brother J[oseph] was obliged to entreat Brother Rigdon, after his exertion in running, while lying by a log to breath more softly if he meant to escape.

When they would run or walk they took each other by the hand and covenanted to live and die together. Owing to the darkness of the night their pursuers had to carry lighted torches which was one means of the escape of our beloved sufferers as they could see them in every direction while they were climbing over fences or traveling through brush or corn fields until about 12 o'clock. When after traveling as they suppose in this manner five or six miles they found the road which led homeward and saw no more of their pursuers. After traveling on foot along muddy slippery roads till near three in the morning they arrived safe at home almost fainting with fatigue.

He, Brother J[oseph], told us that he decreed in his heart when first taken that he would see home before sun rise and thank God so it was. And notwithstanding all he had to endure he appeared in the house of the Lord throughout the Sabbath in excellent spirits and spoke in a very powerful manner and blessed the congregation in the name of the Lord and I do assure you the saints felt the blessing and left the house rejoicing abundantly returning their blessing upon him. Brother Rigdon through his great weariness and a small hurt received from a fall did not attend the house but is now well. I suppose all these things will only add another gem to their crown.

Kenneth W. Godfrey, Audrey M. Godfrey, Jill Mulvay Derr, *Women's Voices: An Untold History of the Latter-day Saints, 1830–1900* (Salt Lake City: Deseret Book Co., 1982), pp. 64–65.

THREE BRIGHT SILVER HALF DOLLARS

MARY ELIZABETH ROLLINS LIGHTNER

I saw the first hay and grain stacks on fire, in Bishop Partridge's lot, and other property destroyed [by the mob in Independence, Missouri]. Uncle Gilbert's store was broken open, and some of the goods strewn on the public square; then the few families living in town went to the temple block, where the bishop and his first counselor, John Corrill, lived, for mutual protection; while the brethren were hiding in the woods, their food being carried to them in the night. Some of our brethren were tied to trees and whipped until the blood ran down their bodies. After enduring all manner of grievances we were driven from the county.

While we were camped on the banks of the Missouri River waiting to be ferried over, they found there was not money enough to take all over. One or two families must be left behind, and the fear was that if left, they would be killed. So, some of the brethren by the name of Higbee thought they would try and catch some fish; perhaps the ferryman would take [the fish as payment for passage across the river]. They put out their lines in the evening; it rained all night and most of the next day. When they took in their lines they found two or three small fish, and a catfish that weighed fourteen pounds. On opening it, what was their astonishment to find three bright silver half dollars, just the amount needed to pay for taking their team over the river. This was considered a miracle, and caused great rejoicing among us.

Leonard J. Arrington and Susan Arrington Madsen, *Sunbonnet Sisters: True Stories of Mormon Women and Frontier Life* (Salt Lake City: Bookcraft, 1984), pp. 14, 17.

My Pocket Bible

LORENZO SNOW

I spent the remainder of the winter in travel and preaching, chiefly in the northern part of Kentucky, with varied success, and treatment—sometimes received in the most courteous manner and listened to with intense interest, and, at other times, abusively and impudently insulted; but in no instance treated worse than was Jesus, whom I profess to follow. He said: "If they have called the master of the house Beelzebub, how much more they of his household?" What a fine test the Gospel is, to prove the hearts of the people!

On one occasion, I was very courteously tendered a court house, and at the close of the services, I was invited home by a member of the legislature—was seated at the head of his table, and otherwise as highly honored, and as hospitably treated, as though I had been a sceptered monarch. Then, on another occasion, one evening, I was preaching in a large room of a private house, and afterwards learned that a portion of my audience had gathered for the purpose of mobbing me. They had arranged with a party that lay concealed at a little distance, and within call, to join them immediately on my leaving the house to return to my lodgings, and all proceed together to execute their schemes of vengeance.

It was a very cold night, and after the close of the services I stood with my back to the chimney fire, with a number of others—some of whom belonged to the mob party. One of the latter persons, amid the jostling of the crowd, accidentally brought his hand in contact with one of the pockets in the skirt of my coat, which struck him with sudden alarm on his feeling, what he supposed to be, a large pistol. He immediately communicated the discovery to his affrighted coadjutors, all of whom directly withdrew, and, to their fellows outside, imparted the astounding news that the "Mormon" Elder was armed with deadly weapons.

That was sufficient—the would-be outlaws abandoned their evil designs for fear of signal punishment; but the supposed pistol which caused their alarm and my protection, was my pocket Bible, a precious gift to me from the dearly beloved Patriarch, Father Joseph Smith.

Eliza R. Snow, *Biography and Family Record of Lorenzo Snow* (Salt Lake City: Deseret News Co., 1884), pp. 37–38.

HONORING THE PRIESTHOOD

WILFORD WOODRUFF

I was once moved upon to go and warn old Father Hakeman, living on Petty-John Creek, Arkansas. He had been in Jackson County during the persecution period. His wife died there. His family consisted of five sons, all over six feet tall. Most of them had been whipped with hickory gads by mobs, and he went south into Arkansas, taking his sons with him. We went a good deal out of our way for the purpose of visiting Father Hakeman. I had a vision the night previous, in which was manifested to me the trouble that lay before us, but that the Lord would deliver us. We arrived at his house on Sunday morning. He was taking breakfast. We had had breakfast at the place where we stayed overnight. I saw a Book of Mormon on the shelf. He did not seem to pay any attention to us, or to take any interest in us. I took up the Book of Mormon, and said, "You have a very good book here."

"Yes," said he, "but it is a book that came from the devil."

That opened my eyes. He had been an elder; he had been in Zion; had been persecuted there and driven out; but I found that he had apostatized, and he was our enemy. I saw he would do anything he could against us.

We left him and went to Brother Hubbard's and stayed with him three weeks, during which we took our axes and cleared some land for him. I was strongly impressed three times to go up and warn Father Hakeman. At last I did so, according to the commandment of God to me. The third time I met with him, his house seemed to be full of evil spirits, and I was troubled in spirit at the manifestation. When I finished my warning, I left him. He followed me from his house—with the intention of killing me. I have no doubt about his intention, for it was shown to me in vision. When he came to where I was, he fell dead at my feet, as if he had been struck with a thunderbolt from heaven. I was then a priest, but God defended me and preserved my life. I speak of this because it is a principle that has been manifest in the church of God in this generation as well as in others. I had the administration of angels while holding the office of a priest. I had visions and revelations. I traveled thousands of miles. I baptized men, though I could not confirm them because I had not the authority to do it.

I speak of these things to show that a man should not be ashamed of any portion of the priesthood. Our young men, if they are deacons, should labor to fulfill that office. If they do that, they may then be called to the office of a teacher, whose duty it is to teach the people, visit the Saints and see that there is no evil or iniquity carried on. God has no respect for persons in this priesthood any further than as they magnify their callings and do their duty.

Millennial Star 53:641–42.

"GET UP AND MOVE YOUR CARRIAGE"

∽

WILFORD WOODRUFF

In 1848, after my return to Winter Quarters from our pioneer journey, I was appointed by the Presidency of the Church to take my family and go to Boston, to gather up the remnant of the Saints and lead them to the valleys of the mountains.

While on my way east I put my carriage into the yard of one of the brethren in Indiana, and Brother Orson Hyde set his wagon by the side of mine, and not more than two feet from it.

Dominicus Carter, of Provo, and my wife and four children were with me. My wife, one child and I went to bed in the carriage, the rest sleeping in the house.

I had been in bed but a short time when a voice said to me: "Get up, and move your carriage."

It was not thunder, lightning or an earthquake, but the still, small voice of the Spirit of God—the Holy Ghost.

I told my wife I must get up and move my carriage. She asked: "What for?"

I told her I did not know, only the Spirit told me to do it.

I got up and moved my carriage several rods, and set it by the side of the house.

As I was returning to bed, the same spirit said to me, "Go and move your mules from that oak tree," which was about one hundred yards north of our carriage.

I moved them to a young hickory grove and tied them up. I then went to bed.

In thirty minutes a whirlwind caught the tree to which my mules had been fastened, broke it off near the ground and carried it one hundred yards, sweeping away two fences in its course, and laid it prostrate through that yard where my carriage stood, and the top limbs hit my carriage as it was.

In the morning I measured the trunk of the tree which fell where my carriage had stood, and I found it to be five feet in circumference. It came within a foot of Brother Hyde's wagon, but did not touch it.

Thus by obeying the revelation of the Spirit of God to me, I saved my life and the lives of my wife and child, as well as my animals.

Wilford Woodruff, *Leaves from My Journal* (Salt Lake City: Juvenile Instructor's Office, 1882), p. 88.

"DON'T GO ABOARD
THAT STEAMER"

WILFORD WOODRUFF

When I got back to Winter Quarters from the pioneer journey [1847], President Young said to me, "Brother Woodruff, I want you to take your wife and children and go to Boston and stay there until you can gather every Saint of God in New England and Canada and send them up to Zion."

I did as he told me. It took me two years to gather up everybody, and I brought up the rear with a company (there were about one hundred of them). We arrived at Pittsburgh one day at sundown. We did not want to stay there, so I went to the first steamboat that was going to leave.

I saw the captain and engaged passage for us on that steamer. I had only just done so when the Spirit said to me, and that, too, very strongly, "Don't go aboard that steamer, nor your company." Of course, I went and spoke to the captain, and told him I had made up my mind to wait.

Well, that ship started, and had only got five miles down the river when it took fire, and three hundred persons were burned to death or drowned. If I had not obeyed that Spirit, and had gone on that steamer with the rest of the company, you can see what the result would have been.

Wilford Woodruff, *The Discourses of Wilford Woodruff,* edited by G. Homer Durham (Salt Lake City: Bookcraft, 1946), pp. 294–95.

Whisperings of the Spirit

Wilford Woodruff

I will now give an example from my own experience of the result of not obeying the voice of the Spirit.

Some years since I had part of my family living in Randolph, Rich County. I was there on a visit, with my team in the month of December.

One Monday morning my monitor, the Spirit watching over me, said: "Take your team and go home to Salt Lake City."

When I named it to my family who were at Randolph they urged me strongly to stop longer.

Through their persuasion I stayed until Saturday morning, with the Spirit continually prompting me to go home. I then began to feel ashamed to think that I had not obeyed the whisperings of the Spirit to me before.

I took my team and started early on Saturday morning. When I arrived at Woodruff, the Bishop urged me to stop until Monday and he would go with me.

I told him, "No, I have tarried too long already."

I drove on sprightly, and when within fifteen miles of Wasatch, a furious storm overtook me, the wind blowing heavily in my face.

In fifteen minutes I could not see any road whatever, and knew not how or where to guide my horses.

I left my lines loosely on my animals, went inside my wagon, tied down my cover, and committed my life and guidance into the hands of the Lord, trusting to my horses to find the way, as they had twice before passed over that road.

I prayed to the Lord to forgive my sin in not obeying the voice of the Spirit to me, and implored Him to preserve my life.

My horses brought me onto the Wasatch station at 9 o'clock in the evening, with the hubs of my wagon dragging in the snow.

I got my horses under cover, and had to remain there until next Monday night, with the snow six feet deep on the level, and still snowing.

It was with great difficulty at last that I saved the lives of my horses by getting them into a box car and taking them to Ogden; while, if I had obeyed the revelation of the Spirit of God to me, I should have traveled to Salt Lake City over a good road without any storm.

As I have received the good and the evil, the fruits of obedience and disobedience, I think I am justified in exhorting all my young friends to always obey the whisperings of the Spirit of God, and they will always be safe.

Wilford Woodruff, *Leaves from My Journal* (Salt Lake City: Juvenile Instructor's Office, 1882), pp. 90–91.

DANGERS AND
HAIRBREADTH ESCAPES

⌒

WILFORD WOODRUFF

Varied and diverse are the lives and fortunes of men; while the paths of some are strewn with flowers and ease from the cradle to the grave, with naught to disturb their peace, others are marked victims of varied misfortunes, accidents and dangers. The last-named class is the one in whose ranks I have stood through my infancy, childhood, youth and manhood, up to the present time, so much so, that it has seemed as though some invisible power or fate was watching my footsteps, in order to find some opportunity to take my life from the earth. I can only attribute the continuation of my life to the present time to a merciful God, whose hand has been stretched out, and rescued me from death in the midst of the many dangers and hairbreadth escapes I have passed through, some of which I will here mention.

When three years of age, I fell into a caldron of boiling water, was instantly caught out, but was so badly scalded, that it was nine months before I was considered out of danger.

At five years of age, I fell from the great beam of a barn, striking my face upon the floor, which came near breaking my neck.

Three months afterwards, I broke one of my arms, by falling down stairs. I soon after broke my other arm, by falling out of a high stoop upon a pile of timber.

When six years of age, I came near being killed by a surly bull. My father and I were feeding pumpkins to the cattle, a surly bull drove my cow away from the one she was eating. I took the pumpkin he had left, upon which he pitched at me. My father told me to throw down the pumpkin and run. I ran down a steep hill, and took the pumpkin with me, being determined that the cow should have her rights. The bull pursued. As he was about to overtake me, I stepped into a posthole and fell; the bull leaped over me, after the pumpkin, and tore it to pieces with his horns, and would have served me in the same way, had I not fallen.

During the same year, I went into my father's sawmill, with several others. I got upon the head-block to take a ride, while the carriage was running back, not anticipating any danger; my leg was caught between the head-block and the fender-post, and broke both bones of my leg below the knee. I was taken to the house, and lay nine hours before my bones were set, suffering severe pain; but being young, my bones soon knit together, and I was upon my feet again. During my confinement by this lameness, my brother Thompson was also confined in the same room with the typhus fever.

When seven years of age, I was riding on the top of a load of hay, which my uncle, Ozan Woodruff, was driving to the barn; he turned the load over upon me; I was nearly suffocated for the want of air, before the hay was removed.

At eight years old, I was riding in a one-horse wagon with several others, the horse took fright, ran down a steep hill, and turned the wagon over upon us; but again, while in the midst of danger, my life was preserved; none of us were seriously injured.

When nine years old, I climbed into an elm tree to obtain bark. I stepped upon a dry limb, which broke, and I fell about fifteen feet upon my back, which beat the breath out of my body. A cousin ran and told my parents I was dead. Before they arrived at the spot, I came to my senses, and met them.

When twelve years of age, I was drowned in Farmington River, and sunk in thirty feet of water, and after carrying one person to the bottom with me, I was miraculously saved by a young man named Bacon diving to the bottom, and carrying with him a large stone, to hold him down until he obtained my body, not expecting to save me alive. I suffered much in being restored to life.

At thirteen years of age, while passing through Farmington meadows, in the depth of winter, the roads were drifted with snow; and in an exceedingly blustering day, I became so chilled and overcome with cold, that I could not travel. I crawled into the hollow of a large apple tree. A man in the distance seeing me go in, hastened to my rescue, realizing my danger more fully than I did. When he arrived at the spot, I had fallen asleep, and was nearly insensible; he had much difficulty in arousing me to a sense of my situation. He procured means to carry me to my father's house, and through a kind Providence, my life was again preserved.

At fourteen years of age, I split my left instep open with an ax, which went nearly through my foot; it was nine months getting well.

At fifteen years of age, I was bitten in my left hand by a mad dog in the last stage of hydrophobia. He dented my hand with his teeth, but did not draw blood, and I was again preserved, through the mercies of God, from an awful death.

At the age of seventeen, I was riding a very ill-tempered horse that I was not acquainted with; and while going down a very steep rocky hill, the horse taking advantage of the ground, suddenly leaped from the road, and ran down the steep, amid the rocks, at full speed, and commenced kicking up, and attempted to throw me over his head upon the rocks; but I lodged upon the top of his head, grasped hold of each ear as with a death grip, expecting every moment to be dashed to pieces against the rocks. While in this position, sitting astride of his neck, with no bridle to guide him but his ears, he plunged down the hill under full speed, until he ran against a rock, and was dashed to the ground. I went over both his head and the rocks, about one rod, and struck the ground square on my feet, being the only thing visible that saved my life; for, had I struck upon any other part of my body, it must have killed me instantly; as it was, my bones crushed from under me as though they were reeds. It broke my left leg in two places, and put out both my ankles in a shocking manner, and the horse came near rolling over me in his struggles to get up. My uncle, Titus Woodruff, saw me fall, got assistance, and carried me to his house. I lay from 2 P.M. till 10, without medical aid; then my father arrived, bringing Dr. Swift, of Farmington, with him, who set my bones, boxed up my limbs, and carried me in his carriage eight miles that night to my father's. My sufferings were very great. I had good attention, however, and in eight weeks I was outdoors upon my crutches.

In 1827, while attempting to clear the ice out of a waterwheel, standing upon the wheel with one arm around the shaft, a man hoisted the gate, and let a full head of water upon it. As soon as the water struck the wheel it started, my feet slipped into the wheel, but I immediately plunged head foremost over the rim into about three feet of water, and my weight drew my legs out of the wheel, or I should have been drawn under a shaft and crushed to death.

In 1831, while having charge of the flouring mill in Collinsville, Connecticut, I was standing inside of a breast wheel, 20 feet in diameter, upon one of the arms near the top, clearing out the ice, when a full head of water was let onto it. The wheel immediately started; but I dropped my ax and leaped through it to the bottom, by the shaft and arms, about twenty feet; as I struck the bottom of the wheel, I was rolled out against a ragged stone wall, with only about two feet clearance between it and the wheel. The wheel caught me and rolled me out into the water below, where I found myself without any bones broken, but with some bruises and much fright.

During the winter of 1831, while in New Hartford, Connecticut, I passed through a severe course of lung fever.

In 1833, the day I was baptized, one of my horses, newly sharp shod, kicked my hat off my head, and had he struck two inches lower, would probably have killed me instantly. In ten minutes afterwards, while driving the same team down a hill, on a sleigh without any box, the bottom boards slipped forward under the roller and caught the ground, turned endwise, and fell on the horses' backs, throwing me between the horses; they ran to the bottom of the hill, dragging me with the lines, head foremost, with the sleigh on top of me, about twenty rods over a smooth snow path; I escaped unharmed, however, in the midst of both dangers.

In 1834, while travelling in Zion's Camp in Missouri, a rifle was accidentally discharged, and the ball passed through three tents, with about twelve men in each, and lodged in a wagon axletree, while a man was standing behind it, and injured no one. It passed within a few inches of my breast, and many others escaped as narrowly as myself.

A few months afterwards a musket, heavily loaded with buckshot, was accidentally snapped within a few feet of me, with the muzzle pointed at my breast; it had a good flint and was well primed, but it missfire[d], and my life was again preserved.

In April 1839, in Rochester, Illinois, I was riding upon the running gears of a wagon without a box, sitting upon the forward axletree, when the bolt, fastening the coupling pole, came out, which left the hind wheels; and my weight on the forward bolster and tongue, turned the coupling pole over on to the horses, turning the stakes upside down, and shut me up fast between the bolster and tongue, but in such a manner that my head and shoulders dragged on the ground; my horses took fright, and ran out into an open prairie, and dragged me in this position for about half a mile. I managed to guide them with my left hand, so as to run them into a corner of a high worm fence, where we landed in a pile together. I was considerably bruised, but escaped without any broken bones.

July 23, 1842.—President Joseph Smith [Jr.] sent me from Nauvoo to St. Louis to procure a stock of paper. I went down upon a steamboat; was six days on the way, during which time I was severely attacked with bilious fever. The day I made my purchase, the fever was so high I was scarcely sensible of what I was doing. As soon as I made my purchase and got my freight on board, I took my berth, and lay there until I arrived at Nauvoo on the 10th of August. I was confined to my bed forty days, and passed through the most severe fit of sickness I ever endured; my life was despaired of by many of my friends. I was administered to by President [Joseph] Smith and the Twelve; my life was preserved by the power of God. I took a relapse twice after I began to recover; once while in council with the Presidency and Twelve, my strength left me, my breath stopped, and I felt as though I was struck with death.

September 12, 1843.—At five o'clock P.M., I left Boston on the express train for Portland. While passing through Chesterwoods, six miles south of Kennebunk, after dark, and while going at full speed, we struck one of the rails which some persons had raised by rolling a log under it, and landed in a pile; three cars were filled with passengers, and their lives were saved by having a long train of freight between the passenger cars and the engine; all of them were mashed to pieces; the engineer was killed, some of the passengers had bones broken; I escaped unhurt.

On the 5th of October, 1846, while with the camp of Israel building up Winter Quarters, on the west side of the Missouri River, (then Indian country) I passed through one of the most painful and serious misfortunes of my life. I took my axe and went two and a half miles on to the bluffs to cut some shingle timber to cover my cabin; I was accompanied by two men. While the third tree was falling, which was an oak, over two feet in diameter, I stepped behind it some ten feet, and also to one side the same distance, where I thought I would be entirely out of danger; but when the tree fell, there being a crook in the body of it, which struck a knoll on the ground, the whole body shot endways back of the stump and bounded, and the butt of the tree struck me on the breast and knocked me several feet into the air against a standing oak, and the falling tree followed me in its bound and caught me against the standing tree, and I came down between them; before reaching the earth, however, I was liberated from them, and struck the ground upon my feet in a badly bruised condition. My left thigh, the whole length of it, and my hip and left arm were much bruised; my breast bone and three ribs on my left side were broken; my lungs, vitals and left side were also bruised in a shocking manner.

After the accident I sat upon a log until Mr. John Garrison went a quarter of a mile to get my horse. Notwithstanding I was so badly hurt, I mounted my horse, and rode two and a half miles over a very rough road, dismounting twice in consequence of miry places, my breast and vitals were so badly torn to pieces, that at each step of the horse the pain went through me like an arrow. I continued on horseback until I arrived at Turkey Creek, on the north side of Winter Quarters. I then became exhausted, and was taken off my horse and carried to my wagon in a chair. I was met in the street by Presidents Brigham Young, H[eber] C. Kimball and W[illard] Richards and others, who assisted in carrying me to my family. Before laying me upon my bed, the Presidency laid hands upon me, rebuked my suffering and distress in the name of the Lord, and said I should live and not die. I was then laid upon my bed in my wagon, and as the Apostles prophesied upon my head, so it came to pass. I employed no physician on this occasion, but was administered to by the elders of Israel and nursed by my wife. I lay upon my bed unable to move until my breastbone began to knit together, which commenced on the ninth day. I began to walk about in twenty days; in thirty days from the time I was hurt I again commenced to do hard labor.

July 5th, 1848.—While on a mission to the Eastern States, I drove my carriage, containing myself and family into the dooryard of Brother James Williams in Iowa, to camp for the night. I tied my mules to a large oak tree several rods from the carriage. As we were about to lay down in the carriage for the night, I was strongly impressed to go and move my mules from the oak tree, and also to move my carriage. I followed the dictates of the spirit, and removed my mules to a small hickory grove, also moved my carriage several rods, and retired to rest. In a short time a heavy rainstorm came on, which broke the tree near the ground, and laid it prostrate where my carriage had stood. As it was, the top struck the hind end of the carriage; the tree was two feet in diameter. Thus, by obeying the whisperings of the Spirit, myself and family were preserved.

On the 21st day of April, 1856, while assisting to remove an ox that had died from poison and had been skinned, I inoculated my arm with poison and mortification ensued. The poison worked through my system for seven days before it showed itself outwardly. On the 28th my arm began to swell, was in great pain and showed signs of mortification. I showed it to President [Brigham] Young, who advised me to cleanse my stomach immediately, and put on onion poultices, and anything that would draw the poison from my system into my arm, which counsel I immediately put in execution. The 29th was another trying day to my life; the poison had so thoroughly penetrated my whole system, that my strength left me; I could not stand, I was led to my bed, my bowels and stomach ceased to act, my speech was like that of a drunken man. President [Brigham] Young called, in company with Dr. Sprague, and laid hands upon me, and rebuked the disease and the power of the destroyer which had seized my body, and promised me in the name of the Lord, that I should not die but live to finish my work which was appointed me upon the earth. I soon began to recover. The poison and mortification left my system and centered in my arm, and was drawn from my arm through the aid of charcoal poultices, moistened with a strong decoction of wormwood, ragweed and wild sage; the dead flesh was removed from my arm with instruments and lunar caustic, and in a few days I was well again.

I have occupied considerable space in referring to those peculiar circumstances which have attended me during life, and to sum the matter up it stands thus:—I have broken both legs—one in two places—both arms, my breastbone and three ribs, and had both ankles dislocated. I have been drowned, frozen, scalded and bit by a mad dog—have been in two waterwheels under full head of water—have passed through several severe fits of sickness, and encountered poison in its worst forms—have landed in a pile of railroad ruins—have barely been missed by passing bullets, and have passed through a score of other hairbreadth escapes.

It has appeared miraculous to me, that with all the injuries and broken bones which I have had, I have not a lame limb, but have been enabled to endure the hardest labor, exposures and journeys—have often walked forty, fifty, and on one occasion, sixty miles in a day. The protection and mercy of God has been over me, and my life thus far has been preserved; for which blessings I feel to render the gratitude of my heart to my Heavenly Father, praying that the remainder of my days may be spent in his service and in the building up of his kingdom.

Millennial Star 27:359–60, 374–76, 391–92.

POINT OF THE MOUNTAIN

HANNAH CORNABY

In a few weeks, [my husband] started for Spanish Fork to seek a new home; having heard while in Provo of the advantages it offered to new settlers;—namely, plenty of land, with a good supply of water. This was in August 1856. . . .

We rented a house, purchased a good building site, and built a small room in which to winter. This had just been accomplished when my husband was taken very sick; but he recovered in a month sufficiently to take a journey to Salt Lake City on business. He had just reached his destination when unfortunately he took a heavy chill and became entirely prostrated by rheumatic and lung fever. . . .

At this time, I received a letter from a friend in Salt Lake City, informing me that if I wished to see my husband alive, I must go to him at once; but the difficulties in the way seemed almost insurmountable. The roads were nearly impassable for snow. I was sixty miles from Salt Lake City. . . .

On the third day of January, 1857, the teams started for Salt Lake City, and I with them, having arranged to leave my two eldest children in the care of Sister Isabella Rockhill. The first day we traveled twelve miles, reaching Provo at dark. Greatly to my surprise, I met Brother John B. Milner, with whom we [had become] acquainted in crossing the ocean on board the *Ellen Marie*. He, with his wife, made me welcome for the night, offering the best accommodation their house afforded. The following night I spent at Lehi, at the house of Elder Robert Winter, my husband's brother-in-law, who accompanied me the next day on the journey.

I must mention a very providential deliverance I had that day. We had to pass what is known as the "Point of the Mountain"—the divide separating Utah and Salt Lake Valleys. The ascending grade made it impossible for the teams, six in number, to travel without doubling. This slow operation rendered it very tedious sitting so long in the wagon; and I became so benumbed that, following the advice of the teamster, I dismounted and walked on, with my babe well wrapt. But the piercing wind and blinding snow made it hard work [to keep moving], yet necessity compelled me to walk fast to keep from freezing. This took me so far ahead of the teams that [suddenly I realized I was lost]. I attempted to retrace my steps, but was met by the wind and drifting snow, which I could not face; so I continued on. At length I became so exhausted, I thought I must sit down; but knowing this would mean death, I prayed to God for help and waded through snow, drifted so deep in some places that it was impossible to trace the road. Stupified and benumbed as I was, I wandered into a ravine, sinking down into a deep snow-drift, which nearly covered me.

I had just enough consciousness to wonder whether my babe was alive, and how long it would be until the teams would find me, when a stupor came over me, from which I was aroused by a kindly voice. [Looking up] I saw a horse's head quite close. A man passing with a sleigh had seen me and was trying to lift me out, yet fearing his assistance had come too late. He helped me into the sleigh, and drove to a house about two miles distant. By the time the teams came up, I had quite recovered. My babe was in deep sleep and had not suffered.

We stayed at Draperville that night. Next day, Mr. Winter went ahead of the teams, to inform my husband of my coming, and then sent a sleigh to meet me.

I found my husband very sick, but the worst was over; and in six weeks from that time he was sufficiently convalescent to return.

On reaching home, we found the children all right. They had been well cared for in our absence.

Spring had set in; my husband, as soon as [he was] able, taught the ward school; and we spent the summer very comfortably and began to enjoy country life.

Hannah Cornaby, *Autobiography and Poems* (Salt Lake City: J. C. Graham Co., 1881), pp. 43–49.

SAVED FROM A TRAIN WRECK

CHARLES W. NIBLEY

While [Joseph F. Smith] was a hard-headed, successful business man, yet very few in this dispensation have been more gifted with spiritual insight than he. As we were returning from an eastern trip, some years ago, on the train just east of Green River, I saw him go out to the end of the car on the platform, and immediately return and hesitate a moment, and then sit down in the seat just ahead of me. He had just taken his seat when something went wrong with the train. A broken rail had been the means of ditching the engine and had thrown most of the cars off the track. In the sleeper we were shaken up pretty badly, but our car remained on the track.

The President immediately said to me that he had gone on the platform when he heard a voice saying, "Go in and sit down."

He came in, and I noticed him stand a moment, and he seemed to hesitate, but he sat down.

He said further that as he came in and stood in the aisle he thought, "Oh, pshaw, perhaps it is only my imagination;" when he heard the voice again, "Sit down," and he immediately took his seat, and the result was as I have stated.

He, no doubt, would have been very seriously injured had he remained on the platform of that car, as the cars were all jammed up together pretty badly. He said, "I have heard that voice a good many times in my life, and I have always profited by obeying it."

Joseph F. Smith, *Gospel Doctrine,* 5th ed. (Salt Lake City: Deseret Book Co., 1939), pp. 523–24.

"BRETHREN, I FEEL IMPRESSED . . ."

VIRGINIA BUDD JACOBSEN

It happened in 1921, while President McKay and Elder Hugh Cannon were making a tour of the missions of the world. After a day of inspiring conference meetings in Hilo, Hawaii, a night trip to the Kilauea volcano was arranged for the visiting brethren and some of the missionaries. About nine o'clock that evening, two carloads, about ten of us, took off for the then very active volcano.

We stood on the rim of that fiery pit watching Pele in her satanic antics, our backs chilled by the cold winds sweeping down from snowcapped Mauna Loa and our faces almost blistered by the heat of the molten lava. Tiring of the cold, one of the elders discovered a volcanic balcony about four feet down inside the crater where observers could watch the display without being chilled by the wind. It seemed perfectly sound, and the "railing" on the open side of it formed a fine protection from intense heat, making it an excellent place to view the spectacular display.

After first testing its safety, Brother McKay and three of the elders climbed down into the hanging balcony. As they stood there warm and comfortable, they teased the others of us more timid ones who had hesitated to take advantage of the protection they had found. For quite some time we all watched the ever-changing sight as we alternately chilled and roasted.

After being down there in their protected spot for some time, suddenly Brother McKay said to those with him, "Brethren, I feel impressed that we should get out of here."

With that he assisted the elders to climb out, and then they in turn helped him up to the wind-swept rim. It seems incredible, but almost immediately the whole balcony crumbled and fell with a roar into the molten lava a hundred feet or so below.

It is easy to visualize the feelings of those who witnessed this terrifying experience. Not a word was said—the whole thing was too awful, with all that word means. The only sound was the hiss and roar of Pele, the fire goddess of old Hawaii, screaming her disappointment.

None of us, who were witnesses of this experience could ever doubt the reality of "revelation in our day"! Some might say it was merely inspiration, but to us it was a direct revelation given to a worthy man.

David O. McKay, *Cherished Experiences from the Writings of President David O. McKay,* compiled by Clare Middlemiss (Salt Lake City: Deseret Book Co., 1955), pp. 55–56.

"Someone Laid His Hand upon My Head"

Harold B. Lee

May I impose upon you for a moment to express appreciation for something that happened to me some time ago. I was suffering from an ulcer condition that was becoming worse and worse. We had been touring a mission; my wife, Joan, and I were impressed the next morning that we should get home as quickly as possible, although we had planned to stay for some other meetings.

On the way across the country, we were sitting in the forward section of the airplane. Some of our Church members were in the next section of the airplane. As we approached a certain point en route, someone laid his hand upon my head. I looked up; I could see no one. That happened again before we arrived home, again with the same experience. Who it was, by what means or what medium, I may never know, except I knew that I was receiving a blessing that I came a few hours later to know I needed most desperately.

As soon as we arrived home, my wife very anxiously called the doctor. It was now about 11 o'clock at night. He called me to come to the telephone, and he asked how I was; and I said, "Well, I am very tired. I think I will be all right." But shortly thereafter, there came massive hemorrhages which, had they occurred while we were in flight, I wouldn't be here today talking about it.

I know that there are powers divine that reach out when all

other help is not available. . . . Yes, I know that there are such powers.

Harold B. Lee, *Stand Ye in Holy Places* (Salt Lake City: Deseret Book Co., 1974), pp. 187–88.

HEALING

"I Think I Am Also
Entitled to a Blessing"

HOWARD CORAY

In June, 1841, I met with an accident. The Prophet [Joseph Smith] and I, after looking at his horses and admiring them across the road from his house, started thither. The Prophet at the same time put his arm over my shoulder. When we had reached about the middle of the road, he stopped and remarked, "Brother Coray, I wish you were a little larger, I would like to have some fun with you."

I replied, "Perhaps you can as it is"—not realizing what I was saying. The fact that Joseph was a man of over 200 lb., while I was scarcely 130 lb., made it not a little ridiculous for me to think of engaging with him in anything like a scuffle.

However, as soon as I made this reply, he began to trip me. He took some kind of a lock on my right leg, from which I was unable to extricate it, and throwing me around, broke it some three inches above the ankle joint.

He immediately carried me into the house, pulled off my boot, and found at once that my leg was decidedly broken; then got some splinters and bandaged it. A number of times that day he came in to see me, endeavoring to console me as much as possible.

The next day when he happened in to see me after a little conversation, I said: "Brother Joseph, when Jacob wrestled with the angel and was lamed by him, the angel blessed him. Now I think I am also entitled to a blessing."

To that he replied, "I am not the Patriarch, but my father is, and when you get up and around, I'll have him bless you." . . .

In nine days after my leg was broken, I was able to get up and hobble about the house by the aid of a crutch, and in two weeks thereafter I was about recovered—so much so that I went to meeting on foot, a distance of a mile. I considered this no less than a case of miraculous healing.

Hyrum L. Andrus and Helen Mae Andrus, comps., *They Knew the Prophet* (Salt Lake City: Bookcraft, 1974), pp. 135–37.

"HEAL HER
AND WE'LL ALL BELIEVE"

PARLEY P. PRATT

I . . . journeyed in connection with a young Elder, named H. Brown, as far as Henderson County, in northern New York, where lived Elder Brown's father, and where there was quite a branch of the Church. I visited with them for a few days, resting from my toils and ministering among them. Taking leave of these friends, . . . I crossed over the bay to a country neighborhood, called Pillar Point. In this neighborhood there had been some preaching by our Elders; but no branch of the Church organized, though there had been one or two instances of healing, and some few were believing. Here I appointed a meeting for evening in a school house; it was crowded full of people; indeed, all could not get in.

As the meeting closed a man named William Cory stepped forward, and earnestly begged of me to go home with him and minister to his wife, as she was lying at the point of death in consequence of a lingering sickness, not having risen up in her bed for six days without swooning or going into fits. He further said that he was worn out by being up with her every night, and that his neighbors were weary with watching, and it was doubted whether she could survive through the night without relief.

The Spirit would not suffer me to go with him that night, but I promised to call in the morning. At this many voices were heard, saying: "Yes, yes, there's a case in hand; let him heal her and we'll all believe." Others exclaimed: "I wonder if she'll be at his meeting tomorrow! We shall see, and if so, we'll all believe." Expressions like these, joined with my own weakness, only tended to dampen my courage and confidence in the case.

I went home with a friend who invited me to partake of his hospitality for the night. As we entered his house, we found one of his children very sick with a violent pain in the head, to which it had been subject from its birth, and which came at regular periods, and was never relieved till it gathered and broke at his ear— so said his parents. The little fellow was rolling from side to side in his bed, and screeching and screaming with pain. I stepped to the bedside, and laid my hands upon his head in the name of Jesus Christ; he was instantly made whole and went to sleep. Next morning he got up well, and continued so; he said that the pain all left him as soon as my hands touched his head.

In the morning, before I arose, I had a vision, as follows: I saw a log house, and entered it through a door at the northwest corner; in the northeast corner lay a woman sick in bed; in the southeast corner was a small door opening into an adjoining room, and near it a stairway, where stood a ladder; the fireplace being in the south end. As I entered the house and laid my hands on the woman, she rose up and was made whole; the house being crowded, she took her seat near the fire and under the ladder, or near by it, and she praised God with a shout of glory, clapping her hands for joy and exclaimed: "Thank God, I'm every whit whole." I awoke from my vision and related the same to the family where I stayed.

The man harnessed his horses, and with seven or eight persons in the wagon, including myself, we started for meeting, intending to call and see Mrs. Cory on our way, as I had appointed the previous evening. On alighting at her house I saw it was the same that I had seen in the vision; there were the doors, the stairway, ladder, fireplace, bed, and sick woman, just as I had seen and described.

I laid my hands upon the woman, and said: "In the name of Jesus Christ, be thou made whole this instant." I then commanded her to arise and walk. Her husband burst into tears; the people looked surprised; but the woman arose and walked to the fire, and happened to take her seat near the ladder, as I had related in the vision before I saw her. She then clapped her hands for joy, gave a shout of "Glory to God in the highest," and testified that she was every whit whole. We invited her to accompany us to the meeting; she immediately made ready, walked out, helped herself into the wagon, and rode some two miles over a very rough road. She then got out of the wagon, and walked with a strong and quick step into the meeting, where she sat till the discourse was over; when she arose and testified what the Lord had done for her. She then rode home, and was baptized in connection with several others, who came forward and obeyed the fullness of the gospel. We afterwards laid our hands on them for the gift of the Holy Ghost, when it fell upon them in great power, insomuch that all in the room felt its power and influence and glorified God; some spake in tongues, others prophesied and bore testimony to the truth.

The next evening I went over to Sackett's Harbor in order to preach; many of the people from Pillar Point, who had witnessed these things, went with me, and, among others, Mr. Cory with his wife, who had been so miraculously healed. A great rabble came out to hear, or rather to disturb the meeting; and among others, some half dozen clergymen of different orders, who were loud in their challenges and calls for miracles; "give us a miracle—we want a miracle—heal the sick—raise the dead, and then we'll believe." The lying, rage, and confusion excited by these wicked spirits, broke up the meeting, and I had much ado to get out of the crowd without being stoned or torn to pieces.

Parley P. Pratt, *Autobiography of Parley P. Pratt,* edited by Parley P. Pratt Jr., Classics in Mormon Literature ed. (Salt Lake City: Deseret Book Co., 1985), pp. 90–92.

"ARISE AND WALK!"

PARLEY P. PRATT

On the next day we had to cross a plain fifteen miles in length, without a house, a tree, or any kind of shelter; a cold northwest wind was blowing, and the ground covered with snow and ice. We had made two or three miles into the plain when I was attacked with a severe return of my old complaint, which had confined me so many months in Jackson County, and from which I had recovered by a miracle at the outset of this journey—I mean the fever and ague.

I travelled and shook, and shook and travelled, till I could stand it no longer; I vomited severely several times, and finally fell down on the snow, overwhelmed with fever, and became helpless and nearly insensible. This was about seven or eight miles from the nearest house.

Brother John Murdock laid his hands on me and prayed in the name of Jesus; and, taking me by the hand, he commanded me with a loud voice, saying: "In the name of Jesus of Nazareth arise and walk!" I attempted to arise, I staggered a few paces, and was about falling again when I found my fever suddenly depart and my strength come. I walked at the rate of about four miles per hour, arrived at a house, and was sick no more.

Parley P. Pratt, *Autobiography of Parley P. Pratt,* edited by Parley P. Pratt Jr., Classics in Mormon Literature ed. (Salt Lake City: Deseret Book Co., 1985), pp. 60–61.

JOSEPH SMITH HEALS THE SICK

WILFORD WOODRUFF

While I was living in this cabin in the old barracks, we experienced a day of God's power with the Prophet Joseph. It was a very sickly time and Joseph had given up his home in Commerce to the sick, and had a tent pitched in his door-yard and was living in that himself. The large number of Saints who had been driven out of Missouri, were flocking into Commerce; but had no homes to go into, and were living in wagons, in tents, and on the ground. Many, therefore, were sick through the exposure they were subjected to. Brother Joseph had waited on the sick, until he was worn out and nearly sick himself.

On the morning of the 22nd of July, 1839, he arose, reflecting upon the situation of the Saints of God in their persecutions and afflictions, and he called upon the Lord in prayer, and the power of God rested upon him mightily, and as Jesus healed all the sick around Him in His day, so Joseph, the Prophet of God, healed all around on this occasion. He healed all in his house and door-yard, then in company with Sidney Rigdon and several of the Twelve, he went among the sick lying on the bank of the river and he commanded them in a loud voice, in the name of Jesus Christ, to come up and be made whole, and they were all healed. When he healed all that were sick on the east side of the river, they crossed the Mississippi river in a ferry-boat to the west side, to Montrose, where we were. The first house they went into was President Brigham Young's. He was sick on his bed at the time. The Prophet went onto his house and healed him, and they all came out together. As they were passing by my door, Brother Joseph said: "Brother Woodruff, follow me." These were the only words spoken by any of the company from the time they left Brother Brigham's house till we crossed the public square, and entered Brother Fordham's house. Brother Fordham had been dying for an hour, and we expected each minute would be his last.

I felt the power of God that was overwhelming His Prophet.

When we entered the House, Brother Joseph walked up to Brother Fordham, and took him by the right hand; in his left hand he held his hat.

He saw that Brother Fordham's eyes were glazed, and that he was speechless and unconscious.

After taking hold of his hand, he looked down into the dying man's face and said: "Brother Fordham, do you not know me?" At

335

first he made no reply; but we could all see the effect of the Spirit of God resting upon him.

He again said: "Elijah, do you not know me?"

With a low whisper, Brother Fordham answered, "Yes!"

The Prophet then said, "Have you not faith to be healed?"

The answer, which was a little plainer than before, was: "I am afraid it is too late. If you had come sooner, I think I might have been."

He had the appearance of a man waking from sleep. It was the sleep of death.

Joseph then said: "Do you believe that Jesus is the Christ?"

"I do, Brother Joseph," was the response.

Then the Prophet of God spoke with a loud voice, as in the majesty of the Godhead: "Elijah, I command you, in the name of Jesus of Nazareth, to arise and be made whole!"

The words of the Prophet were not like the words of man, but like the voice of God. It seemed to me that the house shook from its foundation.

Elijah Fordham leaped from his bed like a man raised from the dead. A healthy color came to his face, and life was manifested in every act.

His feet were done up in Indian meal poultices. He kicked them off his feet, scattered the contents, and then called for his clothes and put them on. He asked for a bowl of bread and milk, and ate it; then put on his hat and followed us into the street, to visit others who were sick.

The unbeliever may ask: "Was there not deception in this?"

If there is any deception in the mind of the unbeliever, there was certainly none with Elijah Fordham, the dying man, nor with those who were present with him, for in a few minutes more he would have been in the spirit world, had he not been rescued. Through the blessing of God, he lived up till 1880, in which year he died in Utah, while all who were with him on that occasion, with the exception of one, are in the spirit world.

Among the number, were Joseph and Hyrum Smith, Sidney Rigdon, Brigham Young, Heber C. Kimball, George A. Smith, Parley P. Pratt and Orson Pratt. Wilford Woodruff is the only one living who was present at the time, and he will soon mingle with those who have gone.

Wilford Woodruff, *Leaves from My Journal* (Salt Lake City: Juvenile Instructor's Office, 1882), pp. 62–66.

"IT REQUIRED A GOOD DEAL OF FAITH"

WILFORD WOODRUFF

Mary Pitt . . . was something like the lame man who lay at the gate of the Temple called "Beautiful" at Jerusalem—she had not been able to walk a step for fourteen years, and confined to her bed nearly half that time. She had no strength in her feet and ankles and could only move about a little with a crutch or holding on to a chair. She wished to be baptized. Brother Pitt [Mary's brother] and myself took her in our arms, and carried her into the water and I baptized her. When she came out of the water I confirmed her. She said she wanted to be healed and she believed she had faith enough to be healed. I had

had experience enough in this Church to know that it required a good deal of faith to heal a person who had not walked a step for fourteen years. I told her that according to her faith it should be unto her. It so happened that on the day after she was baptized, Brother Richards and President Brigham Young came down to see me. We met at Brother Kington's. Sister Mary Pitt was there also. I told President Young what Sister Pitt wished, and that she believed she had faith enough to be healed. We prayed for her and laid hands upon her. Brother Young was mouth, and commanded her to be made whole. She laid down her crutch and never used it after, and the next day she walked three miles.

Journal of Discourses, 26 vols. (London: Latter-day Saints' Book Depot, 1854–86), 15:344.

JOSEPH'S SILK HANDKERCHIEF

WILFORD WOODRUFF

A man of the world, knowing of the miracles which had been performed, came to [Joseph Smith] and asked him if he would not go and heal two twin children of his, about five months old, who were both lying sick nigh unto death.

They were some two miles from Montrose, [Iowa].

The Prophet said he could not go; but, after pausing some time, he said he would send someone to heal them; and he turned to me and said: "You go with the man and heal his children." He took a red silk handkerchief out of his pocket and gave it to me, and told me to wipe their faces with the handkerchief when I administered to them, and they should be healed. He also said unto me: "As long as you will keep that handkerchief, it shall remain a league between you and me."

I went with the man, and did as the Prophet commanded me, and the children were healed.

I have possession of the handkerchief unto this day.

Wilford Woodruff, *Leaves from My Journal* (Salt Lake City: Juvenile Instructor's Office, 1882), pp. 62–65.

PROVOKING A SNAKE

JOSEPH SMITH

This morning was excessively hot, no air stirring, and traveling in the thick woods, a thunder shower coming on, the brethren caught all the water they could on the brims of their hats, and not catching enough to satisfy their thirst, they drank out of the horse tracks.

Martin Harris having boasted to the brethren that he could handle snakes with perfect safety, while fooling with a black snake with his bare feet, he received a bite on his left foot. The fact was communicated to me, and I took occasion to reprove him, and exhort the brethren never to trifle with the promises of God. I told them it was presumption for any one to provoke a serpent to bite him, but if a man of God was accidentally bitten by a poisonous serpent, he might have faith, or his brethren might have faith for him, so that the Lord would hear his prayer and he might be healed; but when a man designedly provokes a serpent to bite him, the principle is the same as when a man drinks deadly poison knowing it to be such. In that case no man has any claim on the promises of God to be healed.

Joseph Smith, *History of The Church of Jesus Christ of Latter-day Saints,* 7 vols., 2d ed. rev., edited by B. H. Roberts (Salt Lake City: The Church of Jesus Christ of Latter-day Saints, 1932–51), 2:95–96.

"HER SPIRIT LEFT HER BODY"

WILFORD WOODRUFF

December 3rd found my wife very low. I spent the day in taking care of her, and the following day I returned to Eaton to get some things for her. She seemed to be gradually sinking and in the evening her spirit apparently left her body, and she was dead.

The sisters gathered around her body, weeping, while I stood looking at her in sorrow. The spirit and power of God began to rest upon me until, for the first time during her sickness, faith filled my soul, although she lay before me as one dead.

I had some oil that was consecrated for my anointing while in Kirtland. I took it and consecrated it again before the Lord for anointing the sick. I then bowed down before the Lord and prayed for the life of my companion, and I anointed her body with the oil in the name of the Lord. I laid my hands upon her, and in the name of Jesus Christ I rebuked the power of death and the destroyer, and commanded the same to depart from her, and the spirit of life to enter her body.

Her spirit returned to her body, and from that hour she was made whole; and we all felt to praise the name of God, and to trust in Him and to keep His commandments.

While this operation was going on with me (as my wife related afterwards) her spirit left her body, and she saw it lying upon the bed, and the sisters weeping. She looked at them and at me, and upon her babe, and, while gazing upon this scene, two personages came into the room carrying a coffin and told her they had come for her body. One of these messengers informed her that she could have her choice: she might go to rest in the spirit world, or, on one condition she could have the privilege of returning to her tabernacle and continuing her labors upon the earth. The condition was, if she felt that she could stand by her husband, and with him pass through all the cares, trials, tribulation and afflictions of life which he would be called to pass through for the gospel's sake unto the end. When she looked at the situation of her husband and child she said: "Yes, I will do it!"

At the moment that decision was made the power of faith rested upon me, and when I administered unto her, her spirit entered her tabernacle, and she saw the messengers carry the coffin out at the door.

Wilford Woodruff, *Leaves from My Journal* (Salt Lake City: Juvenile Instructor's Office, 1882), pp. 54–55.

"HE CALLED ME BACK"

LEROI C. SNOW

For several long weeks Ella Jensen had lingered, almost between life and death, with scarlet fever. . . . [One evening] towards ten o'clock, Uncle Jake, her father, who was holding his daughter's hand, felt the pulse become very weak. A few moments later he turned to his wife saying: "Althea, she is dead; her pulse has stopped." The heartbroken parents wept and grieved at the loss of their beautiful daughter. . . .

[The story continues in her father, Uncle Jake's, words:]

"We talked the matter over and wondered what we should do. I told my wife that I would go to town, more than a mile from home, and see President Snow, tell him about her death and have him arrange for the funeral.

"I went out to the barn, hitched up, and drove to the tabernacle where . . . President Lorenzo Snow, whom we all loved so much, was in meeting. I went into the vestry, behind the main hall, wrote a note and had it sent to [President Snow], who was speaking to the congregation. When the note was placed upon the pulpit, President Snow stopped his talking, read the note, and then explained to the Saints that it was a call to visit some people who were in deep sorrow and asked to be excused.

"President Snow came into the vestry, and after I told him what had happened he meditated a moment or two and then said: 'I will go down with you.' Just as we were about to leave, President Snow stopped me, saying: 'Wait a moment, I wish you would go into the meeting and get Brother Clawson. I want him to go also.' President Clawson was then the president of the Box Elder Stake. . . ."

President Rudger Clawson . . . being invited by President Snow to go along, [continues the story saying]:

"As we entered the home we met Sister Jensen, who was very much agitated and alarmed. We came to Ella's bedside and were impressed by the thought that her spirit had passed out of the body and gone beyond.

"Turning to me President Snow said: 'Brother Clawson, will you anoint her,' which I did. We then laid our hands upon her head and the anointing was confirmed by President Snow, who blessed her and among other things, used this very extraordinary expression, in a commanding tone of voice, 'Come back, Ella, come back. Your work upon the earth is not yet completed, come back.' . . ."

Uncle Jake, Ella's father, continues his account:

"After President Snow had finished the blessing, he turned to my wife and me and said, 'Now do not mourn or grieve any more. It will be all right. . . .'"

As already stated, it was ten o'clock in the morning when Ella died. It was towards noon when Jacob Jensen [Uncle Jake] reported to President Snow at the tabernacle service, and not long after twelve o'clock, noon, when President Snow and President Clawson left the home after the administration.

Uncle Jake says that he and his wife remained at the bedside. The news of the death spread about the city. Friends continued to call at the home, express their sympathy to the sorrowing parents, and leave. Continuing in Uncle Jake's words:

"Ella remained in this condition for more than an hour after President Snow administered to her, or more than three hours in all after she died. We were sitting there watching by the bedside, her mother and myself, when all at once she opened her eyes. She looked about the room, saw us sitting there, but still looked for someone else. And the first thing she said was: 'Where is he? Where is he?'

"We asked, 'Who? Where is who?'
"'Why, Brother Snow,' she replied. 'He called me back.'"

Improvement Era, September 1929, pp. 881, 883–86.

LORENZO SNOW
SAVED FROM DROWNING

W . W . C L U F F

We arrived at Honolulu, the capital of the islands, about the 27th of March, 1864. On the 29th we sailed for Lahaina, on the schooner *Nettie Merrill,* Captain Fisher, for the island of Maui, a distance of about ninety miles from Honolulu. On the morning of the 31st of March, we came to anchor about one mile from the mouth of the little harbor of Lahaina.

Apostles Ezra T. Benson, Lorenzo Snow, Brother Alma L. Smith, and myself got into the small boat to go on shore. Brother Joseph F. Smith, as he afterwards stated, had some misgivings about going in that boat, but the manifestation was not sufficiently strong to indicate any general accident. He preferred to remain on board the vessel until the boat returned. The boat started for the shore. It contained some barrels and boxes, the captain, a white man, two or three native passengers, and the boat's crew, who were also natives.

The entrance to the harbor is a very narrow passage between coral reefs, and when the sea is rough, it is very dangerous, on account of the breakers. Where the vessel lay, the sea was not rough, but only presented the appearance of heavy swells rolling to the shore.

As we approached the reef it was evident to me that the surf was running higher than we anticipated. I called the captain's attention to the fact. We were running quartering across the waves, and I suggested that we change our course so as to run at right angles with them. He replied that he did not think there was any danger, and our course was not changed. We went but little farther, when a heavy swell struck the boat and carried us before it about fifty yards. When the swell passed it left us in a trough between two huge waves. It was too late to retrieve our error, and we must run our chances. When the second swell struck the boat, it raised the stern so high that the steersman's oar was out of the water, and he lost control of the boat. It rode on the swell a short distance and swung around just as the wave began to break up. We were almost instantly capsized into the dashing, foaming sea.

I felt no concern for myself about drowning, for while on my former mission I had learned to swim and sport in the surf of those shores.

The last I remember of Brother Snow, as the boat was going over, I saw him seize the upper edge of it with both hands. Fearing that the upper edge of the boat, or the barrels, might hit and injure me as the boat was going over, I plunged head foremost into the water. After swimming a short distance, I came to the surface without being strangled or injured.

The boat was bottom upwards, and barrels, hats and umbrellas were floating in every direction. I swam to the boat and as there was nothing to cling to on the bottom, I reached under and seized the edge of it.

About the same time Brother Benson came up near me and

readily got hold of the boat. Brother Alma L. Smith came up on the opposite side of the boat from Brother Benson and myself. He was considerably strangled, but succeeded in securing a hold on the boat.

A short time afterwards the captain was discovered, about fifty yards from ups. Two sailors, one on each side, succeeded in keeping him on the surface, although life was apparently extinct.

Nothing yet had been seen of Brother Snow, although the natives had been swimming and diving in every direction in search of him. We were only about one-fourth of a mile from shore. The people, as soon as they discovered our circumstances, manned a life boat and hurried to the rescue. We were taken into the boat, when the crew wanted to row for the shore, and pick up the captain by the way. We told them that one of our friends was yet missing, and we did not want to leave. We discovered that a second boat had left the shore and could reach the captain as soon as the one we were in. Seeing this, the crew of our boat consented to remain and assist us.

The captain was taken ashore, and by working over him sometime was brought to life. Probably his life would not have been much endangered but for a sack of four or five hundred silver dollars which he held in his hand, the weight of which took him at once to the bottom. The natives dove and brought him up, still clinging to the sack. When his vitality was restored, the first thing he inquired about was the money; intimating to the natives, with peculiar emphasis, that it would not have been healthy for them to have lost it.

Brother Snow had not yet been discovered, and the anxiety was intense. The natives were, evidently, doing all in their power.

Finally, one of them, in edging himself around the capsized boat, must have felt Brother Snow with his feet and pulled him, at least, partly from under it, as the first I saw of Brother Snow was his hair floating upon the water around one end of the capsized boat. As soon as we got him into our boat, we told the boatmen to pull for the shore with all possible speed. His body was stiff, and life apparently extinct.

Brother A. L. Smith and I were sitting side by side. We laid Brother Snow across our laps, and, on the way to shore, we quietly administered to him and asked the Lord to spare his life, that he might return to his family and home.

On reaching the shore, we carried him a little way to some large empty barrels that were lying on the sandy beach. We laid him face downwards on one of them, and rolled him back and forth until we succeeded in getting the water he had swallowed out of him.

During this time a number of persons came down from the town; among them was Mr. E. P. Adams, a merchant. All were willing to do what they could. We washed Brother Snow's face with camphor, furnished by Mr. Adams. We did not only what was customary in such cases, but also what the Spirit seemed to whisper to us.

After working over him for some time, without any indications of returning life, the bystanders said that nothing more could be done for him. But we did not feel like giving him up, and still prayed and worked over him, with an assurance that the Lord would hear and answer our prayers.

Finally we were impressed to place our mouth over his and make an effort to inflate his lungs, alternately blowing in and drawing out the air, imitating, as far as possible, the natural process of breathing. This we persevered in until we succeeded in inflating his lungs. After a little, we perceived very faint indications of returning life. A slight wink of the eye, which, until then, had been open and death-like, and a very faint rattle in the throat, were the first symptoms of returning vitality. These grew more and more distinct, until consciousness was fully restored.

When this result was reached, it must have been fully one hour after the upsetting of the boat. A Portuguese man, living in

Lahaina, who, from the first, rendered us much assistance, invited us to take Brother Snow to his house. There being no Saints in the place, we gladly accepted his kind offer. Every possible attention was given for Brother Snow's comfort.

We will here append my brother's account of the upsetting of the boat, and what he can recollect of the sensations of a man drowning and afterwards coming to life:

"As we were moving along, probably more than a quarter of a mile from where we expected to land, my attention was suddenly arrested by Captain Fisher calling to the oarsmen in a voice which denoted some alarm, 'Hurry up, hurry up!' I immediately discovered the cause of alarm. A short distance behind us, I saw an immense surf, thirty or forty feet high, rushing towards us swifter than a race horse. We had scarcely a moment for reflection before the huge mass was upon us. In an instant our boat, with its contents, as though it were a feather, was hurled into a gulf of briny waters, and all was under this rolling, seething mountain wave. It took me by surprise. I think, however, that I comprehended the situation—in the midst of turbulent waves—a quarter of a mile from the shore, without much probability of human aid.

"I felt confident, however, there would be some way of escape; that the Lord would provide the means, for it was not possible that my life and mission were thus to terminate. This reliance on the Lord banished fear, and inspired me up to the last moment of consciousness. In such extreme cases of excitement, we seem to live hours in a minute, and a volume of thoughts crowd themselves into one single moment. It was so with me in that perilous scene.

"Having been somewhat subject to faint, I think that after a few moments in the water I must have fainted, as I did not suffer the pain common in the experience of drowning persons. I had been in the water only a few moments, until I lost consciousness. The first I knew afterwards, I was on shore, receiving the kind and tender attentions of my brethren. The first recollection I have of returning consciousness, was that of a very small light—the small-est imaginable. This soon disappeared, and I was again in total darkness. Again it appeared much larger than before, then sank away and left me, as before, in forgetfulness. Thus it continued to come and go, until, finally, I recognized, as I thought, persons whispering, and soon after, I asked in a feeble whisper, 'What is the matter?' I immediately recognized the voice of Elder Cluff, as he replied, 'You have been drowned; the boat upset in the surf.' Quick as lightning the scene of our disaster flashed upon my mind. I immediately asked, 'Are you brethren all safe?' The emo-tion that was awakened in my bosom by the answer of Elder Cluff will remain with me as long as life continues: 'Brother Snow, we are all safe.' I rapidly recovered, and very soon was able to walk and accompany the brethren to our lodgings."

Eliza R. Snow, *Biography and Family Record of Lorenzo Snow* (Salt Lake City: Deseret News Co., 1884), pp. 276–81.

"HE COMMANDED HIM TO ARISE"

WILLIAM LOUIS HOWELL

One day Ann saw a multitude of people surrounding the house of a collier, who had just been carried home on a stretcher, apparently dying. A great lump of coal had fallen on his back and broken his spine. . . . He had lately joined the Church but his wife had not. Great sympathy was felt for the man, and several doctors were sent for by various people. They held a consultation and came to the conclusion that the man would only be able to live a couple of hours at the most. But the injured man whispered to his wife to send for the "Mormon" elders. Brother Howell, who was President of the branch, came with his counselors and they administered to the sick man and Brother Howell commanded him in the name of Jesus Christ to arise from his bed. And those who stood around the bed heard the bones of the sick man's body crack as they slid back into their places and the man arose from his bed and gave thanks to God for his mercy.

Donald Q. Cannon and David J. Whittaker, eds., *Supporting Saints: Life Stories of Nineteenth-Century Mormons* (Provo: Brigham Young University Religious Studies Center, 1985), pp. 56–57.

"HE BLESSED ME THAT I MIGHT BE HEALED"

GEORGE ALBERT SMITH

When I was a child I became very ill. The doctor said I had typhoid fever and should be in bed for at least three weeks. He told mother to give me no solid food, but to have me drink some coffee.

When he went away, I told mother that I didn't want any coffee. I had been taught that the Word of Wisdom, given by the Lord to Joseph Smith, advised us not to use coffee.

350

Mother had brought three children into the world and two had died. She was unusually anxious about me.

I asked her to send for Brother Hawks, one of our ward teachers. He was a worker at the foundry and a poor and humble man of great faith in the power of the Lord.

He came, administered to me, and blessed me that I might be healed.

When the doctor came the next morning I was playing outside with the other children. He was surprised. He examined me and discovered that my fever was gone, and that I seemed to be well.

I was grateful to the Lord for my recovery. I was sure that he had healed me.

Jeremiah Stokes, *Modern Miracles* (Salt Lake City: Bookcraft, 1945), p. 135.

John Roothoff Receives His Sight

JOSEPH FIELDING SMITH

It was on the seventh day of August, 1906, that President [Joseph F.] Smith and party arrived in Rotterdam, having come from the boat at Antwerp two days before. There was living in that city a boy of eleven years of age, John Roothoff by name, who had suffered greatly for a number of years with his eyes. His mother was a faithful member of the Church, as also was the boy, who was slowly losing his sight and was unable to attend school. The boy said to his mother: "The Prophet has the most power of any missionary on earth. If you will take me with you to the meeting and he will look into my eyes, I believe they will be healed."

According to his desire he was permitted to accompany his mother to the meeting. At the close of the meeting, as was the custom, President Smith moved towards the door and began to shake hands and speak encouragingly to the people as they passed from the hall. As John Roothoff approached him, led by his mother and his eyes bandaged, President Smith took him by the hand and spoke to him kindly. He then raised the bandage slightly and looked sympathetically into the inflamed eyes, at the same time saying something in English which the boy did not understand. However he was satisfied. President Smith had acted according to the boy's faith; and according to his faith it came to pass. When he arrived home, he cried out with great joy: "Mama, my eyes are well; I cannot feel any more pain. I can see fine now, and far too."

Joseph Fielding Smith, *Life of Joseph F. Smith* (Salt Lake City: Deseret Book Co., 1938), p. 397.

"Save by Prayer and Fasting"

Matthew Cowley

Sometimes we rush in, administer to a person, rush out, and say, "Well, he won't make it. I know he won't." Of course, we have to, in case of an emergency, go immediately. Sometimes I wonder, if we have a little time, if we shouldn't do a little fasting. "This kind cometh not out save by prayer and by fasting."

A little over a year ago a couple came into my office carrying a little boy. The father said to me, "My wife and I have been fasting for two days, and we've brought our little boy up for a blessing. You are the one we've been sent to."

I said, "What's the matter with him?"

They said he was born blind, deaf, and dumb, had no co-ordination of his muscles, couldn't even crawl at the age of five years. I said to myself, this is it. I had implicit faith in the fasting and the prayers of those parents. I blessed that child, and a few weeks later I received a letter: "Brother Cowley, we wish you could see our little boy now. He's crawling. When we throw a ball across the floor, he races after it on his hands and knees. He can see. When we clap our hands over his head, he jumps. He can hear." Medical science had laid the burden down. God had taken over.

Matthew Cowley, *Matthew Cowley Speaks* (Salt Lake City: Deseret Book Co., 1954), pp. 245–46.

"GIVE HIM HIS VISION"

MATTHEW COWLEY

I've told the story about the little baby nine months old who was born blind. The father came up with him one Sunday and said, "Brother Cowley, our baby hasn't been blessed yet; we'd like you to bless him."

I said, "Why have you waited so long?"

"Oh, we just didn't get around to it."

Now, that's the native way; I like that. Just don't get around to doing things! Why not live and enjoy it?

I said, "All right, what's the name?" So he told me the name, and I was just going to start when he said, "By the way, give him his vision when you give him a name. He was born blind."

Well, it shocked me, but then I said to myself, why not? Christ told his disciples when he left them they could work miracles. And I had faith in that father's faith. After I gave that child its name, I finally got around to giving it its vision.

That boy's about twelve years old now. The last time I was back there I was afraid to inquire about him. I was sure he had gone blind again. That's the way my faith works sometimes. So I asked the branch president about him. And he said, "Brother Cowley, the worst thing you ever did was to bless that child to receive his vision. He's the meanest kid in the neighborhood, always getting into mischief." Boy, I was thrilled about that kid getting into mischief!

Matthew Cowley, *Matthew Cowley Speaks* (Salt Lake City: Deseret Book Co., 1954), pp. 247–48.

"HE ANOINTED THE DEAD MAN"

MATTHEW COWLEY

I was called to a home in a little village in New Zealand one day. There the Relief Society sisters were preparing the body of one of our Saints. They had placed his body in front of the Big House, as they call it, the house where the people came to wail and weep and mourn over the dead, when in rushed the dead man's brother.

He said, "Administer to him."

And the young natives said, "Why, you shouldn't do that; he's dead."

"You do it!"

. . . The younger native got down on his knees, and he anointed the dead man. Then this great old sage got down and blessed him and commanded him to rise. You should have seen the Relief Society sisters scatter. And he sat up, and he said, "Send for the elders; I don't feel very well." . . . Well, we told him he had just been administered to, and he said: "Oh, that was it." He said, "I was dead. I could feel life coming back into me just like a blanket unrolling." Now, he outlived the brother that came in and told us to administer to him.

Matthew Cowley, *Matthew Cowley Speaks* (Salt Lake City: Deseret Book Co., 1954), p. 247.

"MAYBE THE LORD
CAN SAVE HER, BUT I CANNOT"

LEGRAND RICHARDS

Following the visit of Elder Melvin J. Ballard at Jacksonville, Florida, on December 8, 1935, one of the elders, with only thirty-five cents in his pocket, started out to return to his field of labor in South Georgia. He attempted to hitchhike on the highway without the usual success, apparently for a wise purpose. About nine o'clock in the evening he found himself still quite a distance from his field of labor, so he decided he would "tract-in" (seek entertainment) for the night.

After being unsuccessful at two homes, he called at the third and was met at the door by a minister of the Gospel. He introduced himself as a Mormon missionary, whereupon he was invited in. The minister explained that he was in deep distress—that his little daughter was very sick and the doctor gave them no hope for her recovery. By this time, they had entered the living room where the family was sitting, and the doctor was at the side of the bed upon which the little girl was lying.

The minister remarked, "You believe in anointing the sick with oil, do you not?" To this the elder replied in the affirmative. He then added, "I wish you would anoint my little girl—I have prayed for her without avail," and he offered the missionary a bottle of olive oil. The elder asked if it had been consecrated, to which the minister replied, "I am afraid I do not understand what you mean"; so the elder suggested that he would use his own oil, as he had a small bottle with him, and he invited the family to kneel

356

with him about the bed to engage in prayer before performing the sacred ordinance. They seemed rather reluctant, as though they had given up all hope. The doctor remarked, "Maybe the Lord can save her, but I cannot." The elder led in prayer and then administered to the little girl, and as he removed his hands from her head she relaxed, and the doctor immediately reached for her pulse as though he feared she was breathing her last.

For about twenty minutes, the elder sat visiting with the minister and his family, at which time the doctor again felt the girl's pulse and remarked, "There is no need of my remaining any longer—your little girl will be all right. I have seen it with my own eyes and yet I cannot believe it."

Addressing the elder, the minister said, "You were seeking a bed for the night, were you not?" and being informed by the missionary that he was, he explained that he was not prepared to accommodate him, but that he was willing to take him to the hotel and pay for his room, or he would drive him in his auto wherever he wanted to go. He explained that his destination was sixty miles from there, but the minister was perfectly willing to take him that distance, and upon reaching his destination, the minister offered the elder ten dollars for what he had done in his home, but he refused to accept the money, explaining the instruction of the Master to the Twelve when he sent them forth: "Freely ye have received, freely give."

Conference Report, April 1936, pp. 117–18.

"THERE WERE NO SCARS"

DAVID O. MCKAY

In the latter part of March, 1916, Ogden River overflowed. It came through the Narrows a raging torrent.

Wednesday noon (about the middle of March 1916) I drove three of my young children up there as far as the Narrows that they might see the river at floodtide and hear the grinding of the stones as they pushed against each other by the force of the water.

Wednesday night my brother, Thomas E., called at the house. Unable to get through the canyon, he called his wife by telephone and asked if she would send a horse down with the road supervisor the next morning so that he (Thomas E.) might get up to the valley. As he hung up the telephone, he turned to my son Lawrence and said: "Will you please drive me up as far as where the road is washed out?" Having been up just that afternoon and knowing the danger, I said: "I think I had better drive you, Thomas E., if you will get up early in the morning so that I can get back in time to catch my train for Salt Lake City."

The next morning several things delayed us, and it was seven o'clock before we started for the canyon. My train left in one hour. I hesitated for a moment, thinking that I should not have time to drive up to the mouth of the canyon and return by eight o'clock. It was then that I received a strong impression to *"go up to the bridge and back."*

We jumped into a little Ford car, dashed through the rain and mud up 21st Street toward the canyon road. Without my having said anything to Thomas E. about my impression, he said: "I think you had better not attempt to cross the bridge."

Notwithstanding these two warnings, as we approached the bridge I thought I could spend another five minutes and take him up as far as I had taken the children the day before. I saw the pile of rocks there at the bridge, and it seemed to be intact just as it had been the day before. So jocularly I said: "I'm going across the bridge, can you swim?" With that I stepped on the gas and dashed across the bridge, only to hear Thomas E. say: "Oh, look out! There's a rope!" The watchman who left at seven o'clock had stretched the derrick rope across the road, and his successor, the day watchman, had not arrived. I reached for the emergency brake but was too late. The rope smashed the window, threw back the top, and caught me just in the chin, severing my lip, knocking out my lower teeth, and breaking my upper jaw. Thomas E. ducked his head and escaped uninjured, but I was left partially senseless.

The engine of the car was unimpaired, and Thomas E. moved me over in the seat, turned the car around, and drove toward home. Just as we neared the top of the hill in Canyon Road, I heard him say: "I think I had better take you to the hospital." I opened my eyes and saw blood in my hand and some loose broken teeth. I said, "No, you had better take me home, something has happened."

About nine o'clock I was on the operating table in care of Dr. Joseph R. Moorell and Dr. Robert S. Joyce. They sewed my upper jaw in place, and took fourteen stitches in my lower lip and lacerated cheek.

One of the attendants remarked: "Too bad; he will be disfigured for life."

Certainly I was most unrecognizable. When I was wheeled back to my room in the hospital, one of the nurses consolingly remarked: "Well, Brother McKay, you can wear a beard," meaning that thus I might hide my scars.

Word of the accident soon spread throughout the city, and at ten o'clock Bishop A. E. Olson, President Thomas B. Evans, and

Heber Scowcroft, three very close friends, called and administered to me. In sealing the anointing, Bishop Olson said: "We bless you that you shall not be disfigured and that you shall not have pain." . . .

Saturday evening Dr. William H. Petty called to see if the teeth that were still remaining in the upper jaw might be saved. It was he who said: "I suppose you are in great pain?" I answered: "No, I haven't *any* pain." He said: "I cannot understand that—I should think that you would have neuralgia pains."

That evening I began to wonder whether or not my nerves were stunned. As I dozed, my arm that I evidently had up at my forehead dropped and hit some of the stitches on my face. Then I knew that my nerves were not stunned, as I felt the pain intensely, for I was aware of the contact of my hand on the stitches.

Sunday morning President Heber J. Grant came up from Salt Lake City. He was then President of the Council of the Twelve. Having noticed the sign on the door, "Visitors Not Allowed," he entered and said: "David, don't talk; I'm just going to give you a blessing."

Among other things he said: "I bless you that you shall not be scarred." Later when he took his hands off my head and looked at me he thought (as he afterwards told me): "My, I've made a promise that cannot be fulfilled!"

On the following Monday morning the doctors removed the stitches from my lower lip, the severed parts having joined together. When Dr. Joyce came in Tuesday morning to take out the stitches from my face, he said: "Well, Mr. McKay, it pays to live a clean life!" Wednesday morning I returned home.

The following October, at a banquet given to the General Authorities on the Roof Garden of the Hotel Utah, I sat at a table near where President Grant was sitting. I noticed that he was look-ing at me somewhat intently, and then he said: "David, from where I am sitting I cannot see a scar on your face!" I answered: "No,

President Grant, there are no scars—your blessing was realized completely!"

David O. McKay, *Cherished Experiences from the Writings of President David O. McKay*, compiled by Clare Middlemiss (Salt Lake City: Deseret Book Co., 1955), pp. 153–56.

MISSIONARY WORK

"WE CALLED AT A
MR. JOSEPH FIELDING'S"

⌐‿⌐

PARLEY P. PRATT

The work soon spread into the country and enlarged its operations in all that region; many were gathered into the Church, and were filled with faith and love, and with the Holy Spirit, and the Lord confirmed the Word with signs following. My first visit to the country was about nine miles from Toronto, among a settlement of farmers, by one of whom I had sent an appointment beforehand. John Taylor accompanied me— this was before he was baptized—we rode on horseback. We called at a Mr. Joseph Fielding's, an acquaintance and friend of Mr. Taylor's. This man had two sisters, young ladies, who seeing us coming ran from their house to one of the neighboring houses, lest they should give welcome, or give countenance to "Mormonism." Mr. Fielding stayed, and as we entered the house he said he was sorry we had come, he had opposed our holding meeting in the neighborhood; and, so great was the prejudice, that the Methodist meeting house was closed against us, and the minister refused, on Sunday, to give out the appointment sent by the farmer.

"Ah!" said I, "why do they oppose Mormonism?"

"I don't know," said he, "but the name has such a contemptible sound; and, another thing, we do not want a new revelation, or a new religion contrary to the Bible."

"Oh!" said I, "if that is all we shall soon remove your preju-

365

dices. Come, call home your sisters, and let's have some supper. Did you say the appointment was not given out?"

"I said, sir, that it was not given out in the meeting house, nor by the minister; but the farmer by whom you sent it agreed to have it at his house."

"Come then, send for your sisters, we will take supper with you, and all go over to meeting together. If you and your sisters will agree to this, I will agree to preach the old Bible gospel, and leave out all new revelations which are opposed to it."

The honest man consented. The young ladies came home, got us a good supper, and all went to meeting. The house was crowded; I preached, and the people wished to hear more. The meeting house was opened for further meetings, and in a few days we baptized Brother Joseph Fielding and his two amiable and intelligent sisters, for such they proved to be in an eminent degree. We also baptized many others in that neighborhood, and organized a branch of the Church, for the people there drank in truth as water, and loved it as they loved life.

Parley P. Pratt, *Autobiography of Parley P. Pratt*, edited by Parley P. Pratt Jr., Classics in Mormon Literature ed. (Salt Lake City: Deseret Book Co., 1985), p. 128.

WILFORD WOODRUFF
CALLED ON A MISSION

⌒‿

WILFORD WOODRUFF

I was still holding the office of a Teacher, and knowing for myself that the fulness of the Gospel of Christ, which God had revealed to Joseph Smith, was true, I had a great desire to preach it to the inhabitants of the earth, but as a Teacher I had no authority to preach the gospel to the world. I went into the forest near Lyman Wight's [in Daviess county, Missouri] one Sunday morning, aside from the abodes of men, and made my desire known unto the Lord. I prayed that the Lord would open my way and give me the privilege of preaching the gospel. I did not make my request expecting any honor from man, for I knew that the preaching of the gospel was attended with hard labor and persecution. While I was praying, the Spirit of the Lord rested upon me, and testified to me that my prayer was heard, and that my request would be granted. I arose to my feet and walked some three hundred yards into a broad road, rejoicing. As I came into the road I saw Judge Elias Higbee standing before me. As I walked up to him he said, "Wilford, the Lord has revealed to me that it is your duty to go into the vineyard of the Lord and preach the gospel." I told him if that was the will of the Lord I was ready to go. I did not tell him that I had been praying for that privilege. I had been boarding at Lyman Wight's with Judge Higbee for months, and it was the first time he had ever named such a thing to me.

B. H. Roberts, *New Witnesses for God* (Salt Lake City: The Deseret News, 1951), pp. 238–39.

BENBOW FARM

WILFORD WOODRUFF

March 1st, 1840, was my birthday, when I was thirty-three years of age. It being Sunday, I preached twice through the day to a large assembly in the City Hall, in the town of Hanley, and administered the sacrament unto the Saints.

In the evening I again met with a large assembly of the Saints and strangers, and while singing the first hymn [I felt] the Spirit of the Lord resting upon me, and the voice of God said to me, "This is the last meeting that you will hold with this people for many days."

I was astonished at this, as I had many appointments out in that district.

When I arose to speak to the people, I told them that it was the last meeting I should hold with them for many days. They were as much astonished as I was.

At the close of the meeting four persons came forward for baptism, and we went down in to the water and baptized them.

In the morning I went in secret before the Lord, and asked him what his will was concerning me.

The answer I got was, that I should go to the south, for the Lord had a great work for me to perform there, as many souls were waiting for the word of the Lord.

On the 3rd of March, 1840, in fulfillment of the word of the Lord to me, I took coach and rode to Wolverhampton, twenty-six miles, and spent the day there.

On the morning of the 4th I again took coach, and rode through Dudley, Stourbridge, Stourport, and Worchester, and then walked a number of miles to Mr. John Benbow's, Hill Farm, Castle Frome, Ledbury, Herefordshire. This was a farming country in the south of England, a region where no elder of the Latter-day Saints had visited.

I found Mr. Benbow to be a wealthy farmer, cultivating three hundred acres of land, occupying a good mansion, and having plenty of means. His wife, Jane, had no children.

I presented myself to him as a missionary from America, an elder of the Church of Jesus Christ of Latter-day Saints, who had been sent to him by the commandment of God as a messenger of salvation, to preach the gospel of life unto him and his household, and the inhabitants of the land.

Mr. Benbow and his wife received me with glad hearts and thanksgiving. It was in the evening when I arrived, having traveled forty-eight miles by coach and on foot during the day, but after receiving refreshments we sat down together, and conversed until two o'clock in the morning.

Mr. Benbow and his wife rejoiced greatly at the glad tidings which I brought unto them of the fulness of the everlasting gospel, which God had revealed through the mouth of his Prophet, Joseph Smith, in these last days.

I rejoiced greatly at the news that Mr. Benbow gave me, that there was a company of men and women—over six hundred in number—who had broken off from the Wesleyan Methodist, and taken the name of United Brethren. They had forty-five preachers among them and had chapels and many houses that were licensed according to the law of the land for preaching in.

This body of United Brethren were searching for light and truth, but had gone as far as they could, and were continually calling upon the Lord to open the way before them, and send them light and knowledge that they might know the true way to be saved.

When I heard these things, I could clearly see why the Lord

had commanded me, while in the town of Hanley, to leave that place of labor and go to the south, for in Herefordshire there was a great harvest-field for gathering many Saints into the kingdom of God.

I retired to my bed with joy after offering my prayers and thanksgiving to God, and slept sweetly until the rising of the sun.

I arose on the morning of the 5th, took breakfast, and told Mr. Benbow I would like to commence my Master's business, by preaching the gospel to the people.

He had a large hall in his mansion which was licensed for preaching, and he sent word through the neighborhood that an American missionary would preach at his house that evening.

As the time drew nigh many of the neighbors came in, and I preached my first gospel sermon in the house. I also preached on the following evening at the same place, and baptized six persons, including Mr. John Benbow and his wife, and four preachers of the United Brethren.

I spent most of the following day in clearing out a pool of water, and preparing it for baptizing in, as I saw many to be baptized there. I afterwards baptized six hundred in that pool of water.

On Sunday, the 8th, I preached at Frome's Hill in the morning, at Standley Hill in the afternoon, and at John Benbow's Hill Farm in the evening.

The parish church that stood in the neighborhood of Brother Benbow's, presided over by the rector of the parish, was attended during the day by only fifteen persons, while I had a large congregation, estimated to number a thousand, attend my meeting through the day and evening.

When I arose in the evening to speak at Brother Benbow's house, a man entered the door and informed me that he was a constable, and had been sent by the rector of the parish with a warrant to arrest me.

I asked him, "For what crime?"

He said, "For preaching to the people."

I told him that I, as well as the rector, had a license for preaching the gospel to the people, and that if he would take a chair I would wait upon him after meeting.

He took my chair and sat beside me. I preached the first principles of the everlasting gospel for an hour and a quarter. The power of God rested upon me, the Spirit filled the house, and the people were convinced.

At the close of the meeting I opened a door for baptism, and seven offered themselves. Among the number were four preachers and the constable.

The latter arose and said, "Mr. Woodruff, I would like to be baptized."

I told him I would like to baptize him. I went down to the pool and baptized seven. We then met together, and I confirmed thirteen and broke bread unto the Saints, and we all rejoiced together.

The constable went to the rector and told him if he wanted Mr. Woodruff taken up for preaching the gospel, he must go himself and serve the writ, for he had heard him preach the only true gospel sermon he had ever listened to in his life.

The rector did not know what to make of it, so he sent two clerks of the Church of England as spies, to attend our meeting, and find out what we did preach.

But they were both pricked in their hearts and received the word of the Lord gladly and were baptized and confirmed members of the Church of Jesus Christ of Latter-day Saints.

The rector became alarmed and did not dare to send anybody else.

The ministers and rectors of the south of England called a convention and sent a petition to the Archbishop of Canterbury, to request Parliament to pass a law prohibiting the "Mormons"

371

from preaching in the British dominion. In this petition the rector stated that one "Mormon" missionary had baptized fifteen hundred persons, mostly members of the English church, during the last seven months.

But the archbishop and council, knowing well that the laws of England gave free toleration to all religions under the British flag, sent word to the petitioners that if they had the worth of souls at heart as much as they had the ground where hares, foxes, and hounds ran, they would not lose so many of their flock.

I continued to preach and baptize daily.

On the 21st day of March I baptized Elder Thomas Kingston. He was the superintendent of both preachers and members of the United Brethren.

The first thirty days after my arrival in Herefordshire, I had baptized forty-five preachers and one hundred-and-sixty members of the United Brethren, who put into my hands one chapel and forty-five houses, which were licensed according to law to preach in.

This opened a wide field for labor and enabled me to bring into the Church, through the blessing of God, over eighteen hundred souls during eight months, including all of the six hundred United Brethren except one person; also including some two hundred preachers of various denominations.

This field of labor embraced Herefordshire, Gloucestershire, and Worcestershire, and formed the conferences of Garway, Godfield, Elm, and Frome's Hill.

I was visited by President Young and Dr. Richards.

Brother Benbow furnished us with 300 pounds to print the first Book of Mormon that was published in England; and on the 20th of May, 1840, Brigham Young, Willard Richards, and I held a council on the top of Malvern Hill, and there decided that Brigham Young go directly to Manchester and publish 3,000 copies of the hymnbook and 3,000 copies of the Book of Mormon, this being the first publication of these books in England.

The power of God rested upon us and upon the mission.

The sick were healed, devils were cast out, and the lame were made to walk. . . .

The whole history of this Herefordshire mission shows the importance of listening to the still small voice of the Spirit of God and the revelations of the Holy Ghost.

The Lord had a people there prepared for the gospel. They were praying for light and truth, and the Lord sent me to them, and I declared the gospel of life and salvation unto them, and some eighteen hundred souls received it, and many of them have been gathered to Zion in these mountains. Many of them have also been called to officiate in the bishopric, and have done much good in Zion. But in all these things we should ever acknowledge the hand of God, and give him the honor, praise and glory, forever and ever. Amen.

Wilford Woodruff, *Leaves from My Journal* (Salt Lake City: Juvenile Instructor's Office, 1882), pp. 77–83.

"HURRAH FOR ISRAEL!"

B . H . ROBERTS

On the fourteenth of September, Brigham Young left his home at Montrose and started for England. He had been prostrated for some time by sickness, and at the time of starting on his mission was so feeble that he had to be assisted to the ferry, only some thirty rods from his house. All his children were sick, and he left his wife with a babe but ten days old, and in the poorest circumstances, for the mobs of Missouri had robbed him of all he had. After crossing the river to the Nauvoo side, Israel Barlow took him on a horse behind him and carried him to the house of Elder Heber C. Kimball, where his strength altogether failed him, and he had to remain there for several days, nursed by his wife, who, hearing that he was unable to get farther than Brother Kimball's, had crossed the river from Montrose to care for him.

On the eighteenth of the month, however, Elder Young, in company with Heber C. Kimball, made another start. A brother by the name of Charles Hubbard sent a boy with a team to take them a day's journey on their way. Elder Kimball left his wife in bed shaking with ague, and all his children sick. It was only by the assistance of some of the brethren that Heber himself could climb into the wagon. "It seemed to me," he remarked afterwards in relating the circumstance, "as though my very inmost parts would melt within me at the thought of leaving my family in such a condition, as it were, almost in the arms of death. I felt as though I could scarcely endure it."

"Hold up!" said he to the teamster, who had just started. "Brother Brigham, this is pretty tough, but let us rise and give them a cheer." Brigham, with much difficulty, rose to his feet, and joined Elder Kimball in swinging his hat and shouting, "Hurrah, hurrah, hurrah for Israel!" Sisters Young and Kimball, hearing the cheer came to the door—Sister Kimball with great difficulty—and waved a farewell; and the two apostles continued their journey without purse, without script, for England.

B. H. Roberts, *A Comprehensive History of The Church of Jesus Christ of Latter-day Saints,* 6 vols. (Salt Lake City: The Church of Jesus Christ of Latter-day Saints, 1930), 2:23–24.

ONE YORK SHILLING

HEBER C. KIMBALL

Brother Brigham had one York shilling left and on looking over our expenses, we found we had paid out over $87.00 out of the $13.50 we had at Pleasant Garden, which is all the money we had to pay our passage with. We had traveled over 400 miles by stage, for which we paid from eight to ten cents a mile, and had taken three meals a day for each of which we were charged fifty cents, also fifty cents for our lodgings. Brother Brigham often suspected that I put the money in his trunk or clothes, thinking I had a purse of money which I had not acquainted him with, but this was not so. The money could only have been put in his trunk by some heavenly messenger who administered to our necessities daily, as he knew we needed.

Woman's Exponent, July 15, 1880, p. 26.

"IS NOT THAT PLENTY?"

B . H . ROBERTS

When Elder Taylor arrived in New York, Elder Woodruff had been there some time, and was all impatience to embark for England, but as yet the former had no means with which to pay for his ocean passage. Although supplied with all the means necessary on his journey thus far, after paying his cab-fare to the house of Brother Pratt he had but one cent left. Still he was the last man on earth to plead poverty, and in answer to inquiries of some of the brethren as to his financial circumstances, he replied that he had plenty of money.

This was reported to Brother Pratt, who the next day approached Elder Taylor on the subject:

Elder Pratt: "Brother Taylor, I hear you have plenty of money?"

Elder Taylor: "Yes, Brother Pratt, that's true."

Elder Pratt: "Well, I am about to publish my 'Voice of Warning' and 'Millennial Poems.' I am very much in need of money, and if you could furnish me two or three hundred dollars I should be very much obliged."

Elder Taylor: "Well, Brother Parley, you are welcome to anything I have, if it will be of service to you."

Elder Pratt: "I never saw the time when means would be more acceptable."

Elder Taylor: "Then you are welcome to all I have."

And putting his hand into his pocket Elder Taylor gave him his copper cent. A laugh followed.

"But I thought you gave it out that you had plenty of money," said Parley.

"Yes, and so I have," replied Elder Taylor. "I am well clothed, you furnish me plenty to eat and drink and good lodging; with all these things and a penny over, as I owe nothing, is not that plenty?"

That evening at a council meeting Elder Pratt proposed that the brethren assist Elder Taylor with means to pay his passage to England as Brother Woodruff was prepared and desired to go. To this Elder Taylor objected and told the brethren if they had anything to give to let Parley have it, as he had a family to support and needed means for publishing. At the close of the meeting Elder Woodruff expressed his regret at the course taken by Elder Taylor, as he had been waiting for him, and at last had engaged his passage.

Elder Taylor: "Well, Brother Woodruff, if you think it best for me to go, I will accompany you."

Elder Woodruff: "But where will you get the money?"

Elder Taylor: "Oh, there will be no difficulty about that. Go and take a passage for me on your vessel, and I will furnish you the means."

A Brother Theodore Turley, hearing the above conversation, and thinking that Elder Taylor had resources unknown to himself or Brother Woodruff, said: "I wish I could go with you, I would do your cooking and wait on you."

The passage to be secured was in the steerage—these missionaries were not going on flowery beds of ease—hence the necessity of such service as Brother Turley proposed rendering. In answer to this appeal, Elder Taylor told Brother Woodruff to take a passage for Brother Turley also.

At the time of making these arrangements Elder Taylor had no money, but the Spirit had whispered him that means would be forthcoming, and when had that still, small voice failed him! In that he trusted, and he did not trust in vain. Although he did not ask for a penny of anyone, from various persons in voluntary donations he received money enough to meet his engagements for the passage of himself and Brother Turley, but no more.

Elder Taylor and his two companions embarked on the 10th of December, 1839.

B. H. Roberts, *Life of John Taylor* (Salt Lake City: Bookcraft, 1963), pp. 72–74.

"THE LABORER IS WORTHY OF HIS HIRE"

ANDREW JENSON

When [John Taylor's] means were exhausted, with an inexhaustible store of faith, he would stop and preach the gospel. The Lord would raise up friends who would give him money, with which he would proceed on his journey. In doing this he would never ask a human being for help. He asked the Lord, and his prayers never went unanswered.

When they were about to sail from New York to Liverpool, he and two other brethren were almost destitute of means, not having sufficient to pay one passage, much less three. Notwithstanding their predicament, a very short time before the vessel was to sail Elder Taylor told one of his companions to go and engage passage for all three to Liverpool. His fellow-laborers were non-plussed and asked where on earth could they get means in so short a time. Elder Taylor answered that there was plenty of means in the world and the Lord would send them enough before the vessel sailed to pay their way. His words were most remarkably fulfilled. He asked no person for money, and yet immediately after he made the prediction one after another came to them and proffered assistance, until enough was provided to meet their expenses to Liverpool.

He arrived in Liverpool January 11, 1840, and immediately commenced his missionary work, preaching, baptizing, organizing branches, and with his brethren regulating the Church throughout the British Isles. He introduced the gospel into Ireland and the Isle of Man, extending his labors into Scotland. He published several tracts, setting forth principles of the gospel and refuting falsehoods. He corrected the proof sheets of the Book of Mormon, and with President Young and Elder Parley P. Pratt prepared and published the first edition of the Latter-day Saints' Hymn Book.

While laboring on the Isle of Man he had secured the printing of some tracts, which he wrote in reply to the falsehoods circulated by ministers and others regarding the character and doctrines taught by the Prophet Joseph Smith. When the tracts were ready the printer would not deliver them until every penny was paid which was due him. Elder Taylor did not have sufficient to meet the demand, and being very anxious to obtain the tracts went immediately into a private room, and, kneeling down, told the Lord in plain simplicity exactly how much he needed to pay for the matter he had published in defense of his cause. In a few minutes after his prayer was offered a young man came to the door, and upon being invited to enter handed Elder Taylor an envelope and walked out. The young man was unknown to him. The envelope contained some money and a little note which read: "The laborer is worthy of his hire," and no signature was placed thereon.

In a few minutes later a poor woman engaged as a fish vender came to the house and offered a little money to assist him in his ministerial labors. He told her there was plenty of money in the world and he did not wish to take her money. She insisted that the Lord would bless her the more and she would be happier if he would accept it, whereupon he received the offering, and to his surprise the poor woman's mite, added to what the young man had given him, made exactly the amount sufficient to pay the printer the balance due him.

Andrew Jenson, *Latter-day Saint Biographical Encyclopedia*, 4 vols. (Salt Lake City: Andrew Jenson History Co., 1901), 1:16.

"I TOOK UP ELDER SHELTON'S BIBLE"

H G B

Never shall I forget the first time I was called upon to make an effort to preach the gospel. It was in Pittsylvania County, Virginia, in the month of June, 1844.

I had been ordained an Elder and set apart to take a mission to Virginia, in company with Elder Sebert C. Shelton.

My extreme youth prevented me from realizing the responsibilities of a mission. Being a beardless boy, it never occurred to me that I would be called upon to preach. Up to that time I never had been upon my feet to say a word in public.

At a meeting which had been advertised for two weeks, at the Methodist camp meeting ground, in a grove, in the County before mentioned, were gathered an assemblage of six or seven hundred men, women and children, priests, doctors and lawyers, the largest meeting I had ever witnessed up to that time.

I came to this meeting from one part of the County, and Elder Shelton was expected to come from another quarter. But the time to commence meeting had arrived, and Elder Shelton had not.

The audience was impatient. A party of three or four of the leading citizens waited upon me, to know if I would not address the meeting. There never had been a "Mormon" meeting in that County before, and they could not afford to be disappointed.

I was sitting near the center of the meeting (not realizing that the stand was my place) when these men made the inquiry.

If a battery of artillery had been discharged in our midst, I do not think it would have so startled me, as did this request.

For the first time I began to realize that it was my duty to try to advocate the religion I professed.

Just as I was going to answer that I would make an effort, Elder Shelton walked upon the stand, and this seemed to lift a mountain from my shoulders.

Brother Shelton looked wearied and sick, but opened the meeting with singing and prayer, and sang again before he discovered me in the audience. Then he immediately called upon me to come to the stand and preach, as he was too sick and feeble to attempt it.

To say I was scared would scarcely convey a proper idea of my condition. I was in a tremor from head to feet, and shook like a leaf in a storm, scarcely knowing what I did.

I took up Elder Shelton's Bible which lay upon the front board, and without any premeditation, I opened at the third chapter of John, and read the fifth verse.

By the time I had finished reading, all my trembling had left me, and I felt as calm and collected as the quiet that succeeds the storm. The subjects of the first principles of the gospel were opened to me like print, only plainer and more powerful.

Faith, repentance, baptism for the remission of sins and the laying on of hands for the reception of the Holy Ghost, came to me in succession and in their order. And those priests, doctors, lawyers and people did not appear to me more formidable than so many butterflies.

No miracle ever performed by the power of God, could have had a more convincing effect upon me, than did the help that came to me through the power of the Holy Ghost on that occasion. And I am fully convinced in my own mind that never since have I preached a more effective discourse, nor one accompanied by more of the power of God.

Four Faith Promoting Classics (Salt Lake City: Bookcraft, 1968), pp. 64–65.

"YOU ARE NO PREACHER"

ANDREW JENSON

While on this mission, which [Edwin D. Woolley] was performing in the good old way by traveling without money to pay for the necessaries of life, the following interesting incident occurred. While walking through the country one day he reached a toll gate (common in those times) at

Strasburg, Lancaster county, Pennsylvania. It was customary to allow ministers or preachers to pass through free of charge, and when Bro. Woolley stated that he was a preacher of the gospel, the gate keeper allowed him to pass. He had gone about three miles farther on his journey, when he heard the clatter of horses' hoofs on the road behind him; turning, he saw two horsemen coming down the road at a hard gallop. He was soon overtaken and one of the men, placing his hand on the Elder's shoulder, with an oath claimed him as a prisoner, saying, "You are no d—d preacher, and you have got to go back with us, and not only pay your fare, but a fine as well."

Elder Woolley remarked that if they would procure a hall and furnish an audience, he would show them whether or not he was a preacher. This seemed to suit the men, who at once decided to put him to the test; they provided a hall and gave out notices of the meeting to be held, holding the assumed preacher in custody meanwhile. A large congregation gathered, attracted, no doubt, by the novelty of the occasion, more than from any real desire to learn the truth. The Elder must have had the assistance the Lord usually gives to those who trust in Him, for the men who had him in charge were thoroughly convinced that he was a preacher and released him from custody without toll or fine being paid. He was so well satisfied with the reception he met at this meeting that he remained in that neighborhood for some time, preaching and making converts.

Andrew Jenson, *Latter-day Saint Biographical Encyclopedia,* 4 vols. (Salt Lake City: Andrew Jenson History Co., 1901), 1:631.

"THIS PAPER IS BLANK"

THEODORE B. LEWIS

In the early part of President [Jedediah M.] Grant's ministry in [the South], he gained quite a reputation as a ready speaker, frequently responding to invitations to preach from such subjects or texts as might be selected at the time of commencing his sermon, by those inviting him. In time it became a matter of wonder with many as to how and when he prepared his wonderful sermons. In reply to their queries he informed them that he never prepared his sermons as other ministers did. "Of course, I read and store my mind with a knowledge of gospel truths," said he, "but I never study up a sermon."

Well, they did not believe he told the truth, for, as they thought, it was impossible for a man to preach such sermons without careful preparation. So, in order to prove it, a number of persons decided to put him to test, and asked him if he would preach at a certain time and place and from a text selected by them. They proposed to give him the text on his arrival at the place of meeting, thus giving him no time to prepare. To gratify them he consented. The place selected was Jeffersonville, the seat of Tazewell county, at that time the home of the late John B. Floyd, who subsequently became secretary of war, and many other prominent men. The room chosen was in the court house.

At the hour appointed the house was packed to its utmost capacity. Mr. Floyd and a number of lawyers and ministers were present and occupied front seats. Elder Grant came in, walked to the stand and opened the meeting as usual. At the close of the second hymn, a clerk, appointed for the occasion, stepped forward and handed the paper (the text) to Elder Grant, who unfolded it and found it to be blank. Without any mark of surprise, he held the paper up before the audience, and said:

"My friends, I am here today according to agreement, to preach from such a text as these gentlemen might select for me. I have it here in my hand. I don't wish you to become offended at me, for I am under promise to preach from the text selected; and if any one is to blame, you must blame those who selected it. I knew nothing of what text they would choose, but of all texts this is my favorite one. You see the paper is blank (at the same time holding it up to view). You sectarians down there believe that out of nothing God created all things, and now you wish me to create a sermon from Nothing, for this paper is blank. Now, you sectarians believe in a God that has neither body, parts nor passions. Such a God I conceive to be a perfect blank, just as you find my text is. You believe in a church without prophets, Apostles, Evangelists, etc. Such a church would be a perfect blank, as compared with the Church of Christ, and this agrees with my text. You have located your heaven beyond the bounds of time and space. It exists nowhere, and consequently your heaven is blank, like unto my text."

Thus he went on until he had torn to pieces all the tenets of faith professed by his hearers, and then proclaimed the principles of the gospel in great power. He wound up by asking, "Have I stuck to the text and does that satisfy you?" As soon as he sat down, Mr. Floyd jumped up and said: "Mr. Grant, if you are not a lawyer, you ought to be one." Then turning to the people, he added: "Gentlemen, you have listened to a wonderful discourse, and with amazement. Now, take a look at Mr. Grant's clothes. Look at his coat: his elbows are almost out: and his knees are almost through his pants. Let us take up a collection." As he sat down another eminent lawyer Joseph Stras, Esq., still living in Jeffersonville, arose and said: "I am good for one sleeve in a coat and one leg in a pair of pants, for Mr. Grant."

The presiding elder of the M. E. church, South, was requested to pass the hat around, but he replied that he would not take up a collection for a "Mormon" preacher. "Yes you will," said Mr. Floyd; "Pass it around," said Mr. Stras, and the cry was taken up and repeated by the audience, until, for the sake of peace, the minister had to yield. He accordingly marched around with a hat in his hand, receiving contributions, which resulted in a collection sufficient to purchase a fine suit of clothes, a horse, saddle and bridle for Brother Grant, and not one contributor a member of the Church of Jesus Christ of Latter-day Saints, though some joined subsequently. And this from a sermon produced from a blank text.

Andrew Jenson, *Latter-day Saint Biographical Encyclopedia,* 4 vols. (Salt Lake City: Andrew Jenson History Co., 1901), 1:57–58.

"WHO STANDS AT THE HEAD OF YOUR CHURCH?"

THEODORE B. LEWIS

At another time, Elder [Jedediah M.] Grant was challenged by a very eminent Baptist preacher, named Baldwin, to a discussion. Brother Grant consented. The place chosen was the fine, large church of his proud and imperious antagonist. Mr. Baldwin was described to me, as a man, over-bearing in his manner—a regular browbeater. When the time came for the discussion, the house was densely crowded. Umpires were chosen, and everything was ready to proceed, when Brother Grant arose and said: "Mr. Baldwin. I would like to ask you a question before we proceed any farther."

"Certainly so," said Baldwin.

"Who stands at the head of your church in southwest Virginia?"

Mr. Baldwin very quickly and austerely replied, "I do, sir; I do."

"All right," said Brother Grant; "I wished to know that I had a worthy foe."

Mr. Baldwin looked a little confused for a moment, and then said: "Mr. Grant, I would like to ask you, who stands at the head of your church in southwest Virginia?"

Brother Grant arose and with bowed head replied, "Jesus Christ, sir."

The shock was electrical. This inspired answer completely disarmed the proud foe, and the humble servant of God again came off victor.

Andrew Jenson, *Latter-day Saint Biographical Encyclopedia,* 4 vols. (Salt Lake City: Andrew Jenson History Co., 1901), 1:58.

"I WAS CALLED
TO PERFORM A MISSION"

⌒

ELI H. PEIRCE

On the fifth day of October, 1875, at the Semi-annual Conference of the Church of Jesus Christ of Latter-day Saints, I was called to perform a mission to the United States.

Just why my name was suggested as a candidate for this mission, and presented at conference for approval or rejection by the people, I cannot say. My mind prior to that time had been entirely given up to temporalities. I had never read to exceed a dozen chapters of the Bible in my life, and little more than that from either the Book of Mormon or Doctrine and Covenants, and concerning Church history was entirely ignorant. Had never made but one attempt to address a public audience, large or small, and that effort was no credit to me. Had been engaged in the railroad business for a number of years, and this occupation would have deprived me of meetings and religious services even had my inclinations led in that direction, which I frankly confess they did not. I had become almost an inveterate smoker, and bought cigars by the wholesale, a thousand at a time. Was addicted to the use of language which, if not profane, was at least vulgar and reprehensible. Frequently visited saloons, but was not an habitual drinker. Was not proficient at billiards, but squandered considerable money in acquiring what little knowledge I possessed of the game; and pool frequently cost me more for drinks than my board bill came to. Though these indiscretions were common and frequent, thanks to a mother's sagacious training, they never led to grosser or more alluring ones.

Nature never endowed me with a superabundance of religious sentiment or veneration; my region of spirituality is not high, but below the average. A phrenologist once said to me: "You are too level-headed to ever make a sanctimonious church member." With this list of disqualifications, which serious reflection helped to magnify, is it surprising that I marveled and wondered if the Church were not running short of missionary material?

One of my fellow employees was at the conference; I was not, because I did not care to be. He heard my name called, abruptly left the meeting and ran over to the telegraph office to call and tell me the startling news. This was the first intimation I had received that such a thing was contemplated. At the very moment this intelligence was being flashed over the wires, I was sitting lazily thrown back in an office rocking chair, my feet on the desk, reading a novel and simultaneously sucking an old Dutch pipe, of massive proportions, just to vary the monotony of cigar smoking.

As soon as I had been informed of what had taken place, I threw the novel in the waste basket, the pipe in a corner and started up town to buy a catechism. Have never read a novel nor smoked a pipe from that hour. Sent in my resignation the same day, to take effect at once, in order that I might have time for study and preparation.

Remarkable as it may seem, and has since appeared to me, a thought of disregarding the call, or of refusing to comply with the requirement, never once entered my mind. The question I asked myself a thousand times, and which seemed so all-important, was: "How can I accomplish this mission? How can I, who am so shamefully ignorant and untaught in doctrine, do honor to God and justice to the souls of men, and merit the trust reposed in me by the Priesthood?"

Eliza R. Snow, *Biography and Family Record of Lorenzo Snow* (Salt Lake City: Deseret News Co., 1884), pp. 407–9.

"I BORE HIM
A SOLEMN TESTIMONY"

GEORGE Q. CANNON

When the Presbyterian missionary at Wailuku saw that I had come back there he was displeased. He used all his influence against me among his congregation, and one Sunday he came out in public and delivered a most abusive discourse against the Prophet Joseph and our principles, in which he gave an entirely false statement of the cause of his death, and also warned the people against me.

I happened to be present when this sermon was delivered. While listening to it a variety of emotions agitated me. My first impulse was to jump upon one of the seats as soon as he had got through, and tell the people he had told them a pack of falsehoods. But this I thought would produce confusion, and result in no good. When the services were over, I walked around to the pulpit where he stood. He knew how short a time we had been on the islands, and, I believed, had no idea that I could understand what he had said; when he saw me, therefore, his face turned pale, and to me he looked like a man who had been caught in a mean, low act.

I told him I wanted to give him correct information respecting the things he had told the people that morning, that he might remove the effect of the lies which he had repeated to them; for, I said, they were base lies, and I was a living witness that they were.

He said he did not believe they were lies, and he should not tell the people anything different to what he had said; he thought he had but done his duty, and if the people had been warned against Mahomet in his day, he would not have got so many disciples.

I bore him a solemn testimony respecting the Prophet Joseph, and the truth of the work, and said that I would stand as a witness against him at the judgment seat of God, for having told that people lies and for refusing to tell them the truth when it had been shown to him. . . .

This was the first occurrence of the kind in my experience in which I was personally prominent, and it had an importance in my eyes which it would scarcely have were it to happen today.

Preston Nibley, comp., *Three Mormon Classics,* collector's ed. (Salt Lake City: Bookcraft, 1988), pp. 152–53.

"POI IS MY FOOD"

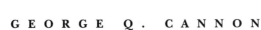

GEORGE Q. CANNON

Before leaving Lahaina [Hawaii], I had tasted a teaspoon of "poi," but the smell of it and the calabash in which it was contained were so much like that of a book-binder's old, sour, paste-pot, that when I put it to my mouth I gagged at it, and would have vomited had I swallowed it. But in traveling among the people I soon learned that if I did not eat "poi" I would put them to great inconvenience; for they would have to cook separate food for me every meal. This would make me burdensome to them, and might interfere with my success [as a missionary]. I, therefore, determined to learn to live on their food, and, that I might do so, I asked the Lord to make it sweet to me. My prayer was heard and answered; the next time I tasted it, I ate a bowlful and I positively liked it. It was my food, whenever I could get it, from that time as long as I remained on the islands.

It may sound strange, yet it is true, that I have sat down to a table on which bread was placed, and though I had not tasted the latter for months, I took the "poi" in preference to the bread; it was sweeter to me than any food I have ever eaten.

Joseph Fielding Smith, *Life of Joseph F. Smith* (Salt Lake City: Deseret Book Co., 1938), p. 172.

"TESTIFY THAT JOSEPH SMITH IS A PROPHET"

DAVID O. MCKAY

My father . . . accepted a call to a mission about 1880. When he began preaching, in his native land, and bore testimony of the restoration of the gospel of Jesus Christ, he noticed that the people turned away from him. They were bitter in their hearts against anything "Mormon," and the name of Joseph Smith seemed to arouse antagonism in their hearts. One day he concluded that the best way to get these people would be to preach just the simple principles, the atonement of the Lord Jesus Christ, the first principles of the gospel, and not bear testimony of the restoration of the gospel. It first came simply, as a passing thought, but yet it influenced his future work. In a month or so he became oppressed with a gloomy, downcast feeling, and he could not enter into the spirit of his work. He did not really know what was the matter, but his mind became obstructed, his spirit became clogged, he was oppressed and hampered; and that feeling of depression continued until it weighed him down with such heaviness that he went to the Lord and said: "Unless I can get this feeling removed, I shall have to go home. I cannot continue my work with this feeling."

It continued for some time after that, when, one morning, before daylight, following a sleepless night, he decided to retire to a cave, near the ocean, where he knew he would be shut off from the world entirely, and there pour out his soul to God and ask why he was oppressed with this feeling, what he had done, and what he could do to throw it off and continue his work. He started out in the dark towards the cave, and he became so eager to get to it that he started to run and was hailed by an officer who wanted to know what was the matter, as he was leaving the town. He gave some noncommittal but satisfying reply and was permitted to go on. Something seemed to drive him; he had to get relief.

He entered that place and said: "Oh, Father, what can I do to have this feeling removed? I must have it lifted or I cannot continue in this work"; and he heard a voice, as distinct as the tone I am now uttering, say: "Testify that Joseph Smith is a Prophet of God."

Remembering, then, what he tacitly had decided six weeks or more before, and becoming overwhelmed with the thought, the whole thing came to him in a realization that he was there for a special mission, and that he had not given that special mission the attention which it deserved. Then he cried in his heart, "Lord, it is enough," and went out from the cave.

Improvement Era, March 1921, p. 405.

"WHATE'ER THOU ART, ACT WELL THY PART"

DAVID O. MCKAY

I remember as a missionary in Scotland fifty-seven years ago, after having been in Stirling only a few weeks, I walked around Stirling Castle with my senior companion, Elder Peter G. Johnston of Idaho. We had not yet secured our lodging in Stirling. I confess I was homesick. I did not like the attitude of the people there as they were so suspicious that we were there for ulterior motives. We had spent a halfday around the castle, and the men out in the field ploughing, that spring day, made me all the more homesick, and took me back to my old home town.

As we returned to the town, I saw an unfinished building standing back from the sidewalk several yards. Over the front door was a stone arch, something unusual in a residence, and what was still more unusual, I could see from the sidewalk that there was an inscription chiseled in that arch.

I said to my companion: "That's unusual! I am going to see what the inscription is." When I approached near enough, this message came to me, not only in stone, but as if it came from One in whose service we were engaged: "Whate'er Thou Art, Act Well Thy Part."

I turned and walked thoughtfully away, and when I reached my companion I repeated the message to him.

That was a message to me that morning to act my part well as a missionary of the Church of Jesus Christ of Latter-day Saints. It is merely another way of saying—what is more precious because it comes from the words of the Savior—"Not every one that saith unto me, Lord, Lord, shall enter into the kingdom of heaven, but he that doeth the will of my Father which is in heaven" (Matthew 7:21).

David O. McKay, *Cherished Experiences from the Writings of President David O. McKay*, compiled by Clare Middlemiss (Salt Lake City: Deseret Book Co., 1955), pp. 182–83.

"You Know What You Had in Your Heart"

DAVID O. MCKAY

It is easy to distinguish between the spirit of slander and the spirit of the Gospel. I remember an instance in England during my late mission that may illustrate my meaning. Two Elders had gone to great expense, for them, in procuring a hall, and in announcing their meeting, in distributing literature, etc. Their hopes were high on Sunday morning when, as they approached that hired hall, they saw a goodly number of persons accepting their invitation. One gentleman who was dressed in the garb of a Christian divine approached the hall and was greeted by the Elder who was standing at the door. The latter extended his hand, but the minister refused, saying contemptuously, "I did not come here to shake hands with you."

"Very well," said the Elder, "you are welcome," and invited him into the hall.

When the Elder reported this to me, he said: "I felt somewhat discouraged and gloomy."

I said: "You ought to be very thankful for the experience that came to you that morning. That gentleman misjudged you. You know he misjudged you. You know your sincerity. You know what you had in your heart. You know also that he was wrong in his accusation and in his feelings towards you and your people. Test that spirit and see if you have not more confidence in the work in which you are engaged than you ever had before."

Conference Report, October 1931, pp. 10–11.

"I BAPTIZED A LITTLE URCHIN"

CLIFFORD E. YOUNG

Brother [Charles A.] Callis was converted over in Wales and was baptized as a small boy into the Church. As he was visiting a stake of Zion, he learned that an old man whom he had known in the mission field was ill. Brother Callis called on him. He found him cynical. Brother Callis tried to encourage him. The man seemed to be beyond encouragement. Then Brother Callis said, "John, do you not remember your missionary labors in Wales? Do you not remember the good you did in the mission field?"

"Oh, I didn't do any good," he said.

"Didn't you ever baptize anyone?"

"No, not that I remember."

Brother Callis said, "Are you sure?"

"Oh," he said, "I baptized a little urchin that used to bother us in our meetings."

Then Brother Callis said, "Brother John, do you know that I was that little urchin?"

Think of the importance of that one baptism! Think of the great work of Brother Callis during his thirty years of service in the Southern States Mission and then his great work as one of the Apostles of the Lord Jesus Christ.

Conference Report, April 1955, p. 74.

"HE REBUKED THE WAVES"

HENRY D. TAYLOR

The Lord has endowed some individuals with a gift and capacity for possessing and exercising great powers of faith. Such a man was Henry A. Dixon. Although married and with a family of many children, when called by the First Presidency to fill a mission to Great Britain, he readily accepted the call without hesitation. With three missionary traveling companions, he embarked from St. John Island at Newfoundland on the steamship *Arizona*.

En route a furious storm arose. As the missionaries were preparing to have their evening prayers prior to retiring, they felt a shocking jolt that caused the entire ship to quiver. As they rushed to the deck they discovered that the ship, traveling at full speed, had rammed a gigantic iceberg. A huge, gaping hole had been torn in the prow of the vessel, which extended even below the water line. The captain advised that only in a calm sea could he and the crew bring the ship to the nearest port, which was some 250 miles away.

The wind and the storm continued unabated. Many hours later and unable to sleep, Elder Dixon arose, dressed, and walked to the deck. Standing there alone in the dark, with deep humility and great faith, by the power of the Holy Priesthood, he rebuked the waves and commanded them to be still.

Thirty-six hours later the ship was able to return and dock at Port St. John. In accordance with Elder Dixon's promise, not a single life had been lost.

When the ship's owner, a Mr. Guion, learned of the accident, and knowing that Mormon missionaries were aboard, he was quoted as saying: "There is nothing to worry about. My line has transported Mormon missionaries for forty years and has never lost a boat with Mormon missionaries aboard!"

Conference Report, October 1970, pp. 19–20.

"ENCLOSED IS SOME MONEY"

THORPE B. ISAACSON

One story is about a young man whom I had the chance to know and interview for his mission, and I had the privilege of setting him apart. I like to write to missionaries. I like to get their letters. I am sure I get more strength from their letters than they do from mine.

This choice boy was sent to Australia. Some weeks ago he sent me a letter, and in that letter there were a number of large bills, greenbacks, currency. I thought he took a chance sending it that way, but it was wrapped well. There were also enclosed an envelope addressed to another elder and a note to this elder.

The missionary in his letter to me said, "Will you put this money and this memorandum in the enclosed envelope, put a stamp on it, and mail it to this elder?" The letter to the missionary to whom the money was to be sent said about these words: "Enclosed is some money that I want you to have so that you can stay and finish your mission. Unsigned."

His missionary companion's folks were having some financial difficulties. This boy had been saving a little money out of his missionary allowance, and he sent that to me to put in an envelope to send back to his companion and he did not want him to know whence it came. Oh, what a lesson!

Conference Report, April 1965, pp. 126–27.

LOVE

"I Got Both Feet in the Mud"

⌒

MARGARETTE
MCINTIRE BURGESS

My older brother and I were going to school, near to the building which was known as Joseph's brick store. It had been raining the previous day, causing the ground to be very muddy, especially along that street. My brother Wallace and I got both feet in the mud, and could not get out, and of course, child-like, we began to cry, for we thought we would have to stay there. But looking up, I beheld the loving friend of children, the Prophet Joseph, coming to us. He soon had us on higher and drier ground. Then he stooped down and cleaned the mud from our little, heavy-laden shoes, took his handkerchief from his pocket, and wiped our tear-stained faces. He spoke kind and cheering words to us and sent us on our way to school rejoicing.

Juvenile Instructor 27:66–67.

"THIS IS NOT MY LITTLE MARY"

MARGARETTE
MCINTIRE BURGESS

Joseph's wife, Sister Emma, had lost a young babe. My mother having twin baby girls, the Prophet came to see if she would let him have one of them. Of course it was rather against her feelings, but she finally consented for him to take one of them, providing he would bring it home each night. This he did punctually himself, and also came after it each morning. One evening he did not come with it at the usual time, and Mother went down to the mansion to see what was the matter, and there sat the Prophet with the baby wrapped up in a little silk quilt. He was trotting it on his knee, and singing to it to get it quiet before starting out, as it had been fretting. The child soon became quiet when my mother took it, and the Prophet came up home with her. Next morning when he came after the baby, Mother handed him Sarah, the other baby. They looked so much alike that strangers could not tell them apart; but as Mother passed him the other baby he shook his head and said, "This is not my little Mary." Then she took Mary from the cradle and gave her to him, and he smilingly carried her home with him. The baby Mary had a very mild disposition, while Sarah was quite cross and fretful, and by this my mother could distinguish them one from the other, though generally people could not tell them apart. But our Prophet soon knew which was the borrowed baby. After his wife became better in health he did not take our baby anymore, but often came in to caress her and play with her. Both children died in their infancy, before the Prophet was martyred.

Juvenile Instructor 27:67.

"I FEEL SORRY
FOR THIS BROTHER TO THE
AMOUNT OF FIVE DOLLARS"

ANDREW WORKMAN

I saw the Prophet Joseph for the first time in May [of 1842]. He was with about a dozen others on the stand in a meeting. I knew him as soon as I saw him. Although I was young I knew him to be a man of God.

A few days after this I was at Joseph's house; he was there, and several men were sitting on the fence. Joseph came out and spoke to us all. Pretty soon a man came up and said that a poor brother who lived out some distance from town had had his house burned down the night before. Nearly all of the men said they felt sorry for the man. Joseph put his hand in his pocket, took out five dollars and said, "I feel sorry for this brother to the amount of five dollars; how much do you all feel sorry?"

Juvenile Instructor 27:641.

JOSEPH'S GENEROSITY

MARY FROST ADAMS

While [Joseph Smith] was acting as mayor of the city, a colored man called Anthony was arrested for selling liquor on Sunday, contrary to law. He pleaded that the reason he had done so was that he might raise the money to purchase the freedom of a dear child held as a slave in a southern state. He had been able to purchase the liberty of himself and wife and now wished to bring his little child to their new home.

Joseph said, "I am sorry, Anthony, but the law must be observed, and we will have to impose a fine."

The next day Brother Joseph presented Anthony with a fine horse, directing him to sell it, and use the money obtained for the purchase of the child.

Young Woman's Journal 17:538.

"LET THEM ALONE—
DON'T HURT THEM!"

JOSEPH SMITH

In pitching my tent we found three massasaugas or prairie rattlesnakes, which the brethren were about to kill, but I said, "Let them alone—don't hurt them! How will the serpent ever lose its venom, while the servants of God possess the same disposition, and continue to make war upon it? Men must become harmless before the brute creation, and when men lose their vicious dispositions and cease to destroy the animal race, the lion and the lamb can dwell together, and the sucking child can play with the serpent in safety."

The brethren took the serpents carefully on sticks and carried them across the creek. I exhorted the brethren not to kill a serpent, bird, or an animal of any kind during our journey unless it became necessary in order to preserve ourselves from hunger.

Joseph Smith, *History of The Church of Jesus Christ of Latter-day Saints,* 7 vols., 2d ed. rev., edited by B. H. Roberts (Salt Lake City: The Church of Jesus Christ of Latter-day Saints, 1932–51), 2:71–72.

"HE LIFTED ME UPON
HIS OWN BROAD SHOULDERS"

JOHN LYMAN SMITH

One evening in the summer of 1837 [my cousin] Joseph [Smith] and I drove a carriage into the little town of Painesville, Ohio, and stopped at the house of a friend for supper. We had scarcely finished our meal when a disturbance arose outside. A mob had gathered; there were angry yells and threats of murder. They demanded that our host bring Joseph and I out to them. Instead, he led us out through a back door, and helped us get away in the darkness. Pretty soon the mob discovered we had escaped, so they dispatched riders to hurry along the road they thought we would take. Bonfires were lighted, sentinels were placed, they hunted the countryside.

Joseph and I did not take the main road, however, but walked through the woods and swamps away from the road. We were helped by the bonfires. Pretty soon I began to falter in our flight. Sickness and fright had robbed me of strength. Joseph had to decide [whether] to leave me to be captured by the mob or to endanger himself by rendering aid. Choosing the latter course, he lifted me upon his own broad shoulders and bore me with occasional rests through the swamp and darkness. Several hours later we emerged upon the lonely road and soon reached safety. Joseph's herculean strength permitted him to accomplish this task and saved my life.

John Lyman Smith, unpublished journal, Special Collections, Brigham Young University.

"I WILL BE
HUNG IN YOUR STEAD"

⌒

F R O M   *H I S T O R Y   O F   T H E   C H U R C H*

5 P.M.—Jailor Stigall returned to the [Carthage] jail, and said that Stephen Markham had been surrounded by a mob, who had driven him out of Carthage, and he had gone to Nauvoo.

Stigall suggested that they would be safer in the cell. Joseph said, "After supper we will go in." Mr. Stigall went out, and Joseph said to Dr. [Willard] Richards, "If we go into the cell, will you go in with us?"

The doctor answered, "Brother Joseph you did not ask me to cross the river with you—you did not ask me to come to Carthage—you did not ask me to come to jail with you—and do you think I would forsake you now? But I will tell you what I will do; if you are condemned to be hung for treason, I will be hung in your stead, and you shall go free."

Joseph said, "You cannot." The doctor replied, "I will."

Joseph Smith, *History of The Church of Jesus Christ of Latter-day Saints,* 7 vols., 2d ed. rev., edited by B. H. Roberts (Salt Lake City: The Church of Jesus Christ of Latter-day Saints, 1932–51), 6:616.

"MY BOY,
COME AND LIVE WITH ME"

B . F . GRANT

My father [Jedediah M. Grant] died when I was only a few weeks old. Mother made moccasins out of deer skins, and sold them to stores at a very small margin of revenue to her. She did housework for different families when it was obtainable. When I was two years old, mother married outside of the Mormon Church. As she was going to Denver, Colorado, to live, grandmother persuaded her to leave me in her care. Grandmother was a cripple. It was difficult for her to care for a little boy and so after a time, she gave me to Beason Lewis, who lived in Richmond, Cache Valley. I remained with this family until I was between eleven and twelve years old. About this time mines were discovered in Montana and trains passed through Utah buying flour, butter, eggs, etc., to be carried to the Montana mines. One of these trains stopped at the Lewis place for a few months to make repairs to their wagons. I made arrangements to run away from home and go with this train to Montana. I remained there until I was 14. The terminus of the Union Pacific was located at Corinne, where the freight from Montana was delivered. I met one of the freighters, who, learning that I was a son of Jedediah M. Grant, invited me to go back to Utah with him. I returned to Salt Lake City when I was between fourteen and fifteen years of age. I went to work in a coal and wood yard.

I had been in Salt Lake City only a short time when in some way President [Brigham] Young learned where I was and what I was doing. President Young's son, Feramorz, and my brother,

410

Heber, at the request of President Young, searched me out and informed me that President Young wanted to see me.

The next day I called on him at his office, and he happened to be alone. I told him who I was, and he did not merely reach out his hand to shake mine, but he arose from his chair and gave me a father's handshake. In so doing, he discovered that the callouses on my hands were hard and thick, and he remarked, "My boy, what kind of work are you doing?" I replied, "I am unloading coal and chopping wood."

He then resumed his seat and continued his inquiry regarding my past life and what I had been doing. He remarked, "Isn't it pretty heavy work, shoveling coal and chopping wood, for a boy of your age?"

I replied, "No, sir, I have been used to hard work all of my life."

He answered, "Wouldn't you like to have something easier than your present work, for instance, a position in a store?"

I replied, "I haven't got sense enough to work in a store."

He said, "What do you mean by that?"

I replied, "I can neither read nor write."

I discovered this good and great man's heart was touched by this remark; I saw tears rolling down his cheek, and he took his handkerchief and wiped them off and said, "My boy, come and live with me; I will give you a home; I will clothe you; I will send you to school; and you can work during the vacation for me."

I accepted his kind offer. He became a father to me. He furnished a home; he clothed me; and provided an opportunity for me to attend school; and he gave me $5.00 a week for spending money, which was a very princely allowance in those days of hardship and trial. His own sons would laughingly tell me they thought I was their father's pet.

Soon after I went to live with President Young, I was given a team and was doing general work on his farm and performing other duties incident to Pioneer life. . . .

In addition to his large family at the time I was living with him, there were six orphaned boys and girls who were being cared for by him. I lived with one of his families and was treated most royally by all the members; in fact, I felt I was indeed a real member of the family so far as treatment was concerned.

During the vacation when I was driving a team, at times breakfast would be served a little late. There was a certain time when every team was supposed to be hooked up and going to its work. When breakfast was late I could not always be on time with my team. The foreman complained to me about this and I told him that I milked the cows and fed the pigs and did the chores, but could not go to work without my breakfast. One morning he became angry and told me if I couldn't get out on time to quit. I, boy like, took his advice without calling on President Young, left, and went to work in the coal yard again.

President Young was soon informed of this and sent for me. When I went into his office he shook hands and wanted to know why I left home. I told him the boss had discharged me.

"Oh," he said, "The boss? Who is he?" I gave the foreman's name.

He laughed, and said, "No, my boy, I am the boss. Didn't I make arrangements for you to come and live with me?"

I replied, "Yes, sir."

He then said, "Remember, when you are discharged I will attend to it myself; now, go back, get your team and go to work."

I replied, "I don't know whether _____ will allow me to go to work now."

"Never mind, my boy," he assured me, "I'll attend to it myself."

The next morning when I went to the barn to get my team I found there was a new foreman. I never did learn why this change was made, but I had a boy's suspicion.

Preston Nibley, *Faith Promoting Stories* (Salt Lake City: Deseret Book Co., 1943), pp. 146–49.

AN INDIAN WAIL

ELLEN R. BRYNER

It was an early fall morning. The air was crisp and cold. The comforts of the impoverished two rooms of log with earthen floor and roof were very few. Caroline Butler awakened after a night of restless anxiety. There were eleven hungry mouths to feed. For days their rations had been scanty. A little wild game had come to them occasionally from members of the camp, while the husband and father, with his teams and wagons, assisted poorer Saints into Winter Quarters. The food in the larder was not sufficient to satisfy the needs for one meal of the hungry, growing family. As the anxious mother placed the last scanty store of food upon the rough table and urged her family to make preparations for their morning meal, her heart was full of entreaty to God to send help from some source that day.

As they were about to partake, an old Indian woman walked into the room and asked for bread. Caroline was conscious of her family's needs for food and of her own physical weakness from lack of it, because she had given most of her portion to satisfy the hunger of her smaller children. "This is all we have," she answered, "but we will share it with you."

The Indian woman partook and went on her way; not far away through the woods she had thriftily stored some food after the Indian fashion.

Caroline learned that day that bread cast upon the water to satisfy the hungry shall come back a hundredfold. Grandmother Indian (as the old Indian was known from day forth) returned with sufficient dried buffalo meat and dried berries to stay the

413

pangs of hunger until other supplies came. Many times during the Butlers' three years' stay in Winter Quarters, she came to the cabin and shared her own savings of food with her adopted family.

Poverty was the order of the day with these driven and much persecuted Latter-day Saints. As many were doing, this large family was planning the long journey westward without sufficient footwear and clothing, a consequence of the confiscation of their possessions and of being driven from their homes.

Hearing that the journey to the mountains was soon to continue, Grandmother Indian determined to make heavy buckskin moccasins for each member of her adopted family. After tedious weeks of labor, all of the moccasins were finished with the exception of a pair for Caroline. Grandmother Indian spent extra time decorating this pair as a visible sign of her deep devotion. Early one morning, knowing that the time for their departure was near, she approached the little log house only to find her loved ones gone. Almost overcome with disappointment and sorrow, she wailed an Indian wail and started to follow the wagon tracks.

The family traveled five miles that first day. After the campfires had burned low and the oxen were cared for, and all the weary travelers were settled in their beds, an Indian wail was heard in the distance, growing louder as it came nearer. Grandmother Indian had followed her newfound family in order to present her last token of love before a final goodbye. With the moccasins she had brought a generous supply of dried pulverized venison in a pouch, and a sack of dried berries.

Leon R. Hartshorn, comp., *Remarkable Stories from the Lives of Latter-day Saint Women* (Salt Lake City: Deseret Book Co., 1975), 2:29–30.

GINGERBREAD TOYS

⌒

HANNAH CORNABY

The recent famine experience had taught me economy, and the little I could procure from the sale of some clothing enabled us to live. I could have made our condition known and have received help, but delicacy forbade; so I made the best of the situation, exerting myself unceasingly for the helpless little ones.

Christmas Eve came, and my darlings, with childish faith, hung up their stockings, wondering if Santa Claus would fill them. With aching heart, which I concealed from them, I assured them they would not be forgotten; and they fell asleep with joyful anticipation for the morrow.

Not having a particle of sweetening, I knew not what to do. They must not, however, be disappointed. I then thought of some squashes in the house, which I boiled, then strained off the liquid; that, when simmered a few hours, made a sweet syrup. With this and a little spice, I made gingerbread dough which, when cut into every conceivable variety of design and baked in a skillet (I had no stove), filled their stockings and pleased them as much as would the most fancy confectionaries.

I sometimes wonder if the children of today enjoy the costly Christmas presents of toys and rich candies with which they are surfeited any more than my little ones did their gingerbread toys.

Hannah Cornaby, *Autobiography and Poems* (Salt Lake City: J. C. Graham Co., 1881), pp. 45–46.

"I WAS STUDYING GRAMMAR"

HEBER J. GRANT

There stand out in my life many incidents in my youth, of wonderful inspiration and power through men preaching the gospel in the spirit of testimony and prayer. I call to mind one such incident when I was a young man, probably seventeen or eighteen years of age. I heard the late Bishop Millen Atwood preach a sermon in the Thirteenth Ward. I was studying grammar at the time, and he made some grammatical errors in his talk.

I wrote down his first sentence, smiled to myself, and said: "I am going to get here tonight, during the thirty minutes that Brother Atwood speaks, enough material to last me for the entire winter in my night school grammar class." We had to take to the class for each lesson two sentences, or four sentences a week, that were not grammatically correct, together with our corrections.

I contemplated making my corrections and listening to Bishop Atwood's sermon at the same time. But I did not write anything more after that first sentence—not a word; and when Millen Atwood stopped preaching, tears were rolling down my cheeks, tears of gratitude and thanksgiving that welled up in my eyes because of the marvelous testimony which that man bore of the divine mission of Joseph Smith, the prophet of God, and of the wonderful inspiration that attended the prophet in all his labors.

Although it is now more than sixty-five years since I listened to that sermon, it is just as vivid today, and the sensations and feelings that I had are just as fixed with me as they were the day I heard it. Do you know, I would no more have thought of using

416

those sentences in which he had made grammatical mistakes than I would think of standing up in a class and profaning the name of God. That testimony made the first profound impression that was ever made upon my heart and soul of the divine mission of the prophet. I had heard many testimonies that had pleased me and made their impression, but this was the first testimony that had melted me to tears under the inspiration of the Spirit of God to that man.

During all the years that have passed since then, I have never been shocked or annoyed by grammatical errors or mispronounced words on the part of those preaching the gospel. I have realized that it was like judging a man by the clothes he wore, to judge the spirit of a man by the clothing of his language. From that day to this the one thing above all others that has impressed me has been the Spirit, the inspiration of the living God that an individual had when proclaiming the gospel, and not the language; because after all is said and done there are a great many who have never had the opportunity to become educated so far as speaking correctly is concerned. Likewise there are many who have never had an opportunity in the financial battle of life to accumulate the means whereby they could be clothed in an attractive manner. I have endeavored, from that day to this, and have been successful in my endeavor, to judge men and women by the spirit they have; for I have learned absolutely, that it is the Spirit that giveth life and understanding, and not the letter. The letter killeth.

Heber J. Grant, *Gospel Standards,* compiled by G. Homer Durham (Salt Lake City: Improvement Era, 1969), pp. 294–97.

"THEY WERE MELTED TO TEARS"

HEBER J. GRANT

I recall one incident showing how song has the power to soothe irritated feelings and bring harmony to the hearts of men who are filled with a contentious spirit. It occurred many years ago and involved a quarrel between two old and faithful brethren whose membership dated back to the days of Nauvoo. These men had been full of integrity and devotion to the work of the Lord. They had been through many of the hardships of Nauvoo, and had suffered the drivings and persecutions of the Saints, as well as the hardships of pioneering, incident to the early settlement of the west. These men had quarreled over some business affairs, and finally concluded that they would try to get President John Taylor to help them adjust their difficulties.

John Taylor was then the president of the Council of the Twelve Apostles. These brethren pledged their word of honor that they would faithfully abide by whatever decision Brother Taylor might render. Like many others, even in these days, they were not willing to accept the conclusions and counsels of their teachers, or bishops, or presidents of stakes, who would have been the authorized persons, in their order, to consult, and which would have been the proper course to pursue. But they must have some higher authority. Having been personally acquainted with President Brigham Young, in the days of Nauvoo, and feeling their importance in their own devotion to the work of the Lord, nothing short of an apostle's advice would seem to satisfy them.

Accordingly they called on President Taylor. They did not immediately tell him what their trouble was, but explained that they had seriously quarreled and asked him if he would listen to their story and render his decision. President Taylor willingly consented. But he said: "Brethren, before I hear your case, I would like very much to sing one of the songs of Zion for you."

Now President Taylor was a very capable singer, and interpreted sweetly and with spirit, our sacred hymns.

He sang one of our hymns to the two brethren.

Seeing its effect, he remarked that he never heard one of the songs of Zion but that he wanted to listen to one more, and so asked them to listen while he sang another. Of course, they consented. They both seemed to enjoy it; and, having sung the second song, he remarked that he had heard there is luck in odd numbers and so with their consent he would sing still another, which he did. Then in his jocular way, he remarked: "Now, brethren, I do not want to wear you out, but if you will forgive me, and listen to one more hymn, I promise to stop singing, and will hear your case."

The story goes that when President Taylor had finished the fourth song, the brethren were melted to tears, got up, shook hands, and asked President Taylor to excuse them for having called upon him, and for taking up his time. They then departed without his even knowing what their difficulties were.

President Taylor's singing had reconciled their feelings toward each other. The spirit of the Lord had entered their hearts, and the hills of difference that rose between them had been leveled and become as nothing. Love and brotherhood had developed in their souls. The trifles over which they had quarreled had become of no consequence in their sight. The songs of the heart had filled them with the spirit of reconciliation.

Heber J. Grant, *Gospel Standards,* compiled by G. Homer Durham (Salt Lake City: Improvement Era, 1969), pp. 285–87.

"THANKS FOR THE ELDERS OF OUR WARD"

LES GOATES

But "as for me and my house" the welfare program began in the Old Field west of Lehi on the Saratoga Road in the autumn of 1918, that terribly climactic year of World War I during which more than 14 million people died of that awful scourge "the black plague," or Spanish influenza.

Winter came early that year and froze much of the sugar beet crop in the ground. My dad and brother Francis were desperately trying to get out of the frosty ground one load of beets each day which they would plow out of the ground, cut off the tops, and toss the beets, one at a time, into the huge red beet wagon and then haul the load off to the sugar factory. It was slow and tedious work due to the frost and the lack of farm help, since my brother Floyd and I were in the army and Francis, or Franz, as everybody called him, was too young for the military service.

While they were thusly engaged in harvesting the family's only cash crop and were having their evening meal one day, a phone call came through from our eldest brother, George Albert, super-intendent of the State Industrial School in Ogden, bearing the tragic news that Kenneth, nine-year-old son of our brother Charles, the school farm manager, had been stricken with the dread "flu," and after only a few hours of violent sickness, had died on his father's lap; and would dad please come to Ogden and bring the boy home and lay him away in the family plot in the Lehi Cemetery.

420

My father cranked up his old flap-curtained Chevrolet and headed for Five Points in Ogden to bring his little grandson home for burial. When he arrived at the home he found "Charl" sprawled across the cold form of his dear one, the ugly brown discharge of the black plague oozing from his ears and nose and virtually burning up with fever.

"Take my boy home," muttered the stricken young father, "and lay him away in the family lot and come back for me tomorrow."

Father brought Kenneth home, made a coffin in his carpenter shop, and mother and our sisters, Jennie, Emma, and Hazel, placed a cushion and a lining in it, and then dad went with Franz and two kind neighbors to dig the grave. So many were dying the families had to do the grave digging. A brief graveside service was all that was permitted.

The folks had scarcely returned from the cemetery when the telephone rang again and George Albert (Bert) was on the line with another terrifying message: Charl had died and two of his beautiful little girls—Vesta, 7, and Elaine, 5, were critically ill, and two babies—Raeldon, 4, and Pauline, 3, had been stricken.

Our good cousins, the Larkin undertaking people, were able to get a casket for Charl and they sent him home in a railroad baggage car. Father and young Franz brought the body from the railroad station and placed it on the front porch of our old country home for an impromptu neighborhood viewing but folks were afraid to come near the body of a black plague victim. Father and Francis meanwhile had gone with neighbors to get the grave ready and arrange a short service in which the great, noble spirit of Charles Hyrum Goates was commended into the keeping of his Maker.

Next day my sturdy, unconquerable old dad was called on still another of his grim missions, this time to bring home Vesta, the smiling one with the raven hair and big blue eyes.

When he arrived at the home he found Juliett, the grief-crazed mother, kneeling at the crib of darling little Elaine, the blue-eyed baby angel with the golden curls. Juliett was sobbing wearily and praying: "Oh, Father in heaven, not this one, please! Let me keep my baby! Do not take any more of my darlings from me!"

Before father arrived home with Vesta the dread word had come again. Elaine had gone to join her daddy, brother Kenneth, and sister Vesta. And so it was that father made another heart-breaking journey to bring home and lay away a fourth member of his family, all within the week.

The telephone did not ring the evening of the day they laid away Elaine nor were there any more sad tidings of death the next morning. It was assumed that George A. and his courageous companion Della, although afflicted, had been able to save the little ones Raeldon and Pauline; and it was such a relief that Cousin Reba Munns, a nurse, had been able to come in and help.

After breakfast dad said to Franz, "Well, son, we had better get down to the field and see if we can get another load of beets out of the ground before they get frozen in any tighter. Hitch up and let's be on our way."

Francis drove the four-horse outfit down the driveway and dad climbed aboard. As they drove along the Saratoga Road, they passed wagon after wagon-load of beets being hauled to the factory and driven by neighborhood farmers. As they passed by, each driver would wave a greeting: "Hi ya, Uncle George," "Sure sorry, George," "Tough break, George," "You've got a lot of friends, George."

On the last wagon was the town comedian, freckled-faced Jasper Rolfe. He waved a cheery greeting and called out: "That's all of 'em, Uncle George."

My dad turned to Francis and said: "I wish it was all of ours."

When they arrived at the farm gate, Francis jumped down off the big red beet wagon and opened the gate as we drove onto the field. He pulled up, stopped the team, paused a moment and scanned the field, from left to right and back and forth—and lo and behold, there wasn't a sugar beet on the whole field. Then it dawned upon him what Jasper Rolfe meant when he called out: "That's all of 'em, Uncle George!"

Then dad got down off the wagon, picked up a handful of the rich, brown soil he loved so much, and then in his thumbless left hand a beet top, and he looked for a moment at these symbols of his labor, as if he couldn't believe his eyes.

Then father sat down on a pile of beet tops—this man who brought four of his loved ones home for burial in the course of only six days: made caskets, dug graves, and even helped with the burial clothing this amazing man who never faltered, nor flinched, nor wavered throughout this agonizing ordeal—sat down on a pile of beet tops and sobbed like a little child.

Then he arose, wiped his eyes with his big, red bandanna handkerchief, looked up at the sky, and said: "Thanks, Father, for the elders of our ward."

Used by permission of L. Brent Goates.

"IOSEPA, IOSEPA"

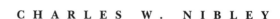

CHARLES W. NIBLEY

When we arrived at the harbor of Honolulu, we were met by the Royal Hawaiian Band. This band was instructed to come up to the "Mormon" meeting house—a quite prominent place in the city of Honolulu, and play for the people in honor of President [Joseph F.] Smith and his company. In the midst of the proceedings, after we were gathered in the meeting house and President Smith was conversing in the native tongue with this one and the other one, and shaking hands with all, there was led into the room an old Hawaiian lady, tottering, blind—led because she could not see. The moment he saw her he turned from everyone else and rushed to this dear old native lady. She was calling "Iosepa, Iosepa"—Joseph, Joseph, her Joseph. He rushed to her and gathered her in his arms, and with tears streaming down his cheeks, said: "My mamma, my mamma, my dear old mamma." And he turned to me, wiping his cheeks, and said, "Charlie, she tended me while I was sick, more than fifty years ago [during his mission in Hawaii], and here she is now; should I not bless her and love her?"

Conference Report, June 1919, p. 62.

VISIT TO PRESIDENT TRUMAN

GEORGE ALBERT SMITH

When the war was over, I went representing the Church, to see the president of the United States. When I called on him, he received me very graciously—I had met him before—and I said: "I have just come to ascertain from you, Mr. President, what your attitude will be if the Latter-day Saints are prepared to ship food and clothing and bedding to Europe."

He smiled and looked at me, and said: "Well, what do you want to ship it over there for? Their money isn't any good."

I said: "We don't want their money." He looked at me and asked: "You don't mean you are going to give it to them?"

I said: "Of course, we would give it to them. They are our brothers and sisters and are in distress. God has blessed us with a surplus, and we will be glad to send it if we can have the co-operation of the government."

He said: "You are on the right track," and added, "we will be glad to help you in any way we can."

I have thought of that a good many times. After we had sat there a moment or two, he said again: "How long will it take you to get this ready?"

I said: "It's all ready."

The government you remember had been destroying food and refusing to plant grain during the war, so I said to him:

"Mr. President, while the administration at Washington were advising the destroying of food, we were building elevators and fill-ing them with grain, and increasing our flocks and our herds, and now what we need is the cars and the ships in order to send considerable food, clothing and bedding to the people of Europe who are in distress. We have an organization in the Church that has over two thousand homemade quilts ready."

[That organization was] . . . the Relief Society. . . . They had two thousand quilts made by their own hands ready to ship. The result was that many people received warm clothing and bedding and food without any delay. Just as fast as we could get cars and ships, we had what was necessary to send to Europe.

Conference Report, October 1947, pp. 5–6.

EZRA TAFT BENSON
ASSISTS THE EUROPEAN SAINTS

FREDERICK W. BABBEL

It was Elder [Ezra Taft] Benson whose phone call . . . had set off the exciting chain of events which had brought me to Europe [in 1946] on a second mission for the Church. The First Presidency had called him to reestablish the European Missions following the long night of war, and to arrange for the distribution of such necessaries as food, clothing and bedding to the distressed saints in Europe. The thrilling assignment was mine to assist him in this great work. . . .

[Our visits to Frankfurt, Germany, were] made in the interest of getting supplies and materials to meet pressing needs for our saints. . . .

We proceeded to the offices of General Joseph T. McNarney, the four-star general in charge of all American forces in Europe. Our first request for an audience was quickly and routinely dismissed. The general's aide, a very businesslike major, advised us that it would be impossible to arrange such a meeting for at least three days.

Somewhat disappointed, we returned to our car where President Benson suggested that we unite our faith in petitioning the Lord. He humbly asked the Lord to be mindful of our situation and to open the way before us.

When we returned to General McNarney's office several minutes later, we were greeted by another officer who was apparently relieving the major. Without mentioning our earlier contact with the major, President Benson requested an audience with the general. . . . Within fifteen minutes we were ushered in for a meeting with the general.

As we entered, it was evident that he regarded this interview as strictly a perfunctory one which he was anxious to terminate as quickly as possible. . . . President Benson warmly shook his hand and stood there looking squarely at him and talking very earnestly. This was a crucial moment. . . .

At first the general seemed visibly annoyed. . . . President Benson continued to gaze intently into the general's eyes as he talked with him, and he spoke with such feeling and conviction that the general's eyes became moist with tears and his cold militaristic manner gave way to a warm, spirited expression of, "Mr. Benson, there's something about you that I like. I want to help you in every way I can!" . . .

As President Benson explained the nature of our mission and the organization of the Church and its welfare program, General

McNarney exclaimed, "Mr. Benson, I have never heard of a church with such vision!"

The general then advised us that for the present time regulations required that all relief supplies be handled and distributed through military channels. However, as he became acquainted with our mission organization and our ability to make our own distribution equitably, he continued to express his amazement . . . [and] suggested that we begin to gather our relief supplies.

When President Benson informed him that we had ninety large welfare storehouses bulging with food and clothing, which could be ready for shipment within twenty-four hours, one could fairly feel the general's astonishment. He then agreed to give us written authorization to make our own distribution through our own channels. In exchange, we agreed to provide a reasonable amount of our foodstuffs for use in the existing child-feeding program.

After this point was reached, General McNarney seemed willing to consider favorably our every request.

Frederick W. Babbel, *On Wings of Faith* (Salt Lake City: Bookcraft, 1972), pp. 2, 43, 45–47.

"U-Dandy Resented Restraint"

DAVID O. MCKAY

Recently I had great pleasure in training a well-bred colt. He had a good disposition, clean, well-rounded eye, was well-proportioned, and all in all, a choice equine possession. Under the saddle he was as willing, responsive, and cooperative as a horse could be. He and my dog "Scotty" were real companions. I liked the way he would go up to something of which he was afraid. He had confidence that if he would do as I bade him he would not be injured.

But "U-Dandy" resented restraint. He was ill-contented when tied and would nibble at the tie-rope until he was free. He would not run away, just wanted to be free. Thinking other horses felt the same, he would proceed to untie their ropes. He hated to be confined in the pasture, and if he could find a place in the fence where there was only smooth wire, he would paw the wire carefully with his feet until he could step over to freedom. More than once my neighbors were kind enough to put him back in the field. He learned even to push open the gate. Though his depredations were provoking and sometimes expensive, I admired his intelligence and ingenuity.

But his curiosity and desire to explore the neighborhood led him and me into trouble. Once on the highway he was hit by an automobile, resulting in a demolished machine, injury to the horse, and slight, though not serious, injury to the driver.

Recovering from that, and still impelled with a feeling of wanderlust he inspected the fence throughout the entire boundary.

He even found the gates wired. So, for awhile we thought we had "U-Dandy" secure in the pasture.

One day, however, somebody left the gate unwired. Detecting this, "U-Dandy" unlatched it, took "Nig," his companion, with him, and together they visited the neighbor's field. They went to an old house used for storage. "U-Dandy's" curiosity prompted him to push open the door. Just as he had surmised, there was a sack of grain. What a find! Yes, and what a tragedy! The grain was poison bait for rodents! In a few minutes "U-Dandy" and "Nig" were in spasmodic pain, and shortly both were dead.

How like "U-Dandy" are many of our youth! They are not bad; they do not even intend to do wrong, but they are impulsive, full of life, full of curiosity, and long to do something. They, too, are restive under restraint, but if they are kept busy, guided carefully and rightly, they prove to be responsive and capable; but if left to wander unguided, they all too frequently find themselves in the environment of temptation and too often are entangled in the snares of evil.

––––––––––

David O. McKay, *Cherished Experiences from the Writings of President David O. McKay*, compiled by Clare Middlemiss (Salt Lake City: Deseret Book Co., 1955), pp. 172–73.

"I Didn't Kiss Ray Good-Bye"

D A V I D   L A W R E N C E   M C K A Y

My father, David O. McKay, served as President of the Church from 1951 to January 1970, when he died at age ninety-six.] During these final years, Mother was always first in Father's heart, even when the Church came first in his time. Some of our sweetest memories from this time are of their continuing love story. Once, after they were both in wheelchairs, Brother Darcey Wright had wheeled Father out of the apartment door and down the hallway. While they were waiting for the elevator, Father suddenly exclaimed, "We have to go back. I didn't kiss [Emma] Ray good-bye." Brother Wright dutifully wheeled him back for this loving ritual that had only become more important as the years passed.

David Lawrence McKay, *My Father, David O. McKay* (Salt Lake City: Deseret Book Co., 1989), p. 264.

"I WAS IN
THE ARMS OF THE PROPHET"

FROM THE *CHURCH NEWS*

A large crowd gathered at the General Authorities' exit of the Tabernacle following the general conference. The visitors, many from out-of-town, were anxious to get a glimpse of President Joseph Fielding Smith or perhaps a warm handshake from the new Church president.

From the crowd, wiggling between legs, came a small girl who made her way to President Smith. Soon she was in his arms for a little hug, and then back into the crowd so quickly that the *Deseret News* photographer was unable to get her name.

The picture, unidentified, appeared in the *Church News*. However, her proud grandmother, Mrs. Milo Hobbs of Preston, Idaho, recognized her and promptly wrote a letter to President Smith to share the information.

"I am so happy that we can identify her as our granddaughter, Venus Hobbs. She has a birthday on April 17 when she will be four years old," Grandmother Hobbs wrote.

On her birthday, little Venus Hobbs, who lives in Torrance, California, received a surprise "happy birthday" call and song from President and Mrs. Smith. President Smith was spending the week in California when he made the call.

The call was a thrill to the W. Odell Hobbs family. Mrs. Hobbs was touched with tears to think that the President of the Church was so kind. Venus was delighted with the song.

The [grandmother's] letter went on to explain, "She was with two of her aunts, but she slipped away. They feared they had lost her in the crowd. When they asked, 'How did you get lost?' 'I wasn't lost!' she said. 'Who found you?' they asked. 'I was in the arms of the Prophet,' was her reply."

Church News, April 25, 1970, p. 3.

HUMOR

Parley P. Pratt
Fools Stu-Boy the Bulldog

⌒‿‿

PARLEY P. PRATT

I was soon ordered to prison, or to pay a sum of money which I had not in the world. It was now a late hour, and I was still retained in court, tantalized, abused and urged to settle the matter, to all of which I made no reply for some time. This greatly exhausted their patience. It was near midnight. I now called on Brother Petersen to sing a hymn in the court. We sung, "O how happy are they." This exasperated them still more, and they pressed us greatly to settle the business, by paying the money.

I then observed as follows: "May it please the court, I have one proposal to make for a final settlement of the things that seem to trouble you. It is this: if the witnesses who have given testimony in the case will repent of their false swearing, and the magistrate of his unjust and wicked judgment and of his persecution, blackguardism and abuse, and all kneel down together, we will pray for you, that God might forgive you in these matters."

"My big bull dog pray for me," says that Judge.

"The devil help us," exclaimed another.

They now urged me for some time to pay the money; but got no further answer.

The court adjourned, and I was conducted to a public house over the way, and locked in till morning; the prison being some miles distant.

In the morning the officer appeared and took me to break-

437

fast; this over, we sat waiting in the inn for all things to be ready to conduct me to prison. In the meantime my fellow travellers came past on their journey, and called to see me. I told them in an undertone to pursue their journey and leave me to manage my own affairs, promising to overtake them soon. They did so.

After sitting awhile by the fire in charge of the officer, I requested to step out. I walked out into the public square accompanied by him. Said I, "Mr. Peabody, are you good at a race?" "No," said he, "but my big bull dog is, and he has been trained to assist me in my office these several years; he will take any man down at my bidding." "Well, Mr. Peabody, you compelled me to go a mile, I have gone with you two miles. You have given me an opportunity to preach, sing, and have also entertained me with lodging and breakfast. I must now go on my journey; if you are good at a race you can accompany me. I thank you for all your kindness—good day, sir."

I then started on my journey, while he stood amazed and not able to step one foot before the other. Seeing this, I halted, turned to him and again invited him to a race. He still stood amazed. I then renewed my exertions, and soon increased my speed to something like that of a deer. He did not awake from his astonishment sufficiently to start in pursuit till I had gained, perhaps, two hundred yards. I had already leaped a fence, and was making my way through a field to the forest on the right of the road. He now came hallooing after me, and shouting to his dog to seize me. The dog, being one of the largest I ever saw, came close on my footsteps with all his fury; the officer behind still in pursuit, clapping his hands and hallooing, "stu-boy, stu-boy—take him—watch—lay hold of him, I say—down with him," and pointing his finger in the direction I was running. The dog was fast overtaking me, and in the act of leaping upon me, when, quick as lightning, the thought struck me, to assist the officer, in sending the dog with all fury to the forest a little distance before me. I pointed my finger in that direction, clapped my hands, and shouted in imitation of the officer. The dog hastened past me with redoubled speed towards the forest; being urged by the officer and myself, and both of us running in the same direction.

Gaining the forest, I soon lost sight of the officer and dog, and have not seen them since.

Parley P. Pratt, *Autobiography of Parley P. Pratt,* edited by Parley P. Pratt Jr., Classics in Mormon Literature ed. (Salt Lake City: Deseret Book Co., 1985), pp. 36–39.

BOGUS BRIGHAM

BRIGHAM YOUNG

I do not profess to be much of a joker, but I do think this to be one of the best jokes ever perpetrated.

By the time we were at work in the Nauvoo Temple, officiating in the ordinances, the mob had learned that "Mormonism" was not dead, as they had supposed. We had completed the walls of the Temple, and the attic story from about half way up of the first windows, in about fifteen months. It went up like magic, and we commenced officiating in the ordinances. Then the mob commenced to hunt for other victims; they had already killed the Prophets Joseph and Hyrum in Carthage jail, while under the pledge of the State for their safety, and now they wanted Brigham, the President of the Twelve Apostles, who were then acting as the Presidency of the Church.

I was in my room in the Temple; it was in the south-east corner of the upper story. I learned that a posse was lurking around the Temple, and that the United States Marshal was waiting for me to come down, whereupon I knelt down and asked my Father in heaven, in the name of Jesus, to guide and protect me that I might live to prove advantageous to the Saints. Just as I arose from my knees and sat down in my chair, there came a rap at my door. I said, "Come in," and Brother George D. Grant, who was then engaged driving my carriage and doing chores for me, entered the room.

Said he, "Brother Young, do you know that a posse and the United States Marshal are here?" I told him I had heard so. On entering the room Brother Grant left the door open. Nothing came into my mind what to do, until looking directly across the hall I saw Brother William Miller leaning against the wall.

As I stepped towards the door I beckoned to him; he came. Said I to him, "Brother William, the Marshal is here for me; will you go and do just as I tell you? If you will, I will serve them a trick." I knew that Brother Miller was an excellent man, perfectly reliable and capable of carrying out my project. Said I, "Here, take my cloak;" but it happened to be Brother Heber C. Kimball's; our cloaks were alike in color, fashion and size. I threw it around his shoulders, and told him to wear my hat and accompany Brother George D. Grant. He did so. I said to Brother Grant, "George, you step into the carriage and look towards Brother Miller, and say to him, as though you were addressing me, 'Are you ready to ride?' You can do this, and they will suppose Brother Miller to be me, and proceed accordingly," which they did.

Just as Brother Miller was entering the carriage, the Marshal stepped up to him, and, placing his hand upon his shoulder, said, "You are my prisoner." Brother William entered the carriage and said to the Marshal, "I am going to the Mansion House, won't you ride with me?" They both went to the Mansion House. There were my sons Joseph A., Brigham Jr., and Brother Heber C. Kimball's boys, and others who were looking on, and all seemed at once to understand and partake of the joke. They followed the carriage to the Mansion House and gathered around Brother Miller, with tears in their eyes, saying, "Father, or President Young, where are you going?" Brother Miller looked at them kindly, but made no reply; and the Marshal really thought he had got "Brother Brigham."

Lawyer Edmonds, who was then staying at the Mansion House, appreciating the joke, volunteered to Brother Miller to go to Carthage with him and see him safe through. When they arrived within two or three miles of Carthage, the Marshal with his posse stopped. They arose in their carriages, buggies and waggons, and, like a tribe of Indians going into battle, or as if they were a pack of demons, yelling and shouting, they exclaimed, "We've got him! We've got him! We've got him!"

When they reached Carthage the Marshal took the supposed Brigham into an upper room of the hotel, and placed a guard over him, at the same time telling those around that he had got him. Brother Miller remained in the room until they bid him come to supper. While there, parties came in, one after the other, and asked for Brigham. Brother Miller was pointed out to them. So it continued, until an apostate Mormon, by the name of Thatcher, who had lived in Nauvoo, came in, sat down and asked the landlord where Brigham Young was. The landlord, pointing across the table to Brother Miller, said, "That is Mr. Young." Thatcher replied, "Where? I can't see any one that looks like Brigham." The landlord told him it was that fat, fleshy man eating. "Oh, h___!" exclaimed Thatcher, "that's not Brigham; that is William Miller, one of my old neighbors."

Upon hearing this the landlord went, and, tapping the Sheriff on the shoulder, took him a few steps to one side, and said, "You have made a mistake, that is not Brigham Young; it is William

Miller, of Nauvoo." The Marshal, very much astonished, exclaimed, "Good heavens! and *he* passed for Brigham." He then took Brother Miller into a room, and, turning to him, said, "What in h___ is the reason you did not tell me your name?"

Brother Miller replied, "You have not asked me my name."

"Well," said the Sheriff, with another oath, "What is your name?"

"My name," he replied, "is William Miller."

Said the Marshal, "I thought your name was Brigham Young. Do you say this for a fact?"

"Certainly I do," said Brother Miller.

"Then," said the Marshal, "why did you not tell me this before?"

"I was under no obligations to tell you," replied Brother Miller, "as you did not ask me."

Then the Marshal, in a rage, walked out of the room, followed by Brother Miller, who walked off in company with Lawyer Edmonds, Sheriff Backenstos, and others, who took him across lots to a place of safety; and this is the real pith of the story of "Bogus" Brigham, as far as I can recollect.

Journal of Discourses, 26 vols. (London: Latter-day Saints' Book Depot, 1854–86), 14:218–19.

THE BULLY OF LA HARPE

⌒

CALVIN W. MOORE

It was at the time Porter Rockwell was in jail, in Missouri. His mother went to see him at the jail, and the Missourians told her that if she would raise a certain amount of money and give them they would let her son go. Joseph [Smith] started out to get the money. He came to a large crowd of young men who were wrestling, that being the popular sport in those days. Among the boys there was a bully from La Harpe, I believe. He had thrown down everyone on the ground who took hold of him. When Joseph came to the crowd he told them what he wanted, passed around the hat, raised what money he could and then went into the ring to take part with the young men and boys in their games. So he was invited to wrestle with this bully. The man was eager to have a tussle with the Prophet, so Joseph stepped forward and took hold of the man. The first pass he made Joseph whirled him around and took him by the collar and seat of his trowsers and walked out to a ditch and threw him in it. Then, taking him by the arm, he helped him up and patted him on the back and said, "You must not mind this. When I am with the boys I make all the fun I can for them."

Juvenile Instructor 27:255.

"IT MAKES ME LAUGH"

ORSON F. WHITNEY

It is a common remark to this day that such prayers are seldom heard as were wont to issue from the heart and lips of Heber C. Kimball. Reverence for Deity was one of the cardinal qualities of his nature. Nevertheless, it was noticeable that the God to whom he prayed was a being "near at hand and not afar off." He worshiped not as "a worm of the dust," hypocritically meek and lowly, or as one conscious of naught but the meanness of his nature and the absence of merit in his cause. But in a spirit truly humble, confessing his sins, yet knowing something of the nobility of his soul, he talked with God "as one man talketh with another"; and often with the ease and familiarity of an old-time friend.

On one occasion, while offering up an earnest appeal in behalf of certain of his fellow creatures, he startled the kneeling circle by bursting into a loud laugh in the very midst of his prayer. Quickly regaining his composure and solemn address, he remarked, apologetically: "Lord, it makes me laugh to pray about some people."

Orson F. Whitney, *Life of Heber C. Kimball,* 2d ed. (Salt Lake City: Stevens & Wallis, 1945), pp. 426–27.

THE "CAMP SHIRKS"

⌒

JAMES A. LITTLE

The first company of Elders sent on foreign missions from Utah left Great Salt Lake City on the 19th of October and carried the last mail sent east in 1849. It was under the leadership of Jedediah M. Grant.

With this company went Edward Hunter, Bishop of the thirteenth ward of Great Salt Lake City. He was sent by the chief authorities of the Church to the Missouri river as agent of the P. E. Fund Company, with $30,000 in gold to gather up as many as possible of the Saints remaining of the Nauvoo exodus and bring them to Utah. His character peculiarly adapted him for the work of gathering the poor.

Aside from his excellent business qualifications, nature had endowed him with humane and self-sacrificing principles. Under the unavoidable hardships of traveling, in that early period, he not only manifested a kindly regard for the comfort of others but, as well, ever carried his full share of the general burden. What was said of the Prophet Joseph Smith was, as well, applicable to him, "He was always willing to carry his part of the burden, and to share in any suffering or deprivation inflicted upon his friends."

The following incidents, related by Charles F. Decker who traveled with him illustrate this trait of his character and also his detestation of "camp shirks":

He had a good natured way of making such characters ashamed rather than angry. It was necessary to cross the Platte river. The quicksand was bad and it was thought necessary for those in a condition to do so to wade the river and thus lighten the loads. It was, no doubt, a chilling operation at that altitude in the month of November. It appeared to require a general lively effort to insure the crossing of the teams in safety. Some persons in poor health, whom the strong brethren proposed should remain in the wagons, refused to do so, while others, in good health seriously objected to wetting their lower extremities.

The brethren began to roll at the wheels of a wagon, the team of which appeared to have more than it could contend with in the quicksand. In the wagon was a Brother J. who, although enjoying very good health, objected to getting out for fear of catching his death cold. Bishop Hunter, having hold of one of the hind wheels, quietly remarked, "Brethren, I think this wagon will have to be tipped over before it will go out." Suiting action to the idea he raised his side of the wagon until it appeared to be going over. Mr. J., inside, anticipating such a catastrophe, cried out, with some energy "Oh let me get out first!" and sprang into the water. The Bishop quietly remarked, "Well, well, brethren, I think the wagon will go along now, suppose we try it."

One cold evening the company encamped on the bank of the Platte river. Wood for camp purposes could only be obtained by crossing a considerable branch of the river on to an island. It was very unpleasant to ford the stream, but of two evils this seemed the least. The more ambitious of the men took their axes and started, at once, for the island. Mr. J. and another similar character remained on the bank to take wood from those who might bring it through the water. Bishop Hunter discovering the situation, as he came from camp passed between them, seized one with each arm and took both with him into the water, good naturedly remarking, "Come brethren, we are wet now, let us go and get some wood."

James A. Little, *From Kirtland to Salt Lake City* (Salt Lake City: James A. Little, 1890), pp. 213–15.

MIXED MEMORIES OF JUNY

ALBERT L. ZOBELL JR.

He [Joseph Fielding Smith] learned to work on the family farm in Taylorsville, Salt Lake County. An early memory is of milking the family cow without permission "before I was baptized." Milking was a task that had been given to an older sister, but apparently he did it well enough that he soon found himself given the job.

He learned early to work with animals, with nature, with men, and with God. His own growing testimony was aided by the faith and works of his father, who had been a full-time missionary at fifteen and an apostle ten years before Joseph Fielding was born, and who had been called as second counselor in the First Presidency when his namesake son was only four years of age.

Another of the family tasks that fell his lot was that of being stable boy for his mother in her capacity as a licensed midwife. At all hours of the night he was called from his deep boyhood sleep to harness a horse so she could go where she was needed. He would light a kerosene lantern and go to the barn, and soon the horse would be ready.

Reflecting on those early years, he has mixed memories of Juny, a fine horse that his father had purchased from President George Q. Cannon of the First Presidency:

"She was so smart she learned how to unlock one kind of corral fastener after another that I contrived, until Father said to me, half humorously, that Juny seemed to be smarter than I was. So Father himself fastened her in with a strap and buckle. As he did so, the mare eyed him coolly; and, as soon as our backs were turned, she set to work with her teeth until she actually undid the buckle and followed us out, somewhat to my delight. I could not refrain from suggesting that I was not the only one whose head compared unfavorably with the mare's."

Improvement Era, March 1970, pp. 4–5.

JOSEPH FIELDING
RECEIVES A WHIPPING

JOSEPH FIELDING SMITH

It wasn't much of a whipping . . . [my father] did it because he thought I had lied to him. He didn't do it because I had done something wrong, but because he thought I hadn't told him the truth. And so he gave me a cut or two across the back. Years afterwards I said to him one day, "Do you remember when you gave me a lashing?" and told him the circumstances, "because you thought I had told you an untruth?"

"Now," he said," "I don't know that I remember a thing like that."

"Well," I said, "it happened. . . ."

"Oh, well," he said, "we'll let that apply on something you did when you didn't get caught."

Joseph F. McConkie, *True and Faithful: The Life Story of Joseph Fielding Smith* (Salt Lake City: Bookcraft, 1971), pp. 19–20.

ESCAPADES WITH BUD

HUGH B. BROWN

A n] influence on my upbringing was my older brother Bud. One day Bud and I saw a weasel. The little animal ran into his hole, and we got a spade and began to dig him out. We dug down quite a ways, and Bud said, "I think I can hear him down there, we are pretty close to him. Maybe you'd better reach in and see what he's doing." I rolled up my sleeve and reached down into the hole. Well, the weasel got me by the finger, and I still have a scar.

On another occasion, Bud and I went out to the barn, where he helped me up until I could get ahold of the rafters across the top with my hands. Bud said, "I will swing you back and forth. When you get going pretty good, I will tell you when to let loose of that rafter and when to grab the next one." He gave me a good long swing and then said, "Now." I let loose of the rafter, but the other one was not within reach. It took me six hours to wake up as I landed on the back of my head. Needless to say, mother was very concerned for my welfare.

So things went on between Bud and me. But I never felt any animosity or ill-will towards him. It seemed to be part of my education, although he certainly had me in trouble most of the time. But the time soon came when I wanted to get even with Bud for all of his mischief. I had read a story in which a man died, was put in a big vault, and then came to life again. He got out of his casket in the night and walked around, trying to find his way out, but he kept placing his hands on the faces of the other dead men around him. It was a terrible, horrifying story. I knew if I could get

Bud to read it he would react as I had. So I asked him to read it. As he read and marked the book I watched him carefully. When he got to the place where the man was walking around among the dead men, Bud was very excited, to say the least.

At the time, we slept on some hay in the basement of a big barn at Lake Breeze (where my father managed a fourteen-acre orchard between North Temple and 200 South streets on Redwood Road). When Bud got to this place in the book, I said, "Leave your book now and we'll go to bed." He put it down reluctantly and we went out to the barn. I pulled the barn door open. Inside was as dark as a stack of black cats. I had previously arranged for a cousin to be in the basement in a sheet. When we opened the door and he saw this ghost standing at the bottom of the steps, Bud gave an unearthly scream and started to run. I overtook him and brought him back. "That's just the result of the book you've been reading," I said. "Don't be so foolish. I'll show you there's no ghost there." I went down the steps, felt all around, and could not feel the ghost.

Bud decided to trust me. He went down, got into bed, and covered up his head, but he was shaking all over. I said, "Don't be so foolish, Bud. Uncover your head and look around you. You'll see that there are no ghosts here." He uncovered his head and the ghost was standing right at the foot of his bed. He let out another unearthly scream, covered his head again, and began to pray. I felt very guilty because he told the Lord all the bad things he had done and promised never to do any more. Finally, the ghost went away. I guess Bud's prayer had a great effect on him, as well.

Edwin B. Firmage, ed., *An Abundant Life: The Memoirs of Hugh B. Brown* (Salt Lake City: Signature Books, 1988), pp. 2–4.

"I JUST WANTED TO SHAKE HANDS"

⌒

FRANCIS M. GIBBONS

President David O. McKay] entered the elevator in the Hotel Utah one day to find a boy who shook the president's hand with admiring awe. The young man got off the elevator a floor below Brother McKay's apartment. But when the Prophet, who moved very slowly with the help of a companion, finally exited on his floor, he was surprised to see the same boy standing in the hall panting from his race up the stairway, and with his hand extended for another shake. "I just wanted to shake hands with you once more before you die," the boy explained.

Francis M. Gibbons, *David O. McKay: Apostle to the World, Prophet of God* (Salt Lake City: Deseret Book Co., 1986), pp. 232–33.

Ida's Hearing

FROM MARION G. ROMNEY

President Marion G. Romney's good-humored love for his wife Ida was manifested in many ways. He delighted in telling of her hearing loss. Once he tried to get Ida to go to her doctor for a hearing check-up, but she didn't think she needed one. Convinced that there was a problem, but not being able to convince Ida, he finally decided to go see her doctor himself and consult about what should be done.

President Romney explained, "He asked me how bad it was, and I said I didn't know. He told me to go home and find out. The doctor instructed me to go into a far room and speak to her. Then I should move nearer and nearer until she did hear." In this way he could learn how bad the hearing loss was. President Romney went home to try his experiment.

"Following the doctor's instructions, I spoke to her from the bedroom while she was in the kitchen—no answer. I moved nearer and spoke again—no answer. So I went right up to the door of the kitchen and said, 'Ida, can you hear me?'

"She responded, 'What is it, Marion? I've answered you three times.'"

Adapted from F. Burton Howard, *Marion G. Romney: His Life and Faith* (Salt Lake City: Bookcraft, 1988), pp. 144–45.

"Don't You Squeeze Me!"

E D W A R D   L .   K I M B A L L   A N D
A N D R E W   E .   K I M B A L L   J R .

O nce because of airplane trouble it took [President Spencer W. Kimball] twelve hours to get home across the Great Plains. He wryly noted that he had new sympathy for the pioneers.

An airplane hostess asked, "Would you like something to drink?" Spencer asked, "What do you have?" She mentioned coffee, tea, Coca Cola. He shook his head, then rejoined, "Do you have any lemonade?" "No, but I could squeeze you some." Spencer quickly said, in mock horror, "Don't you squeeze me!"

Edward L. Kimball and Andrew E. Kimball, Jr., *Spencer W. Kimball* (Salt Lake City: Bookcraft, 1977), p. 333.

CHURCH OXEN

J. GOLDEN KIMBALL

Joe Morris was the best man with oxen I ever saw. One time when we were hauling some of those temple logs to the sawmill, he turned the whip over to me. There were six yoke. I had never tackled half so many. "You can't learn younger, go ahead," Joe said to me. So I took the whip and started in. The oxen, dumb as they were, knew a change had been made. Immediately they lagged and some of them turned around to look at me. I fancied they were all laughing at my shrill voice. Joe stood by and laughed; he wouldn't help a bit. I spoke quite respectable for a time to those oxen, but what good did it do? Then I started to cuss. (It was after the manifesto on swearing too, but I was mad and had to turn loose. I never did it again; that was the last time.) And, boy, how I did cuss! Did I wax eloquent! I'm afraid I did. But, did those oxen sit up and take notice? They sure did; every one of them got down to business. You see, they were Church oxen, and when you talked that language to them they understood it.

Claude Richards, *J. Golden Kimball: The Story of a Unique Personality* (Salt Lake City: Bookcraft, 1966), p. 34.

"You'll Get Justice"

J . G O L D E N K I M B A L L

I am not going to announce any blood-and-thunder doctrine to you today. I have not been radical for four long months, not since I had appendicitis. I came very nearly to being operated upon. I thought I was going to die for a few hours. People said to me, "Well, Brother Kimball, you needn't be afraid, you'll get justice."

"Well," I said, "that is what I am afraid of."

Thomas E. Cheney, *The Golden Legacy: A Folk History of J. Golden Kimball* (Santa Barbara and Salt Lake City: Peregrine Smith, 1974), p. 51.

"It Has Been Proposed . . ."

A U S T I N F I F E A N D A L T A F I F E

Once [the] task [of conducting sustainings at conference] fell to [J. Golden] Kimball's lot. "It has been proposed," he said, "that we sustain Brother Heber J. Grant as prophet, seer, and revelator of The Church of Jesus Christ of Latter-day Saints. All in favor make it manifest by the raising of the right hand . . . Opposed, if any, by the same sign . . . It has been proposed that we sustain Brother Anthony W. Ivins as . . ." On and on it went, monotonous and tiresome like the ticking of a clock. J. Golden looked up from his list and noticed that his audience was nodding, on the verge of sleep. In the same monotonous tone he continued: "It has been proposed that Mount Nebo be moved from its present site in Juab County and be placed on the Utah-Idaho border. All in favor make it manifest by raising the right hand; opposed, by the same sign." Guffaws from the few who were still awake revived the congregation and the ritual was completed in due course.

Claude Richards, *J. Golden Kimball: The Story of a Unique Personality* (Salt Lake City: Bookcraft, 1966), p. 305.

SUBSCRIPTIONS TO THE *ERA*

THOMAS E. CHENEY

J. Golden was on a trip in September with Apostle Francis M. Lyman. . . . They came to Panaca, Nevada. We had not seen an apostle for twenty years, and it was Sunday, a fast day. Meetings were begun in the morning and they kept them up all day, and we were fasting. I was starved and anxious to go at four o'clock. After four Brother Lyman said, "Now, Brother Kimball, get up and tell them about the *Era*." He had done a good deal of talking himself about the *Era*. Golden got up and said, "All you

456

men that will take the *Era* if we will let you go home, raise your right hand." There was not a single man who did not raise his hand and subscribed and paid $2.00 cash for the *Era*. In that campaign they got 400 subscribers. Golden said later, "I do not claim that was inspiration; it was good psychology. Really they paid $2.00 to get out."

Thomas E. Cheney, *The Golden Legacy: A Folk History of J. Golden Kimball* (Santa Barbara and Salt Lake City: Peregrine Smith, 1974), p. 81.

JONAH AND THE WHALE

THOMAS E. CHENEY

An acquaintance met J. Golden [Kimball] on the street one day and in conversation asked, "Do you believe that Jonah was swallowed by the whale?"

"When I get to heaven I'll ask Jonah," J. Golden answered.

"But," said the man, "what if Jonah is not there?"

"Then you will have to ask him," Golden quickly replied.

Thomas E. Cheney, *The Golden Legacy: A Folk History of J. Golden Kimball* (Santa Barbara and Salt Lake City: Peregrine Smith, 1974), p. 109.

INDEX